RECEIPTS

TASCHI BELT

2017 - 2024

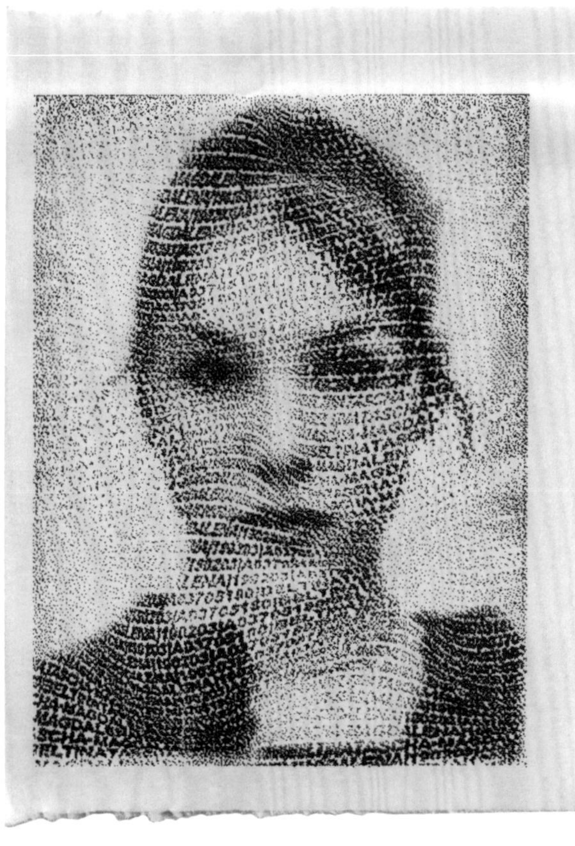

I want to acknowledge these images as my past in physical form and let go of them. This book has gone through several iterations, and the people and pictures that have remained are entirely deliberate. It would've felt dishonest to present an abstract of the past couple of years without including them.

I thank everyone who has given me joy, laughter, excitement, heartbreak, and brought new meanings to my tears. And I especially want to thank Lexie Robinson for showing me what family means, what friendship doesn't, and what can happen if I stay in my seat.
Larisa Sterling, for emotionally (and somewhat physically) pinning me down to my seat on October 31st, 2022. To my amazing parents, David and Antonia. And most of all, my big sister Stella, whom I would be nothing without.

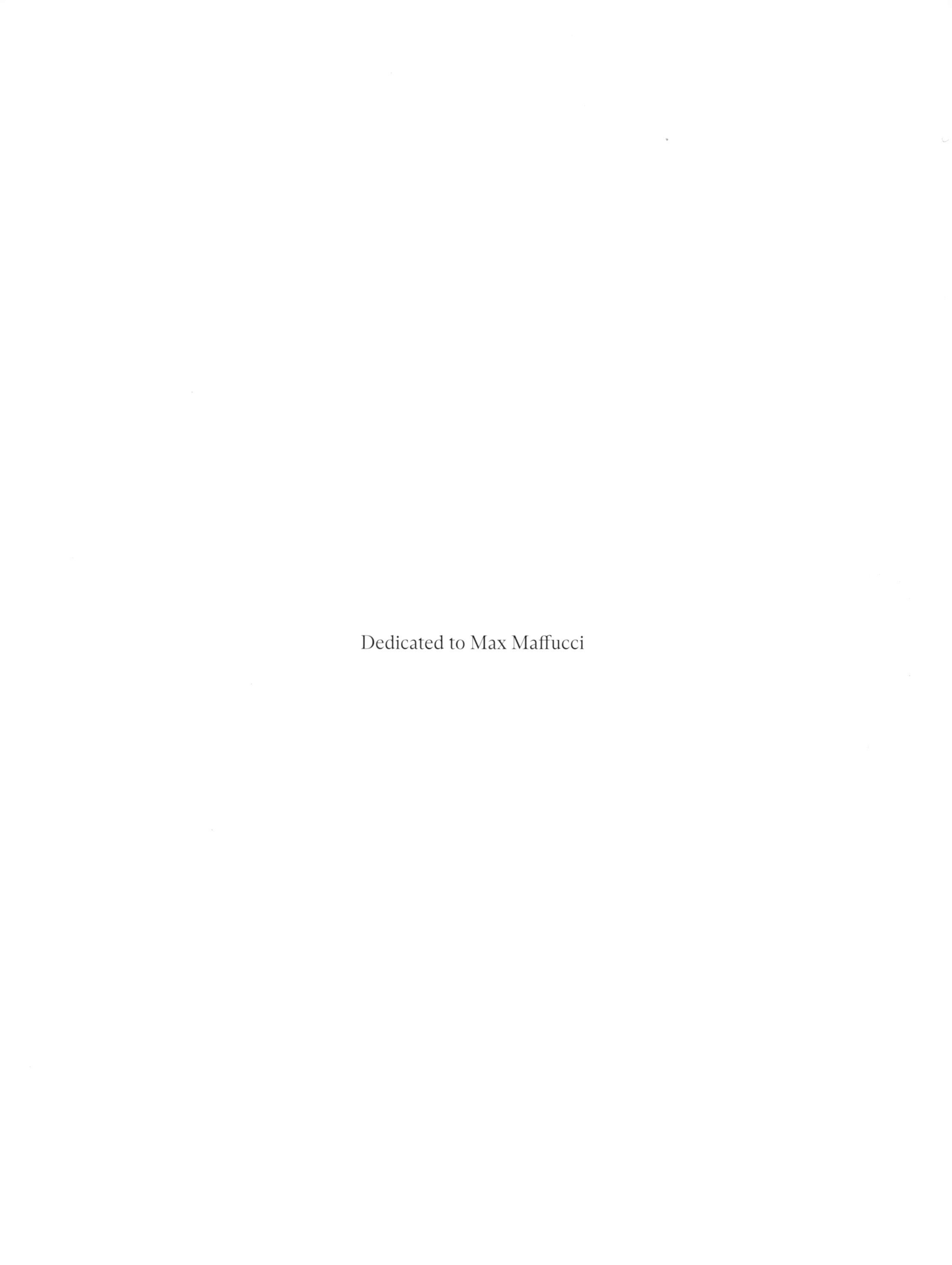

Dedicated to Max Maffucci

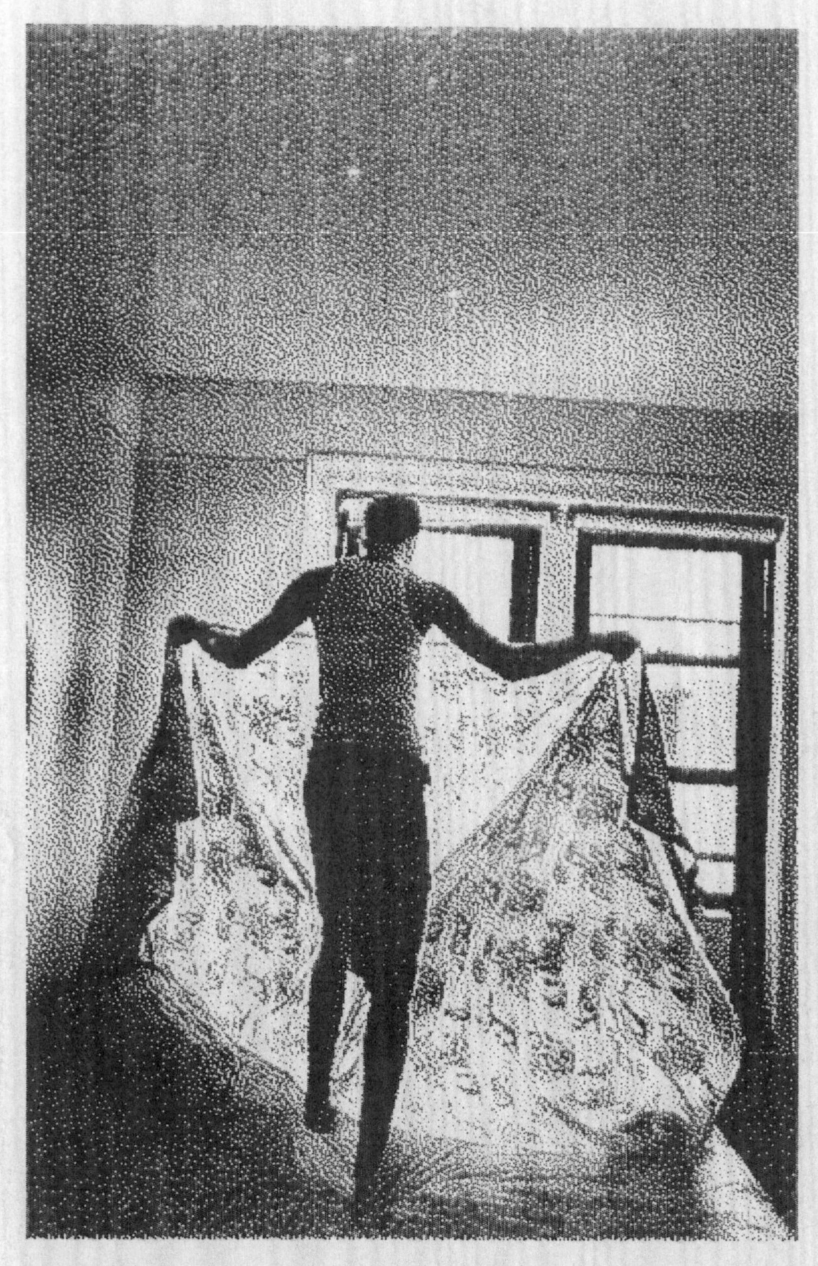

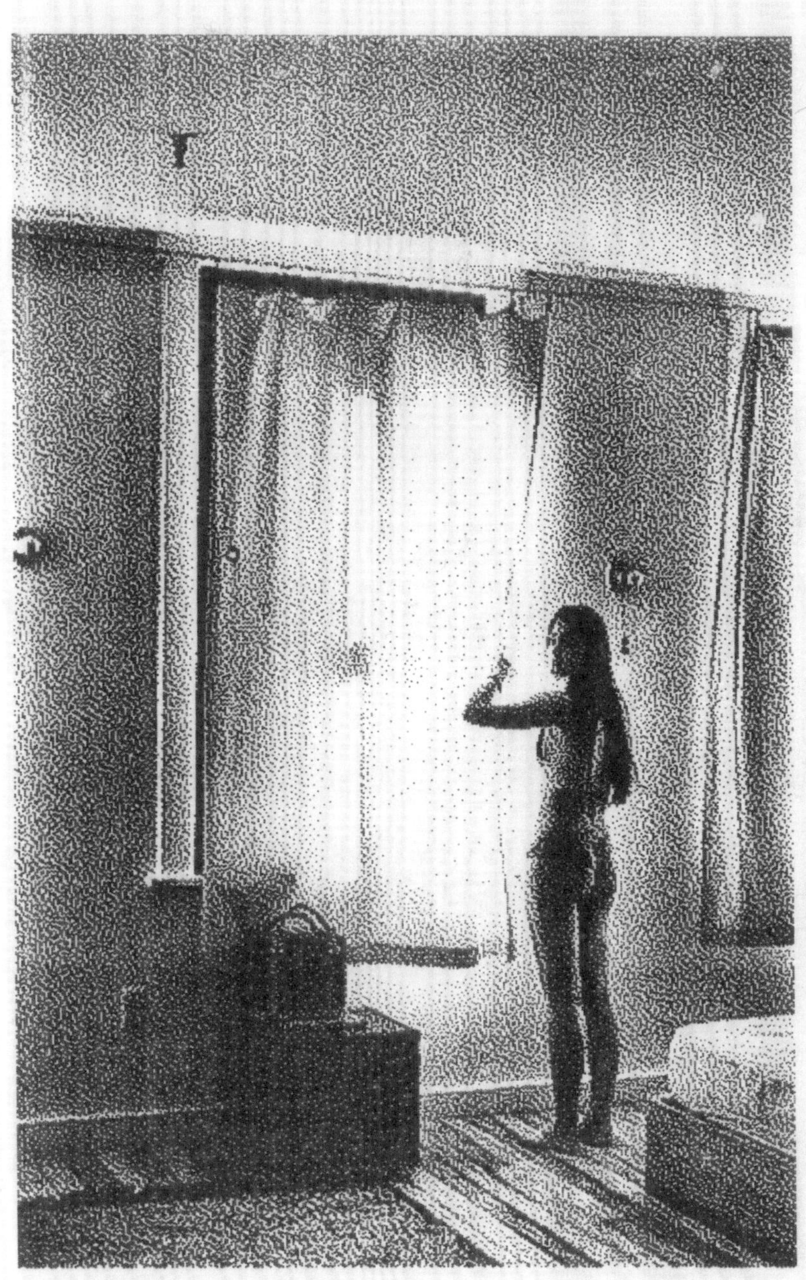

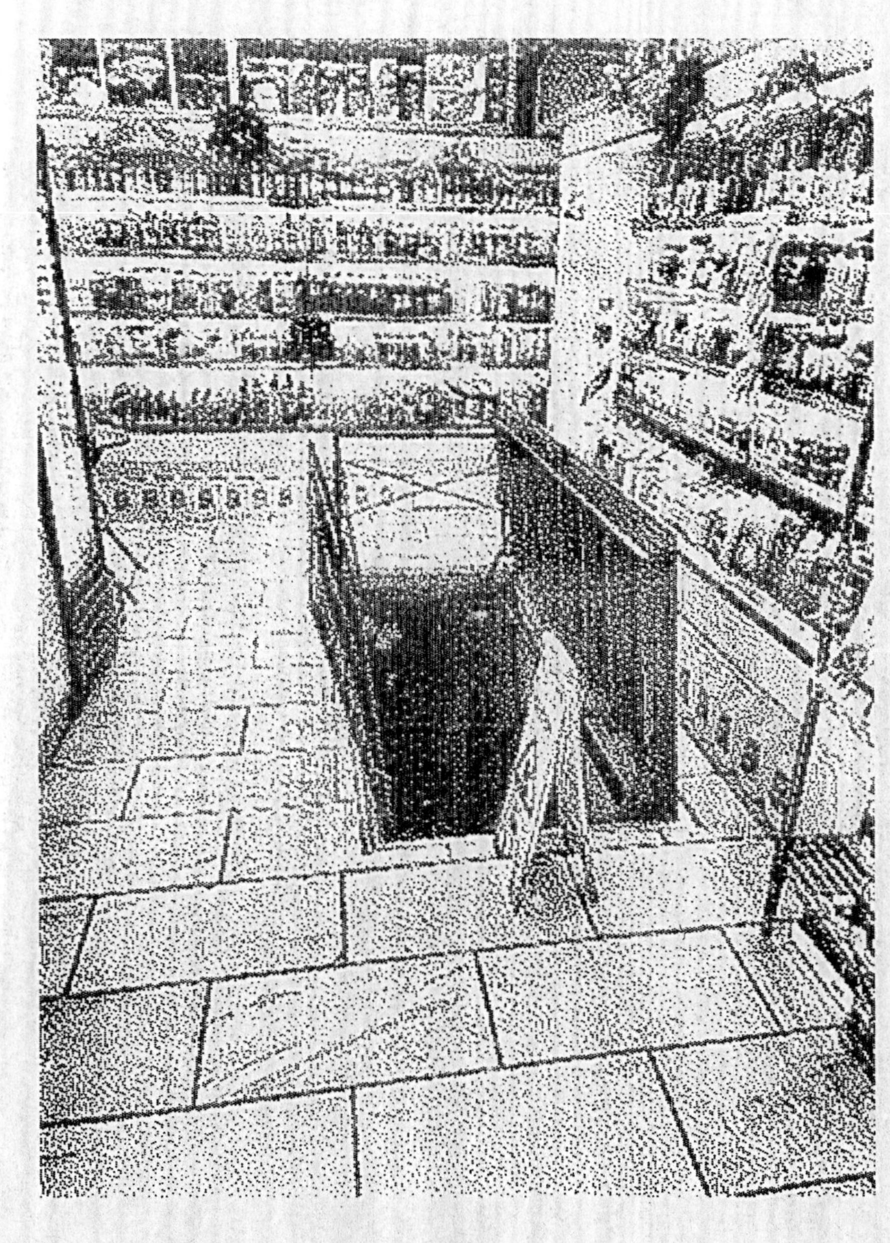

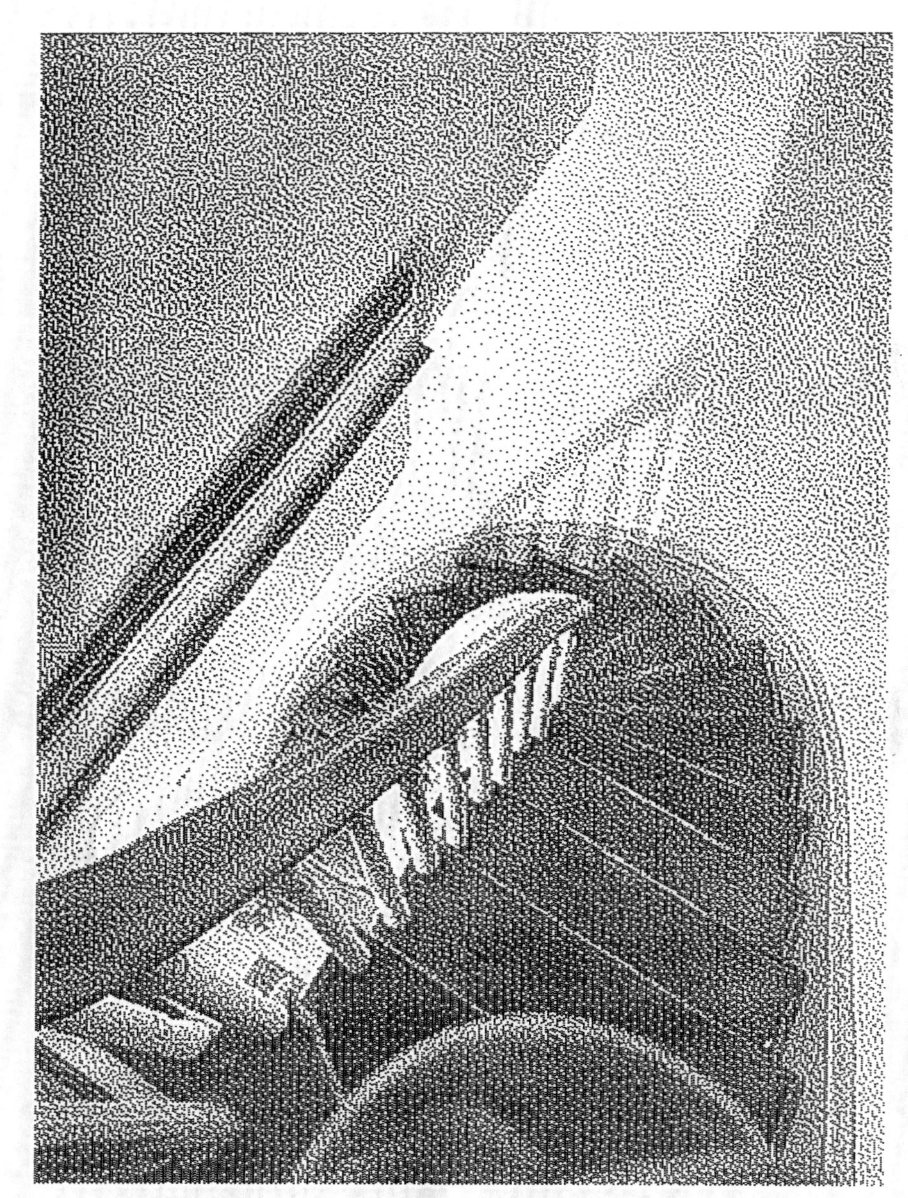

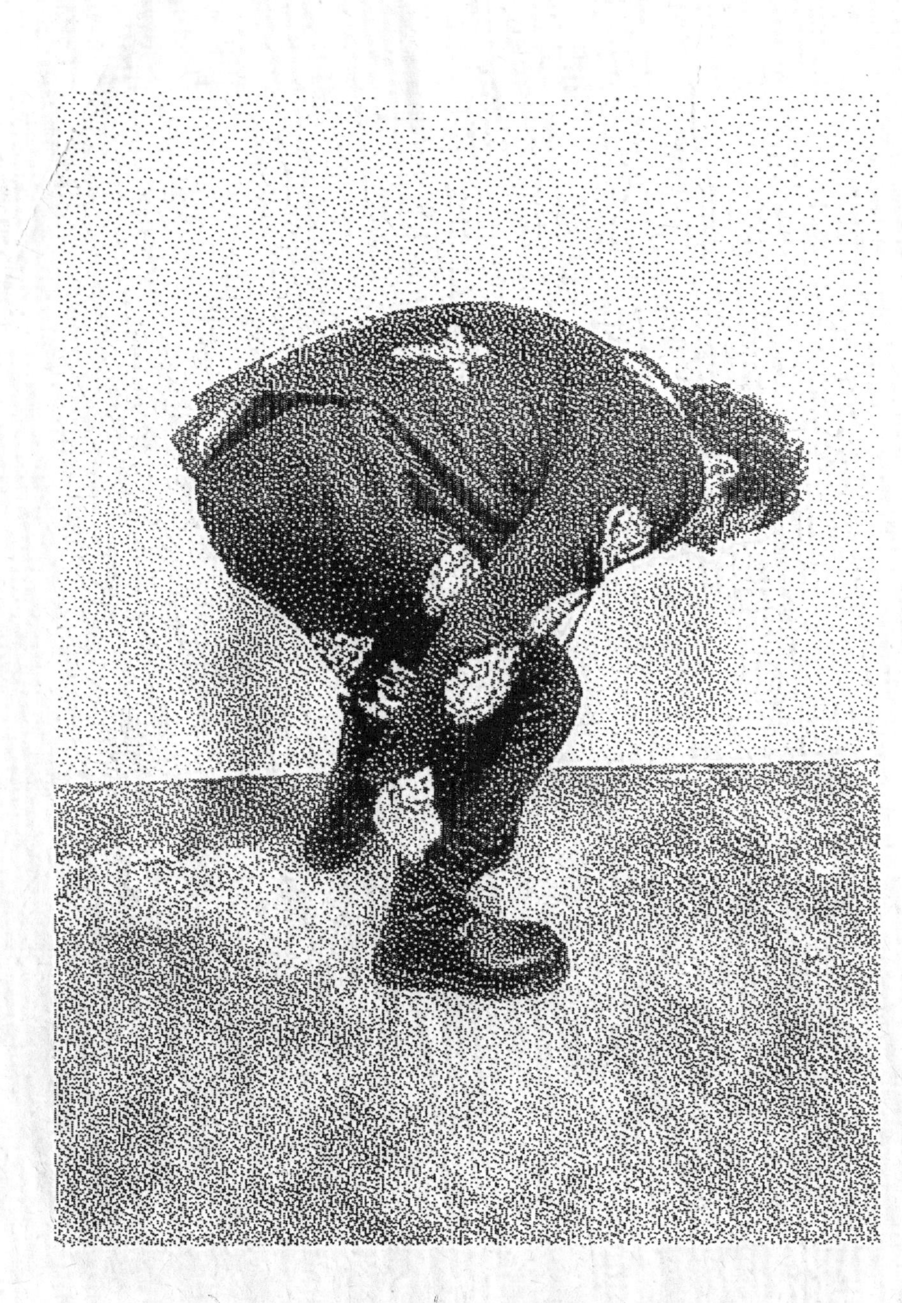

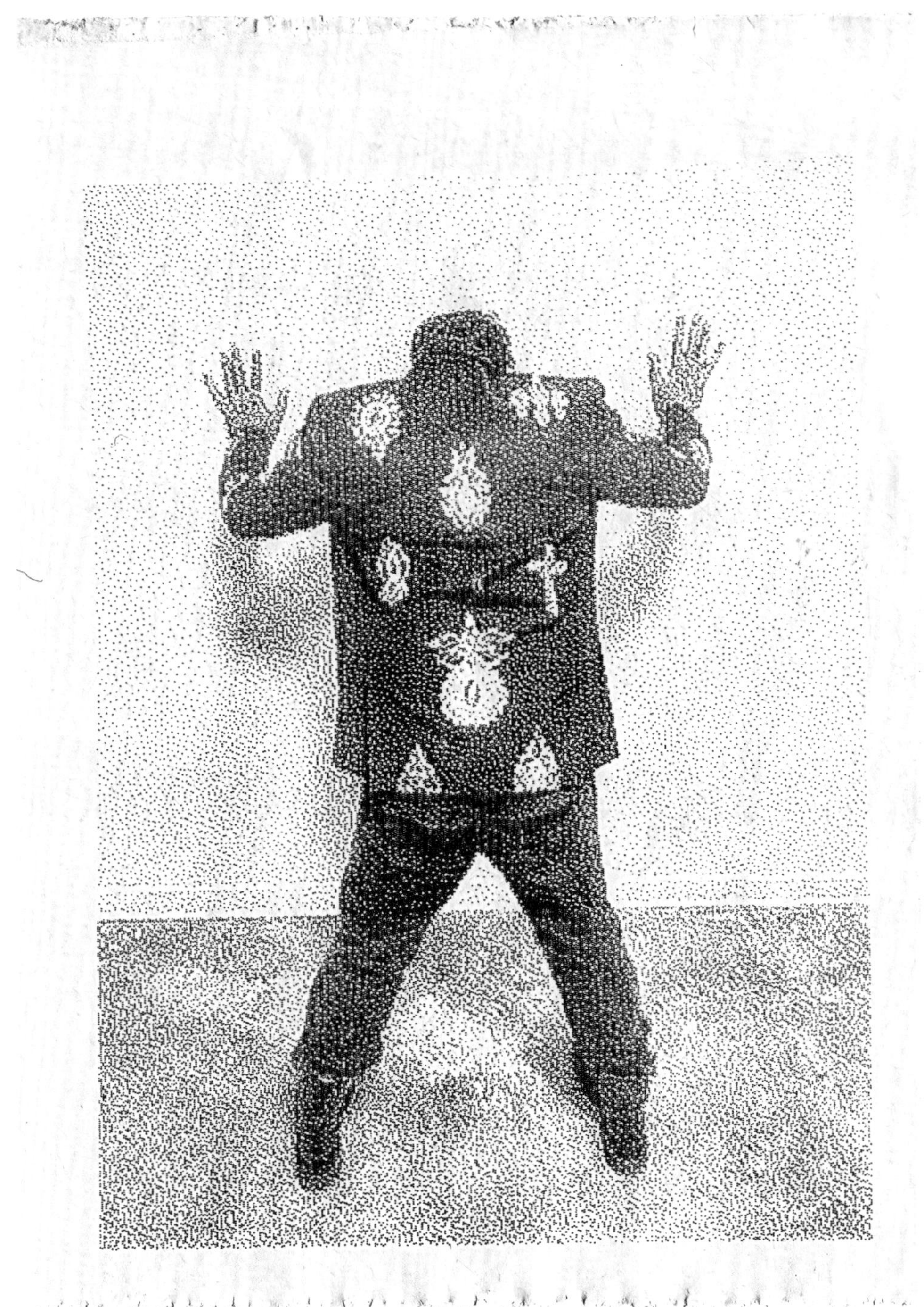

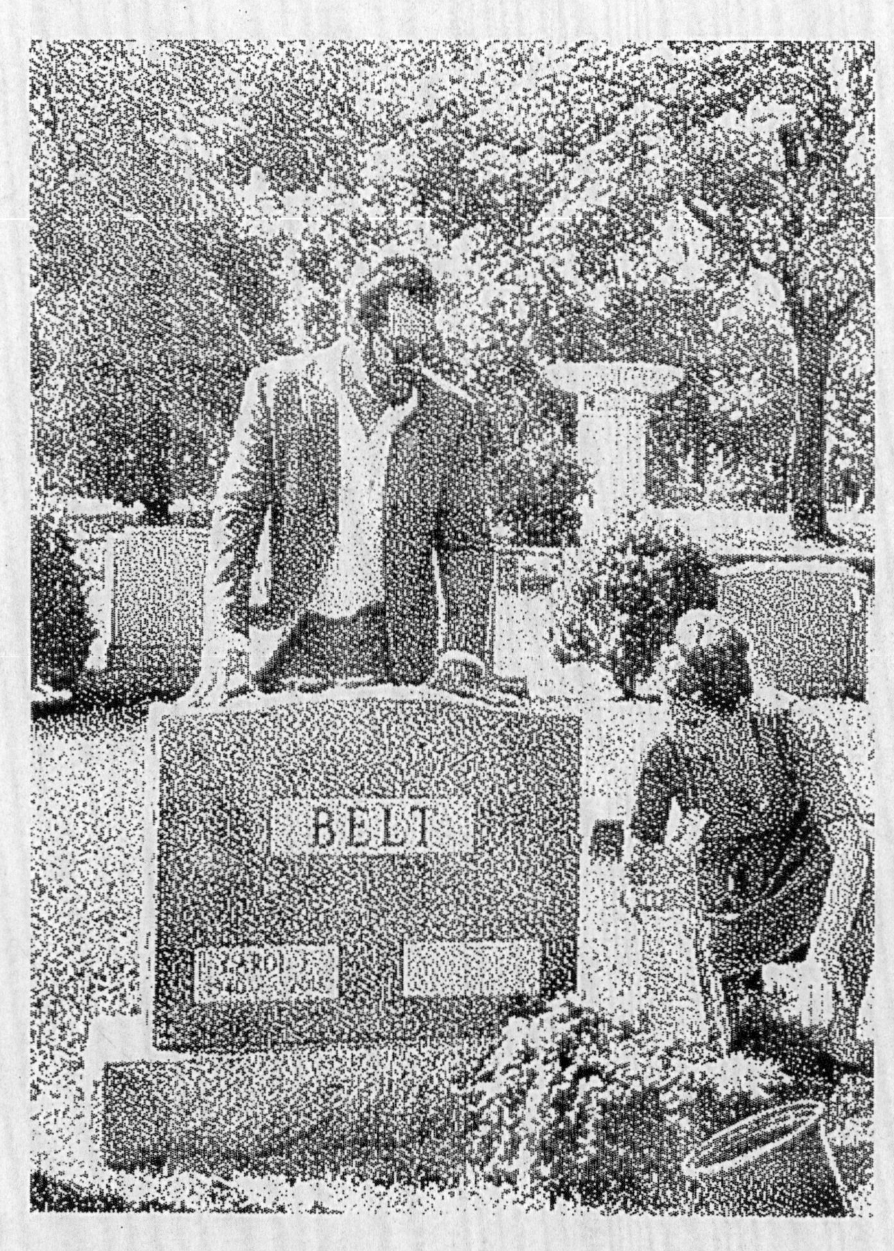
BELT

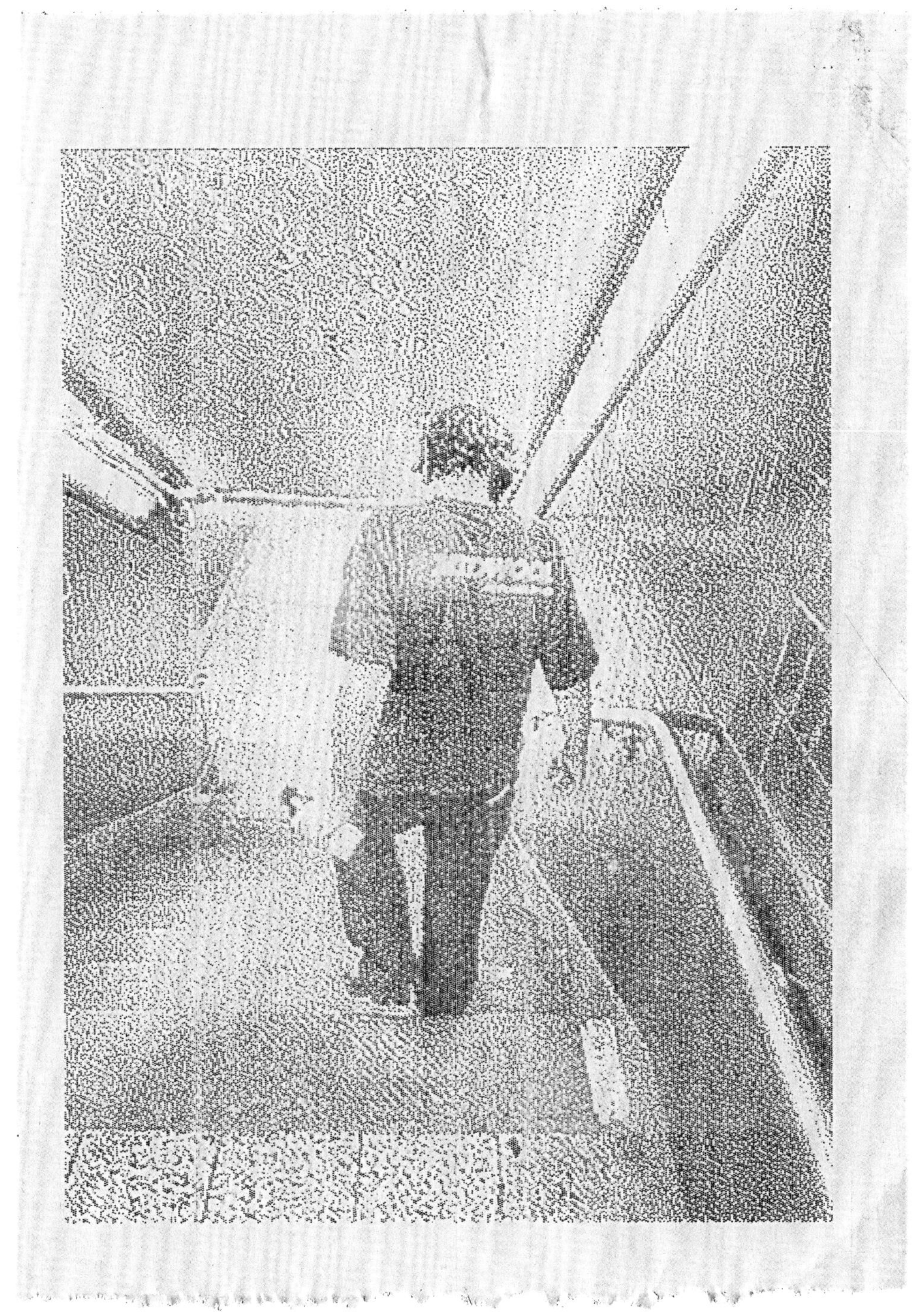

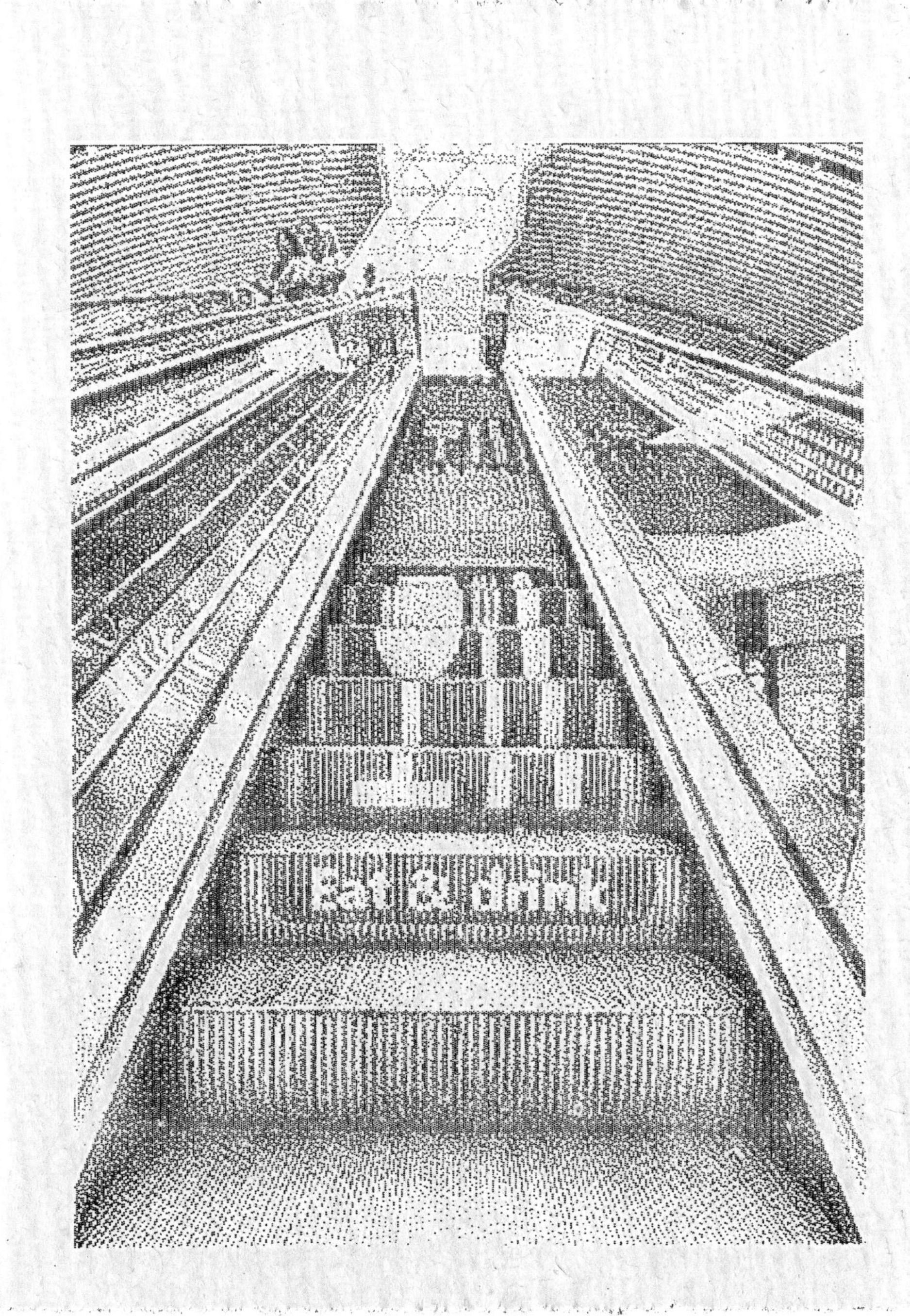
Eat & drink

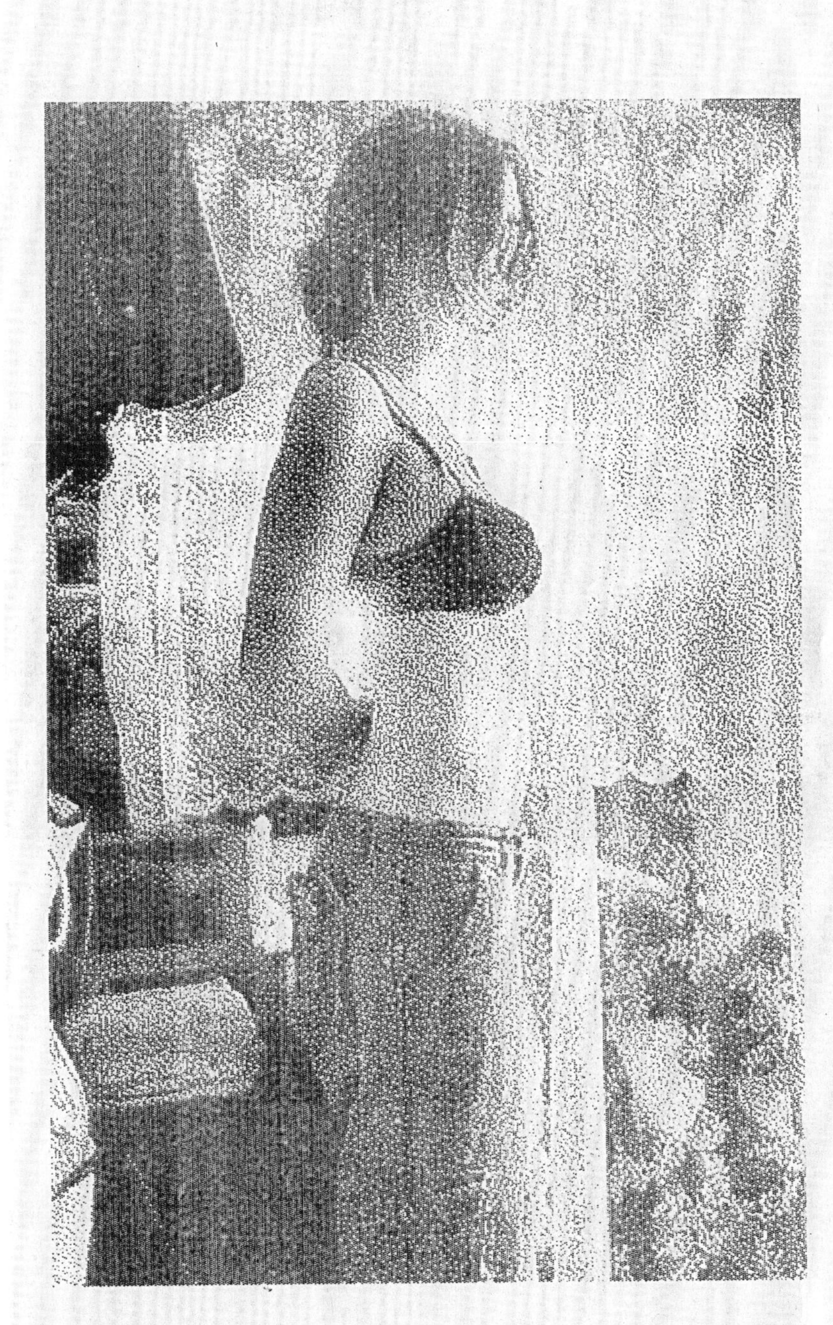

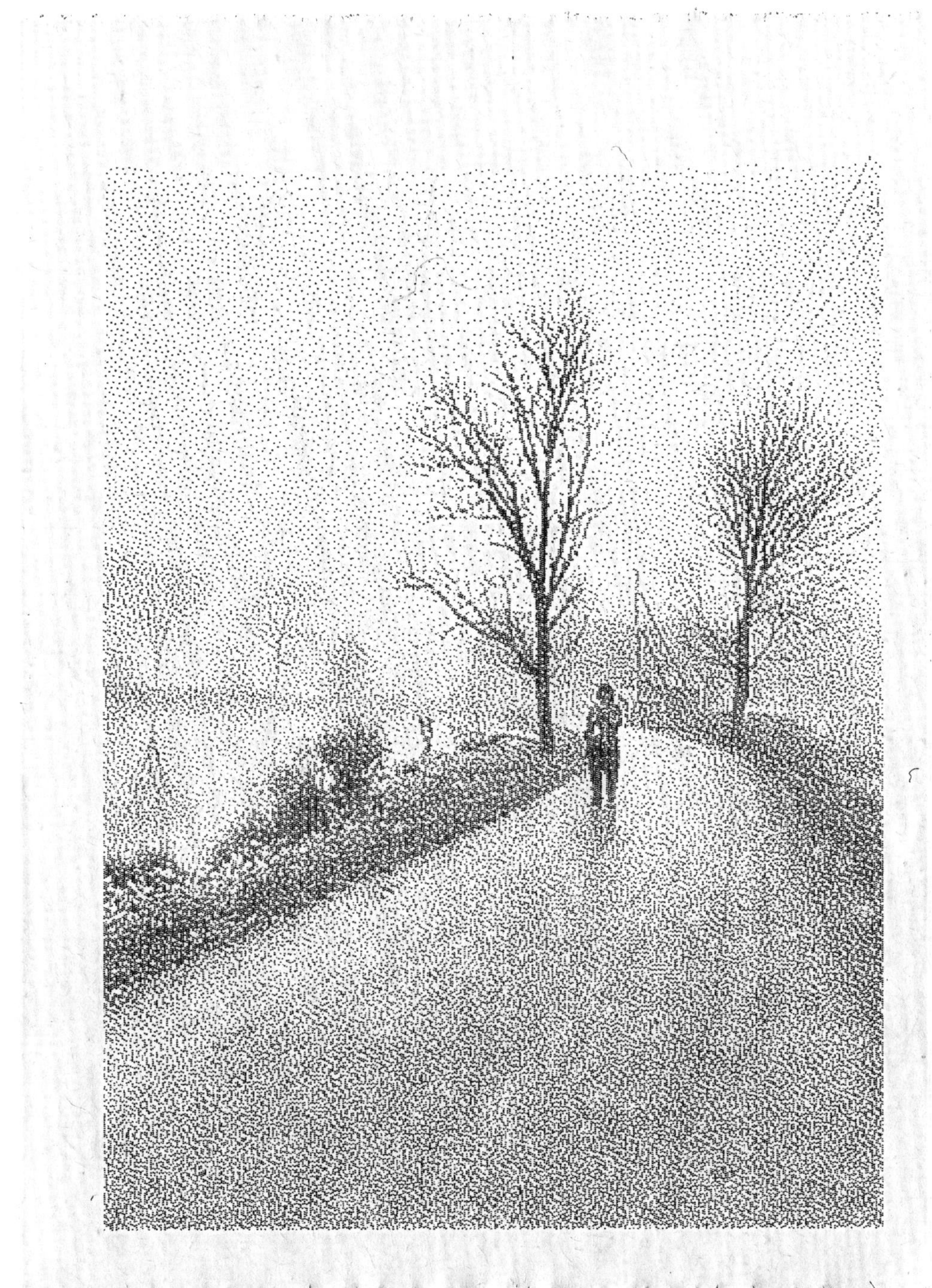

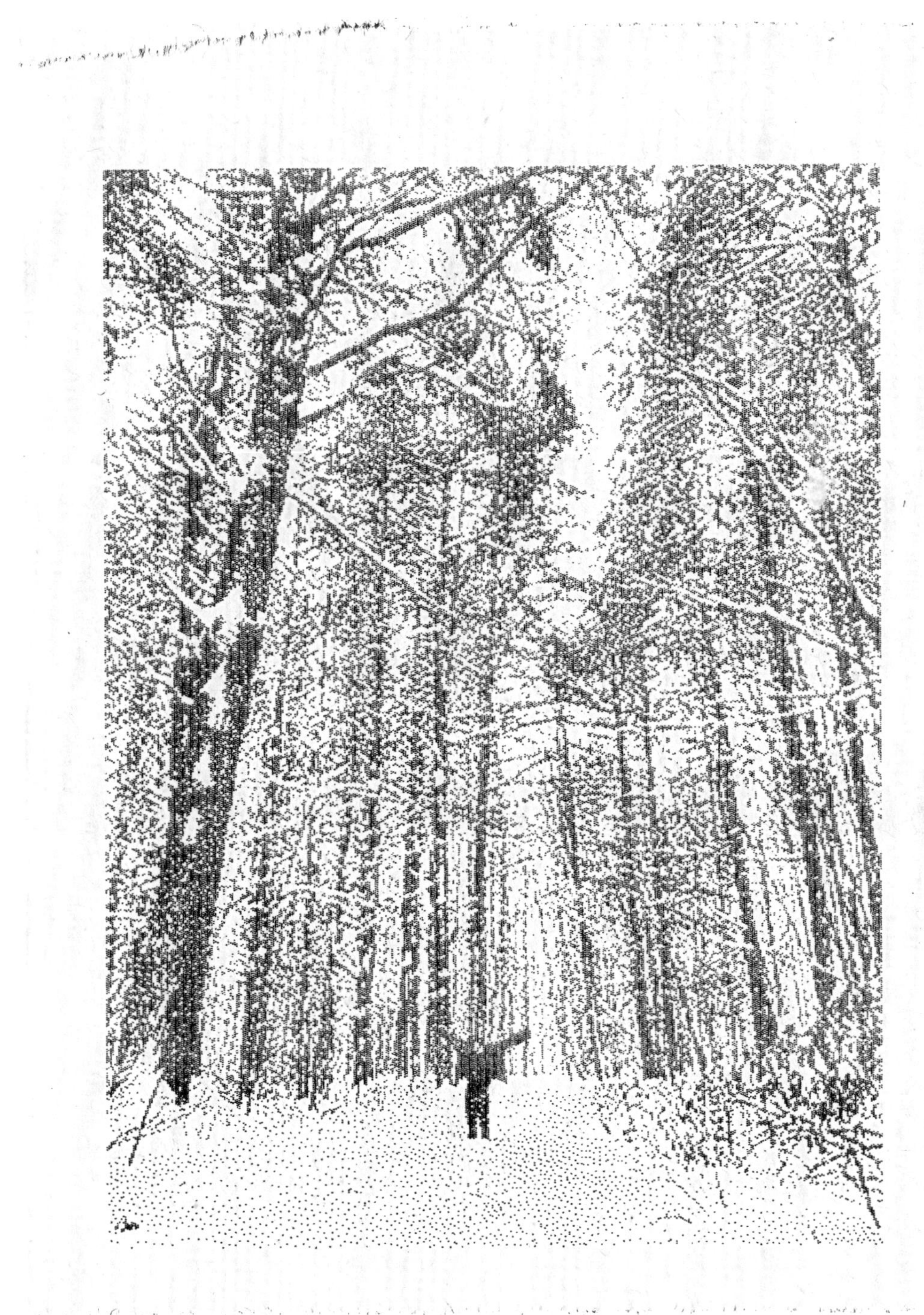

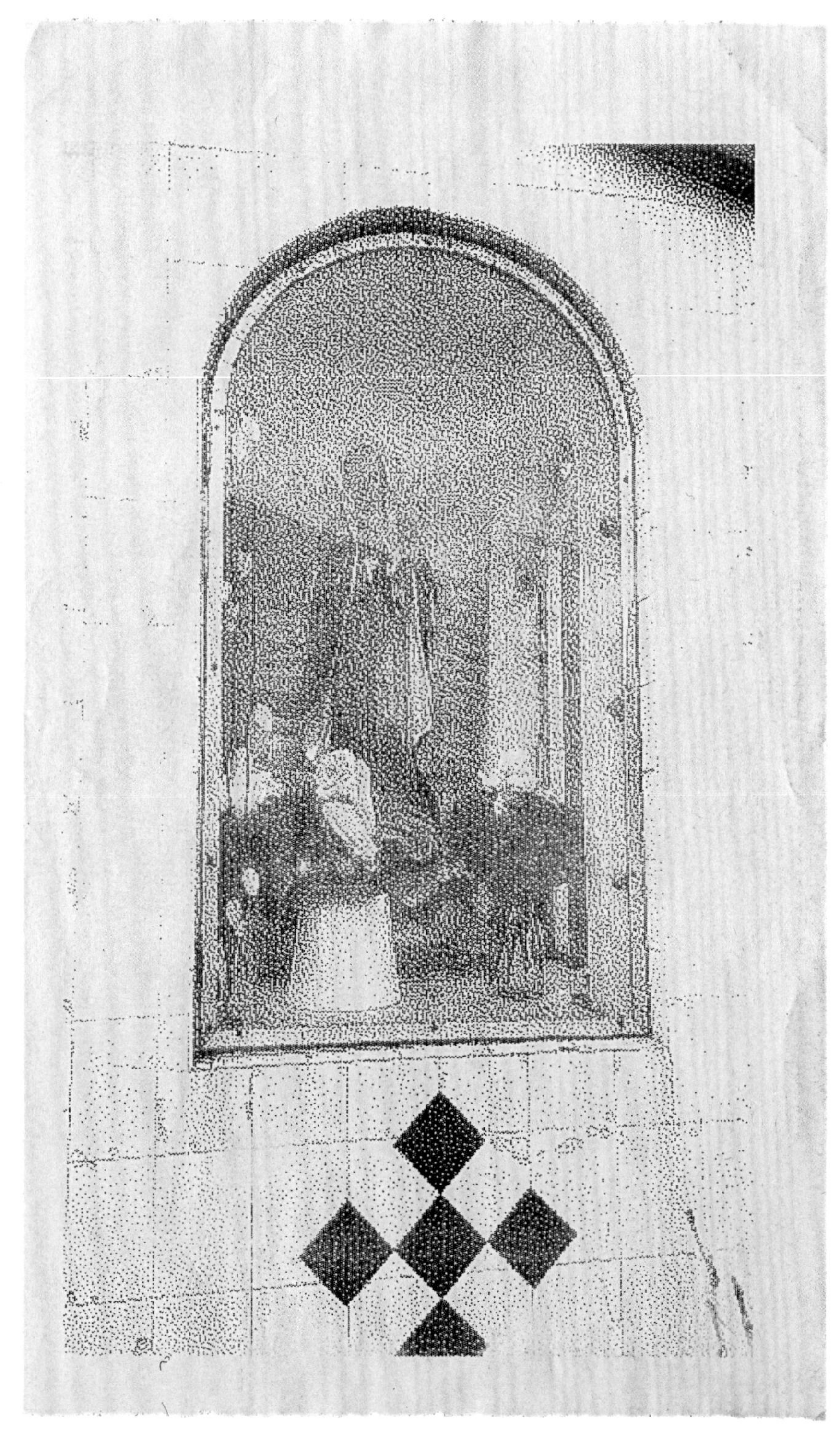

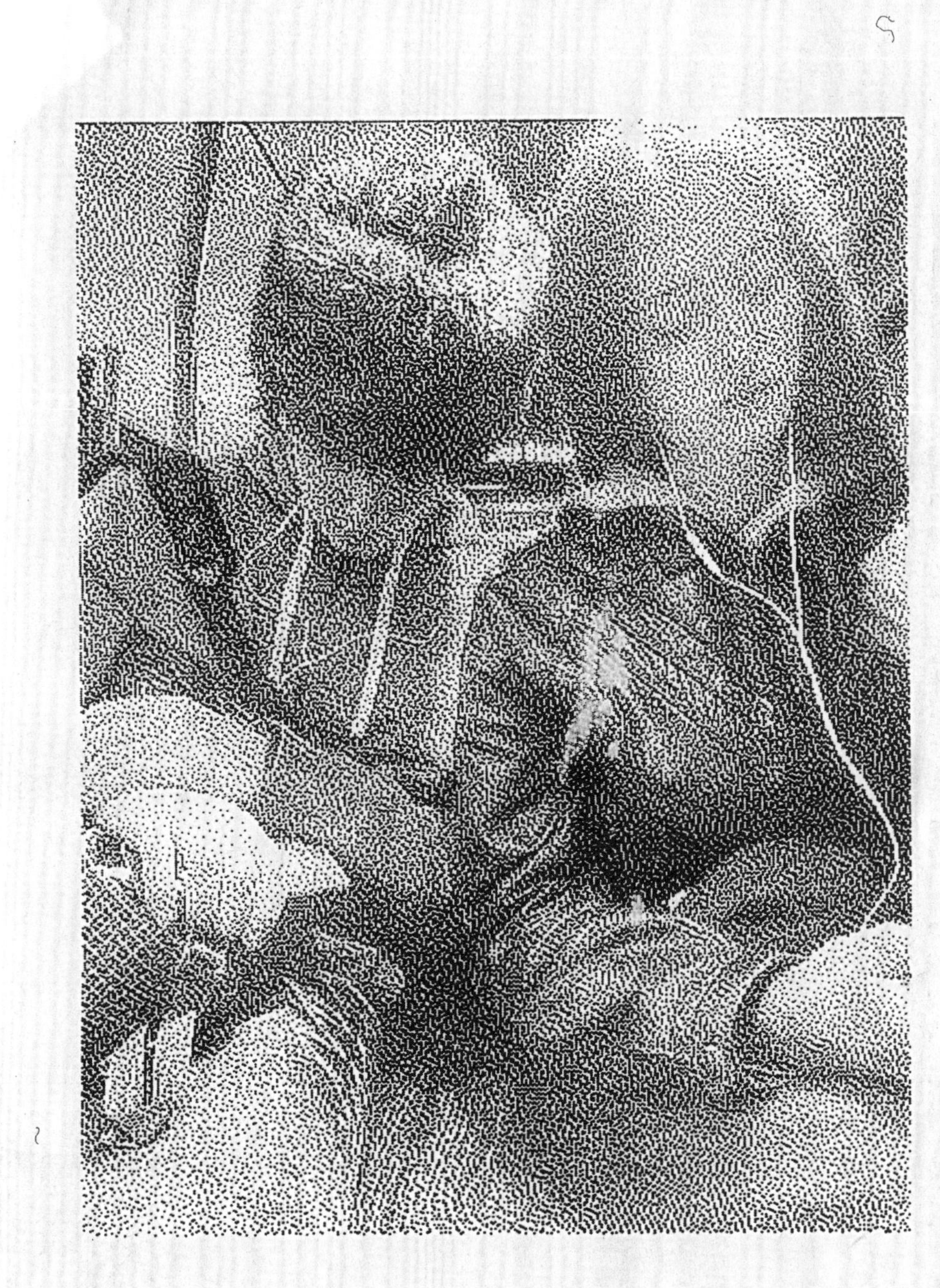

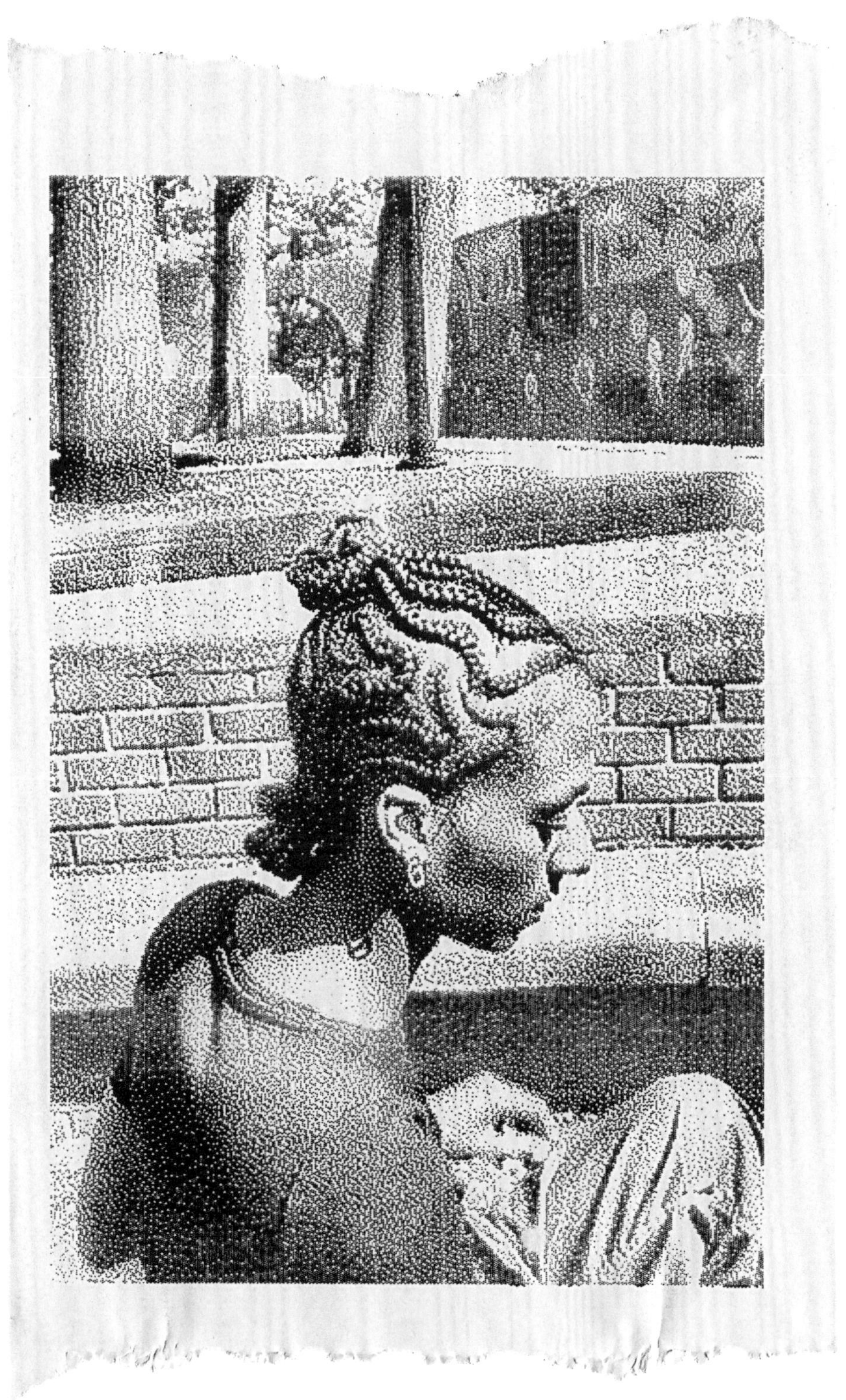

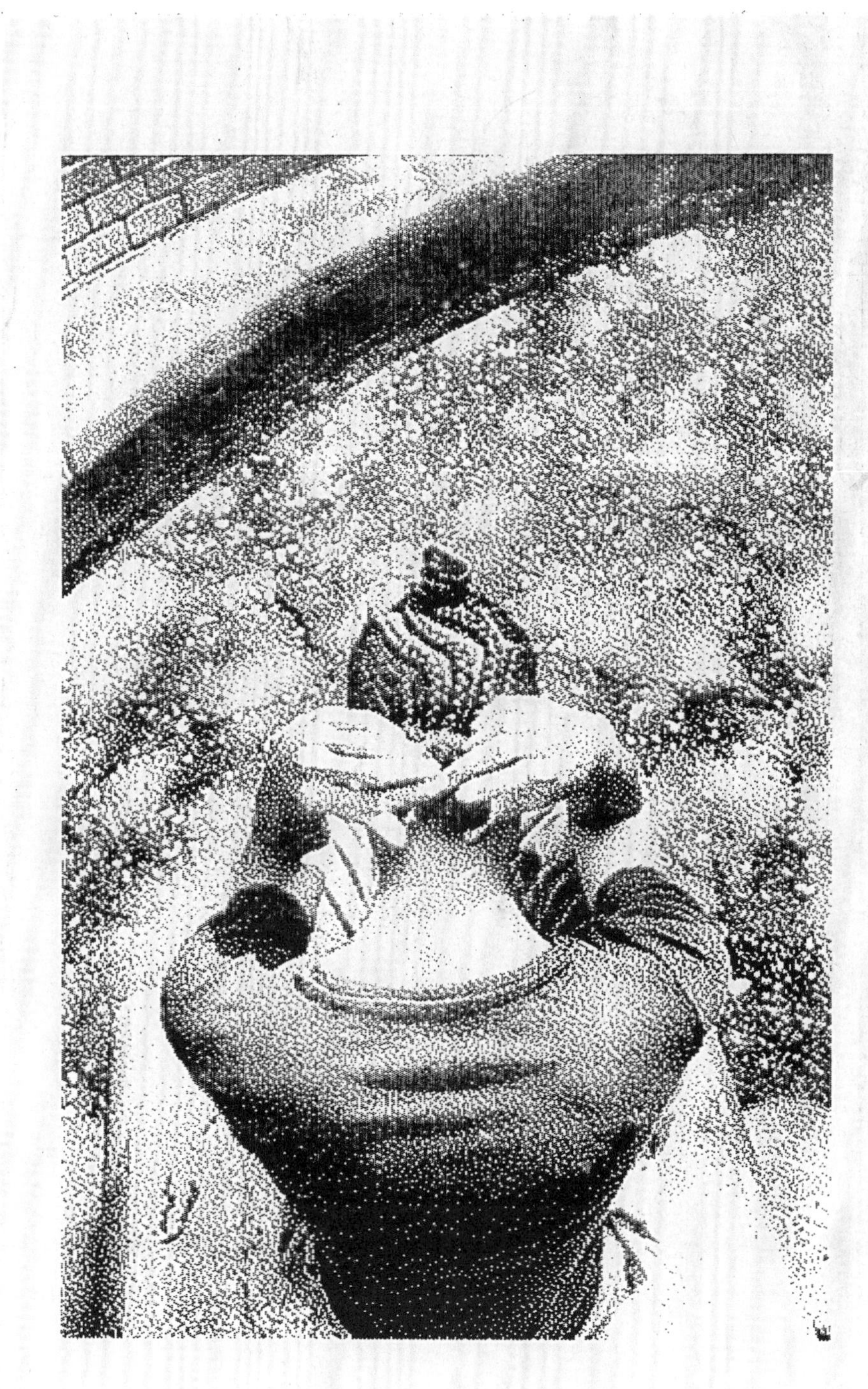

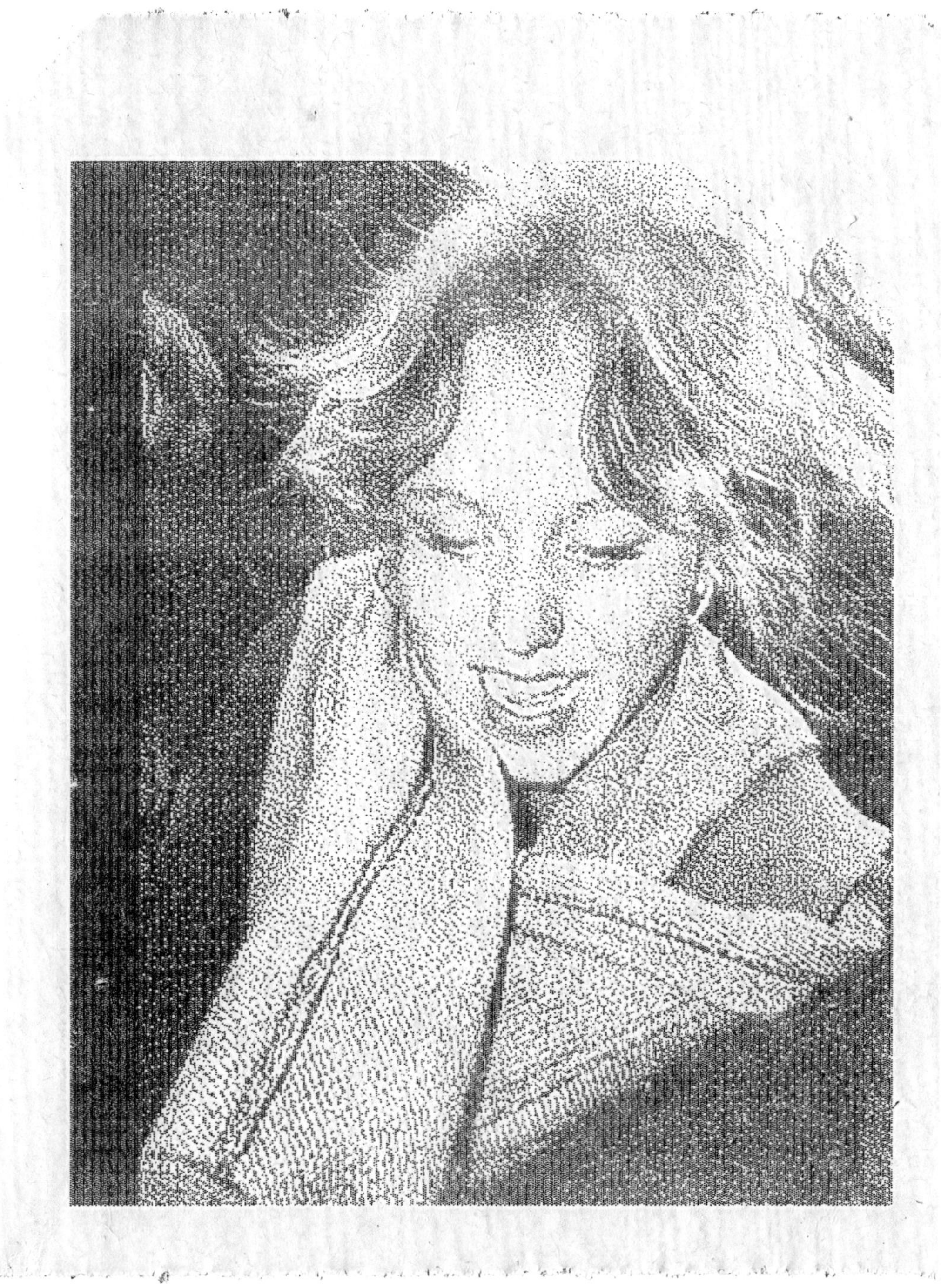

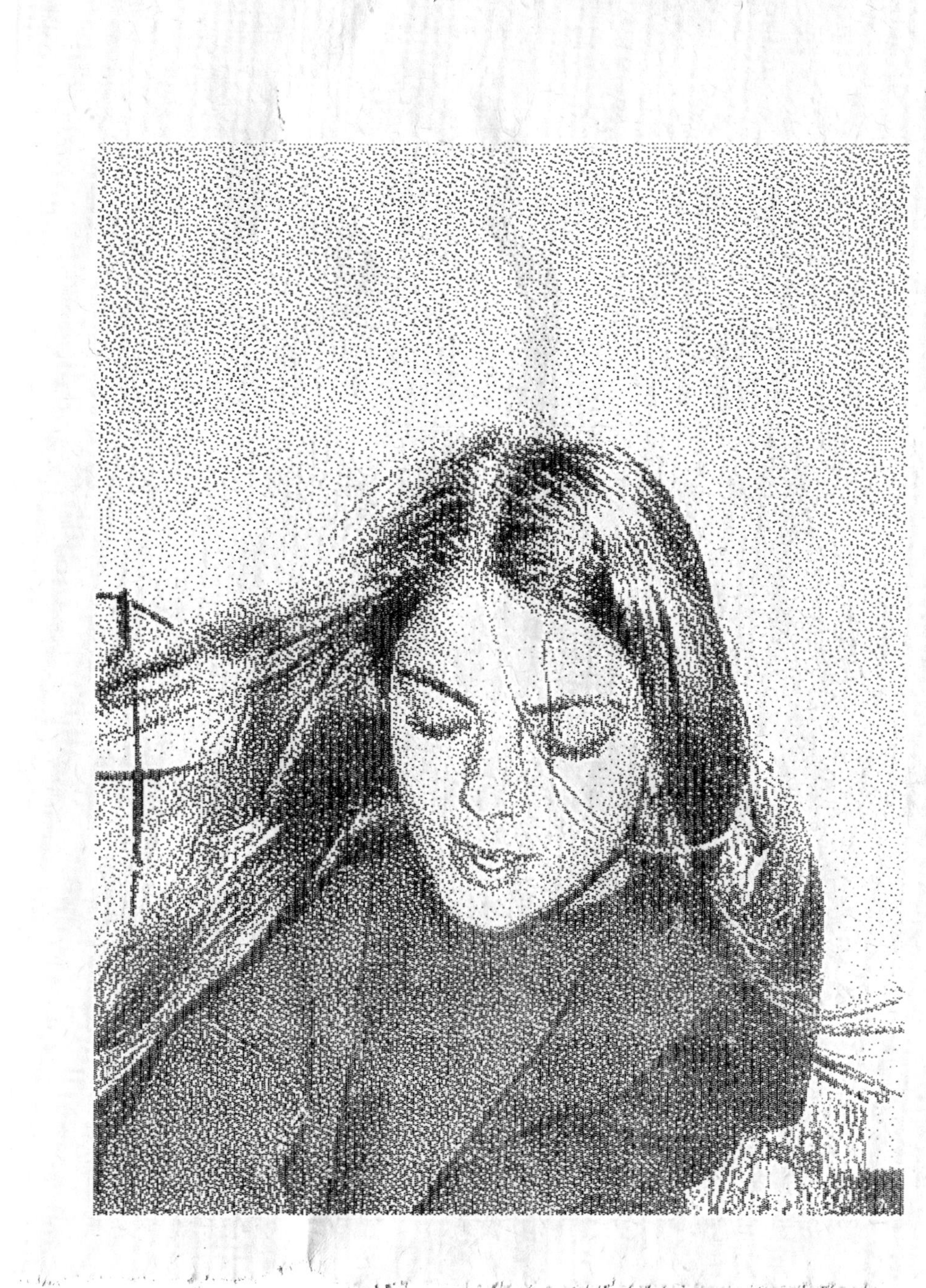

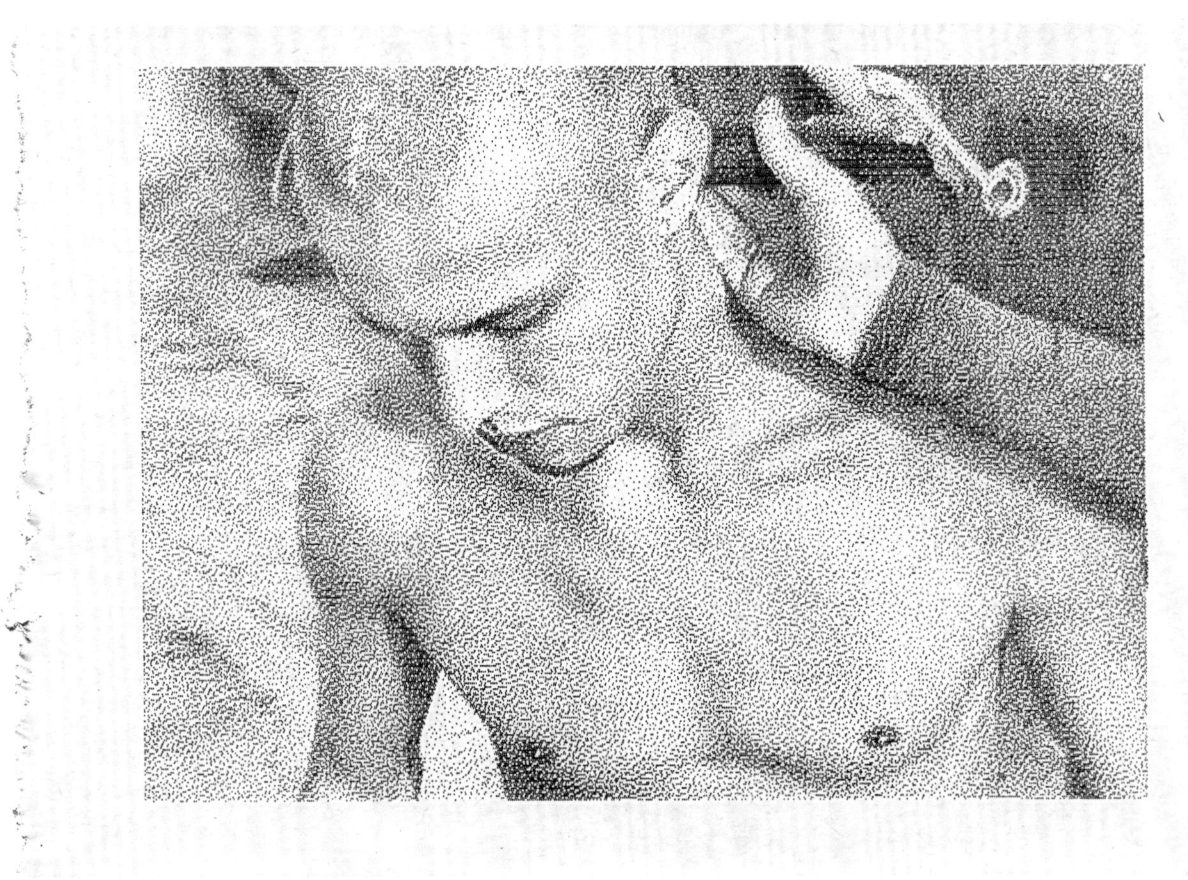

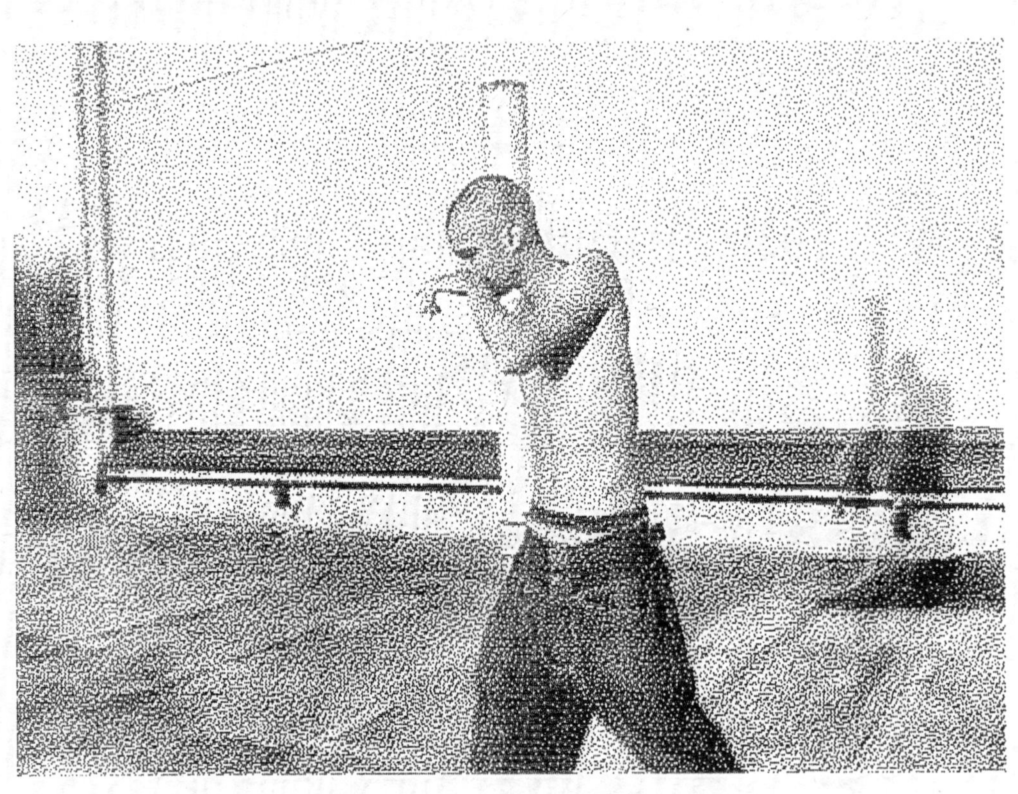

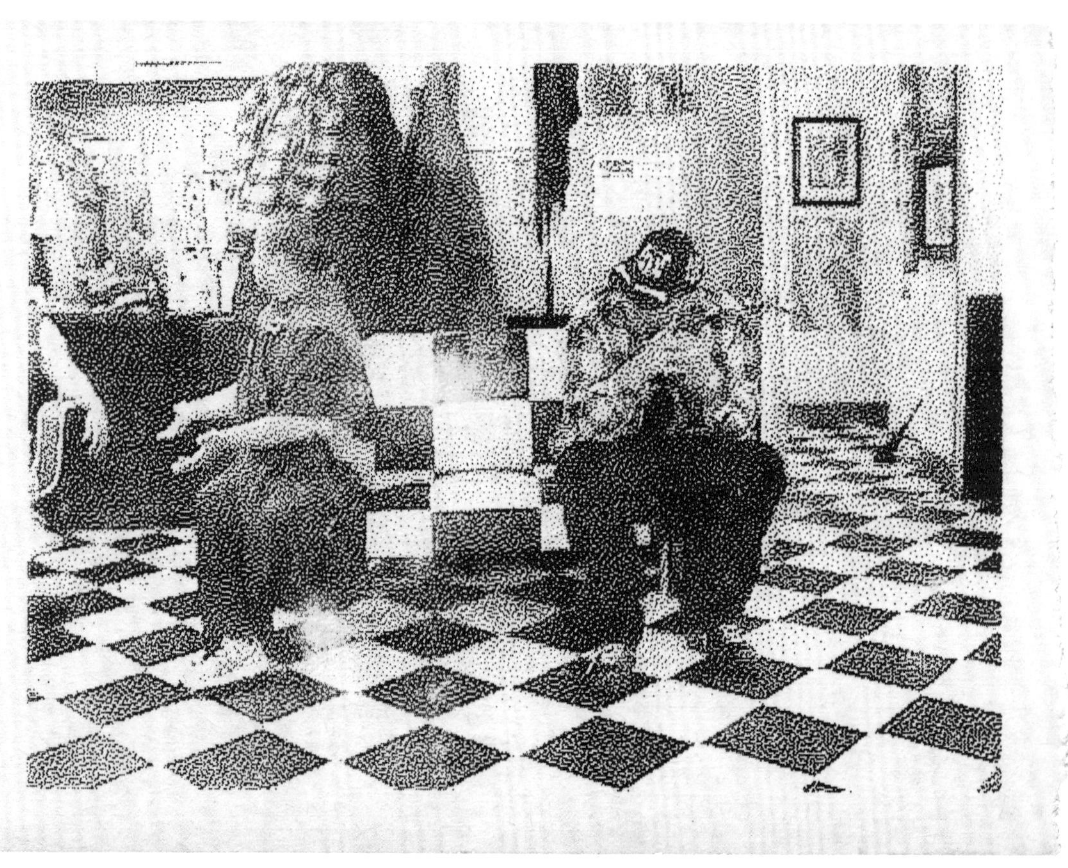

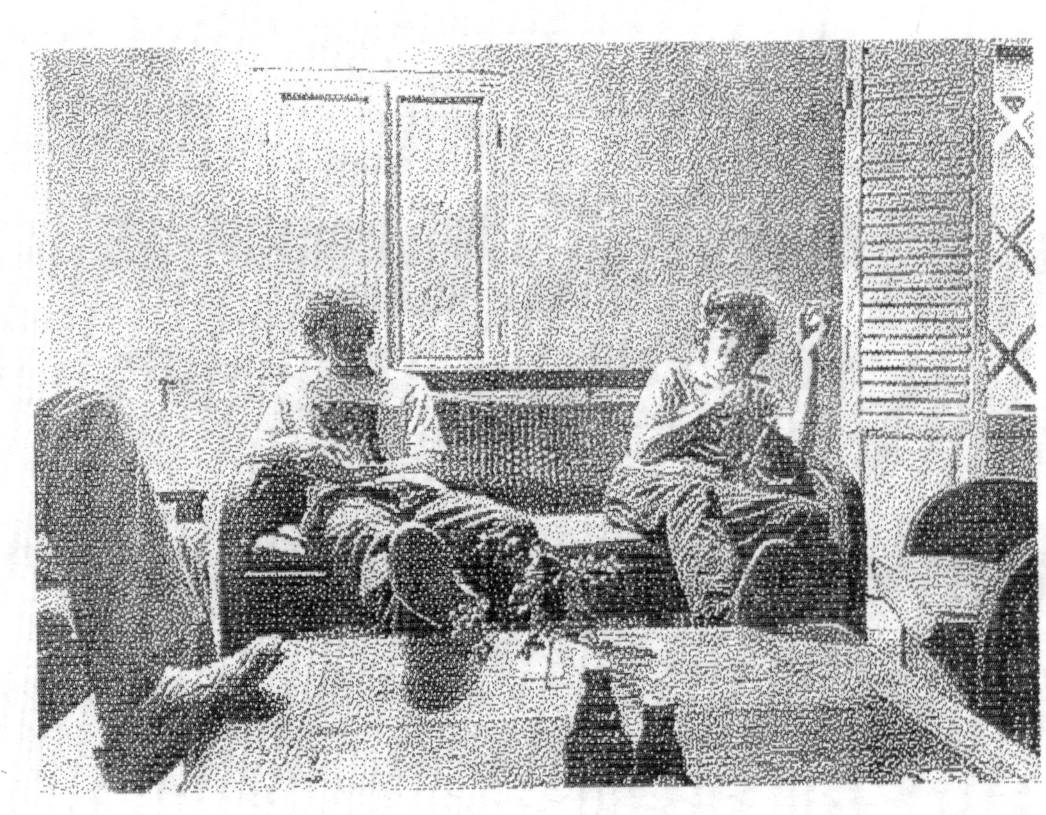

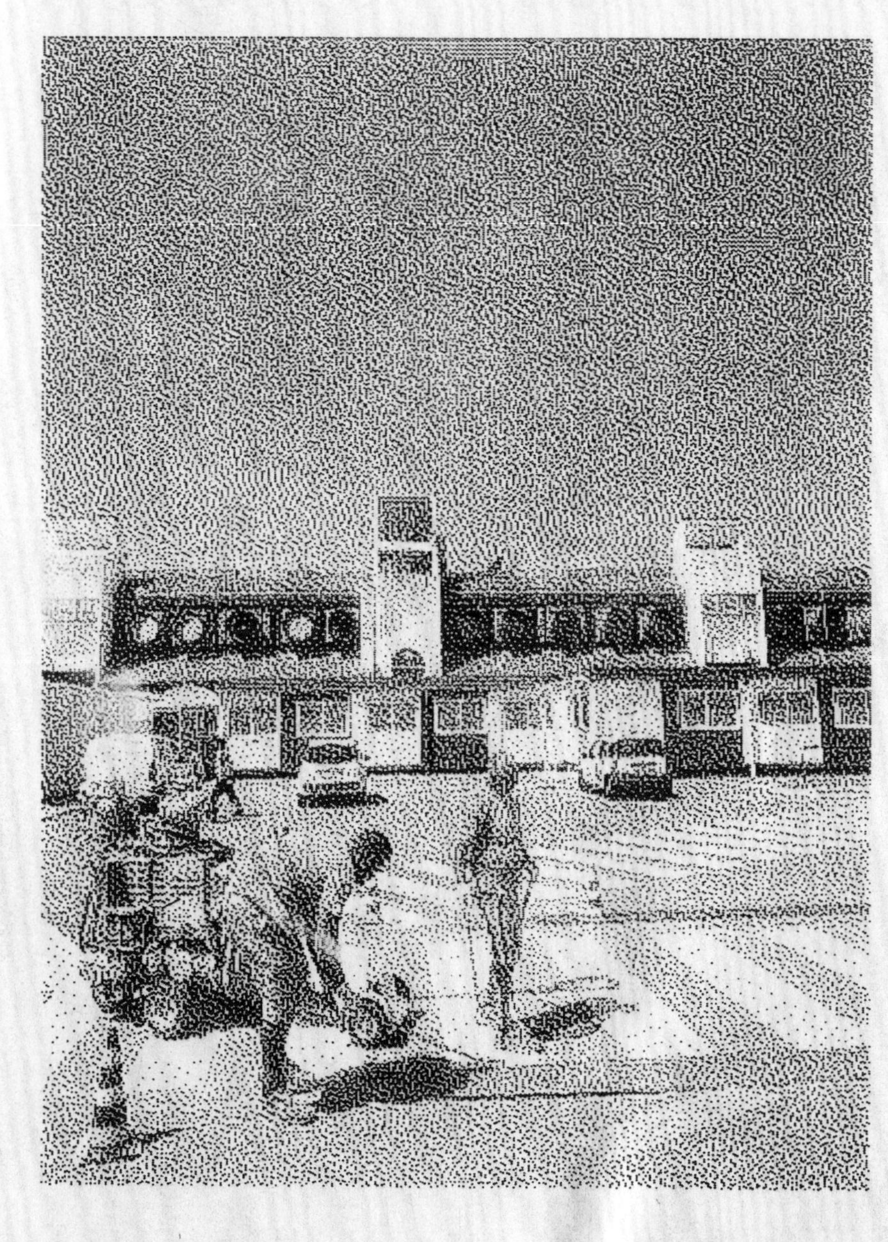

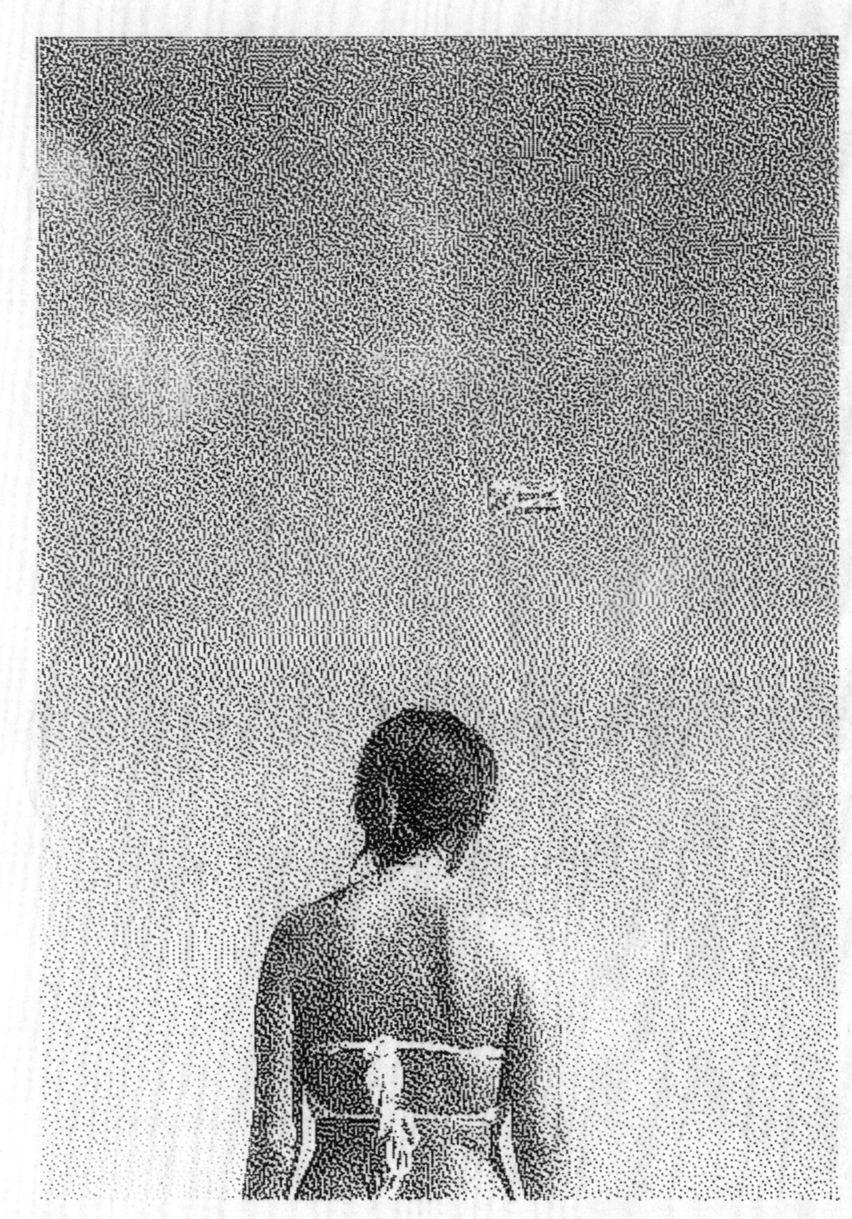

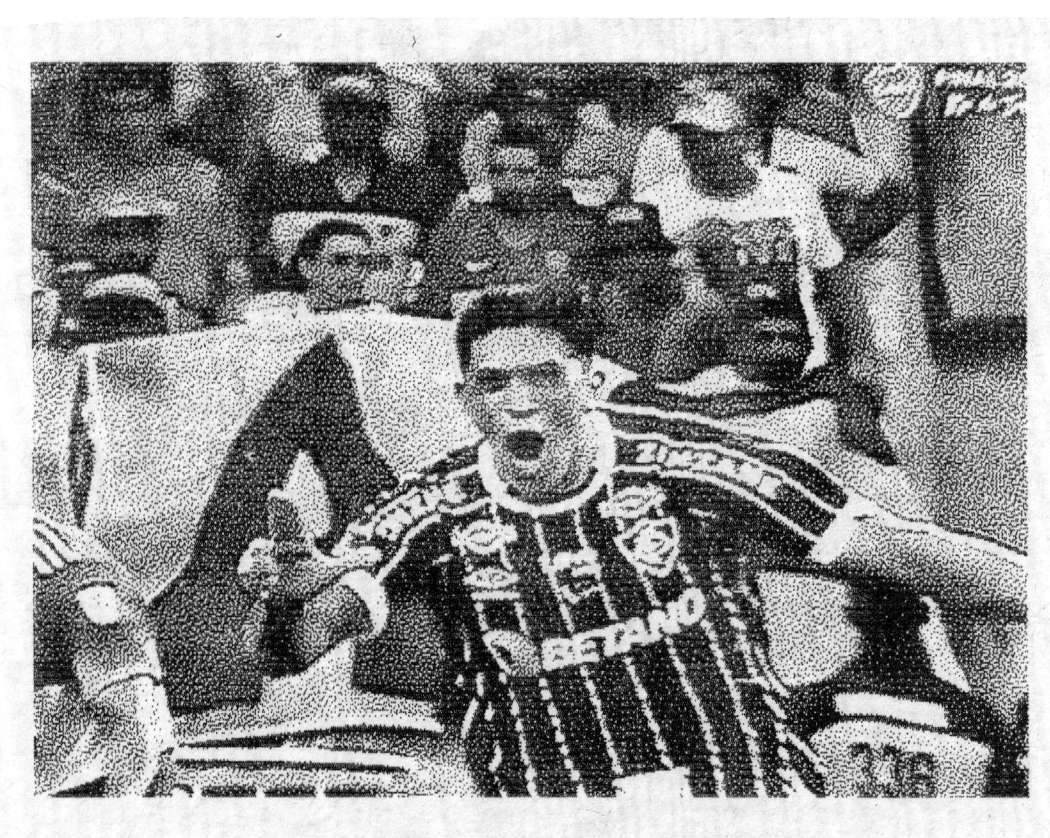
BETANO

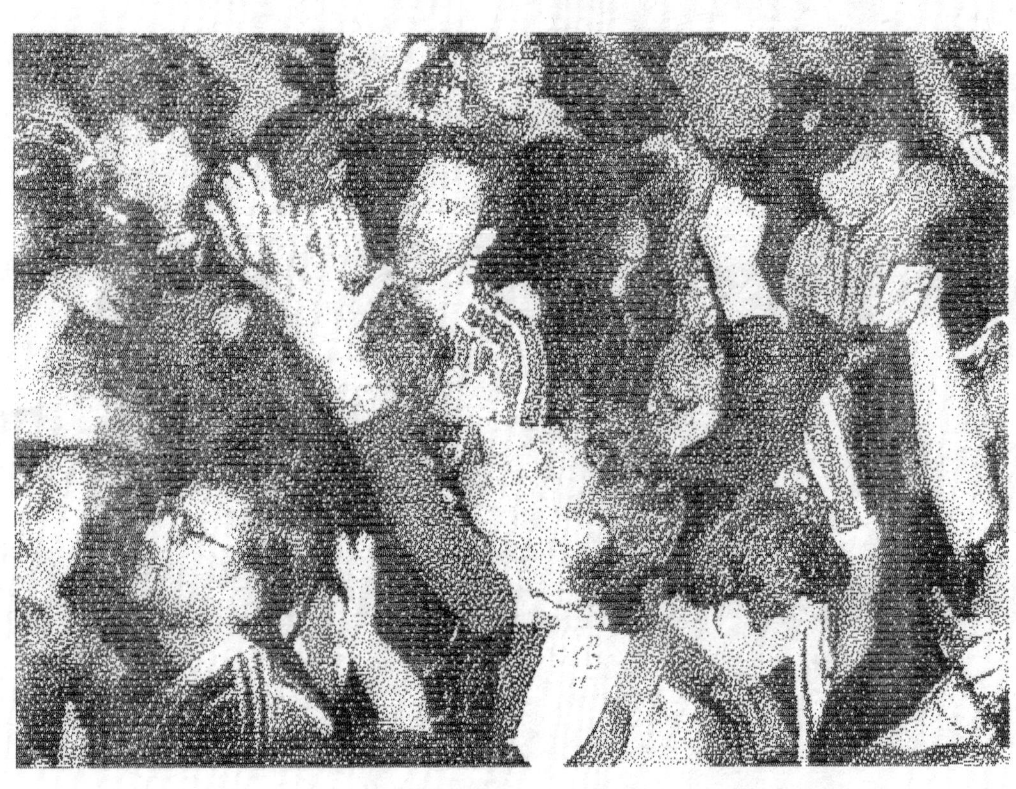

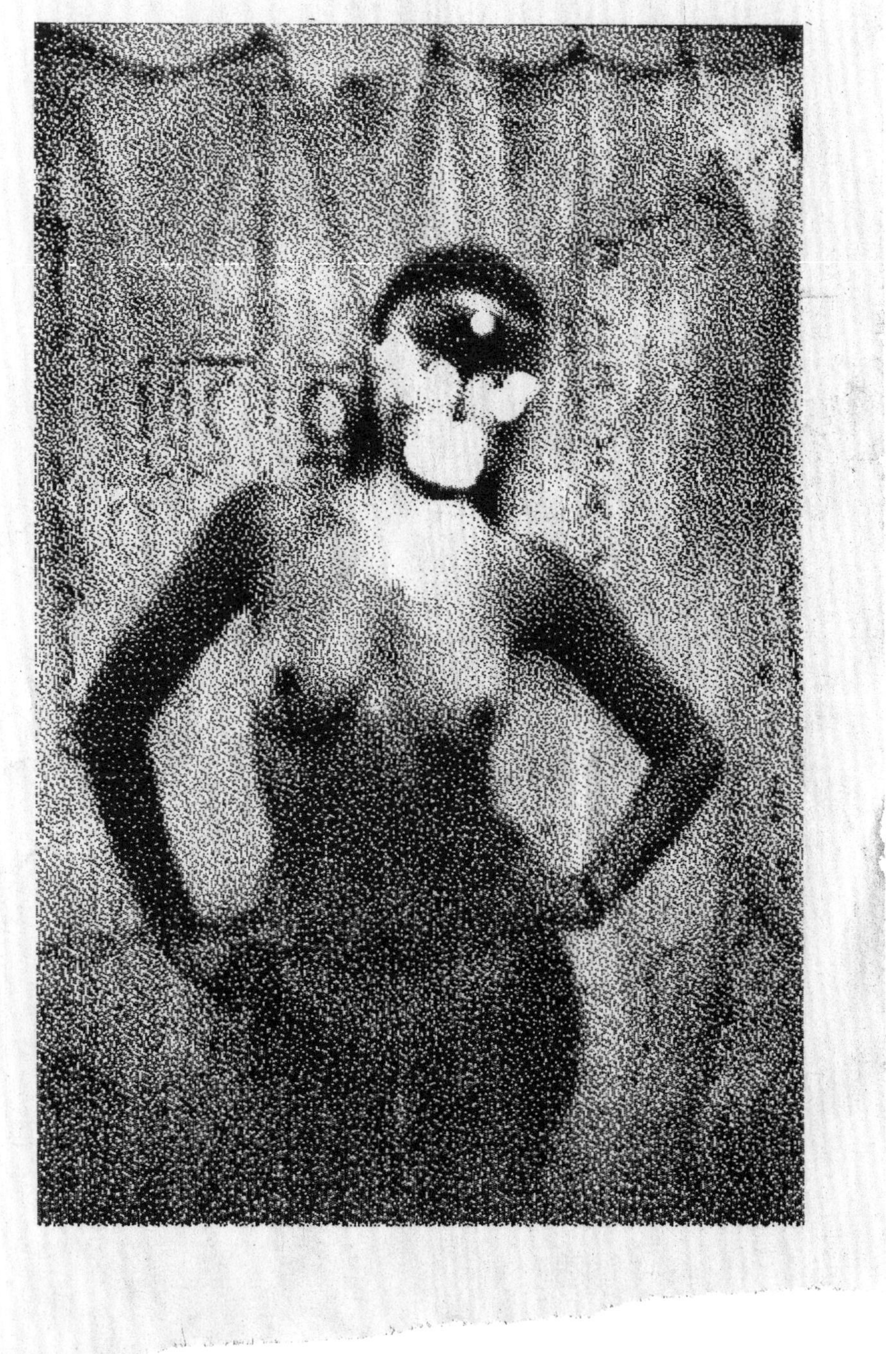

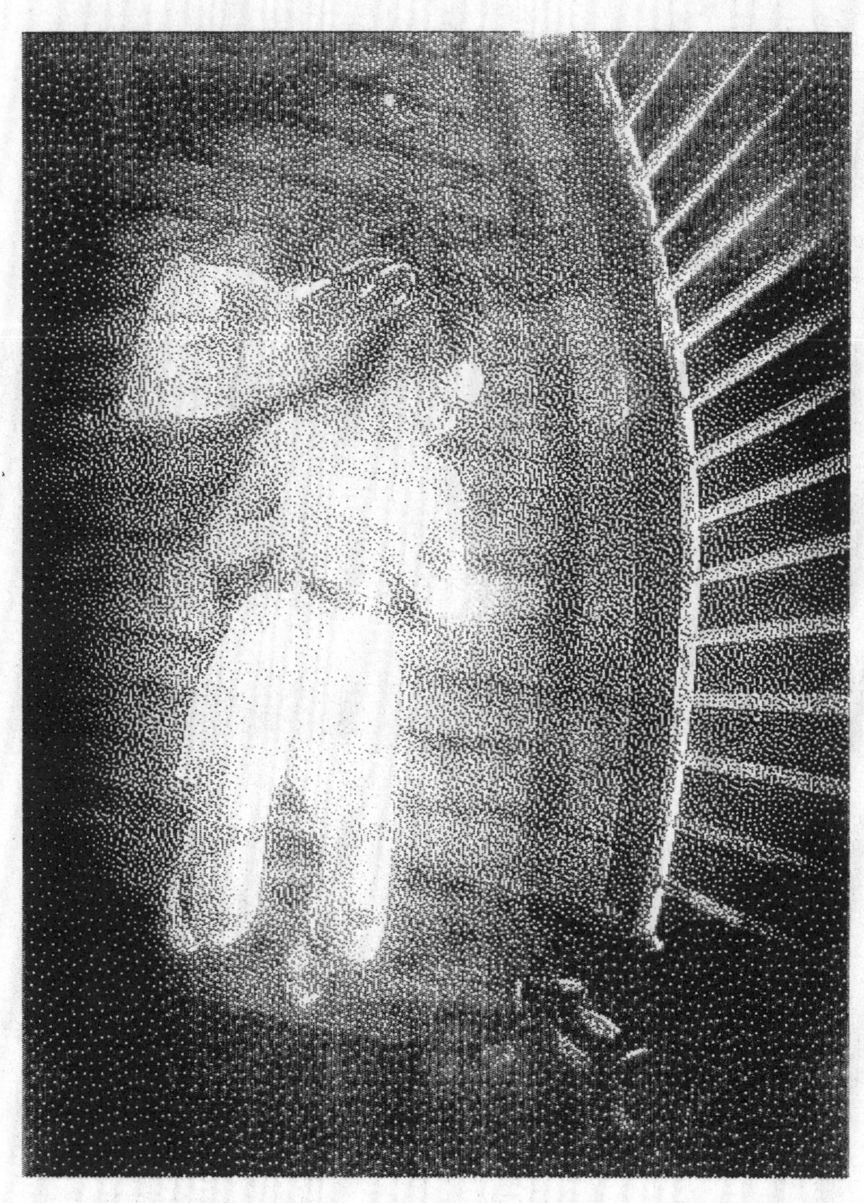

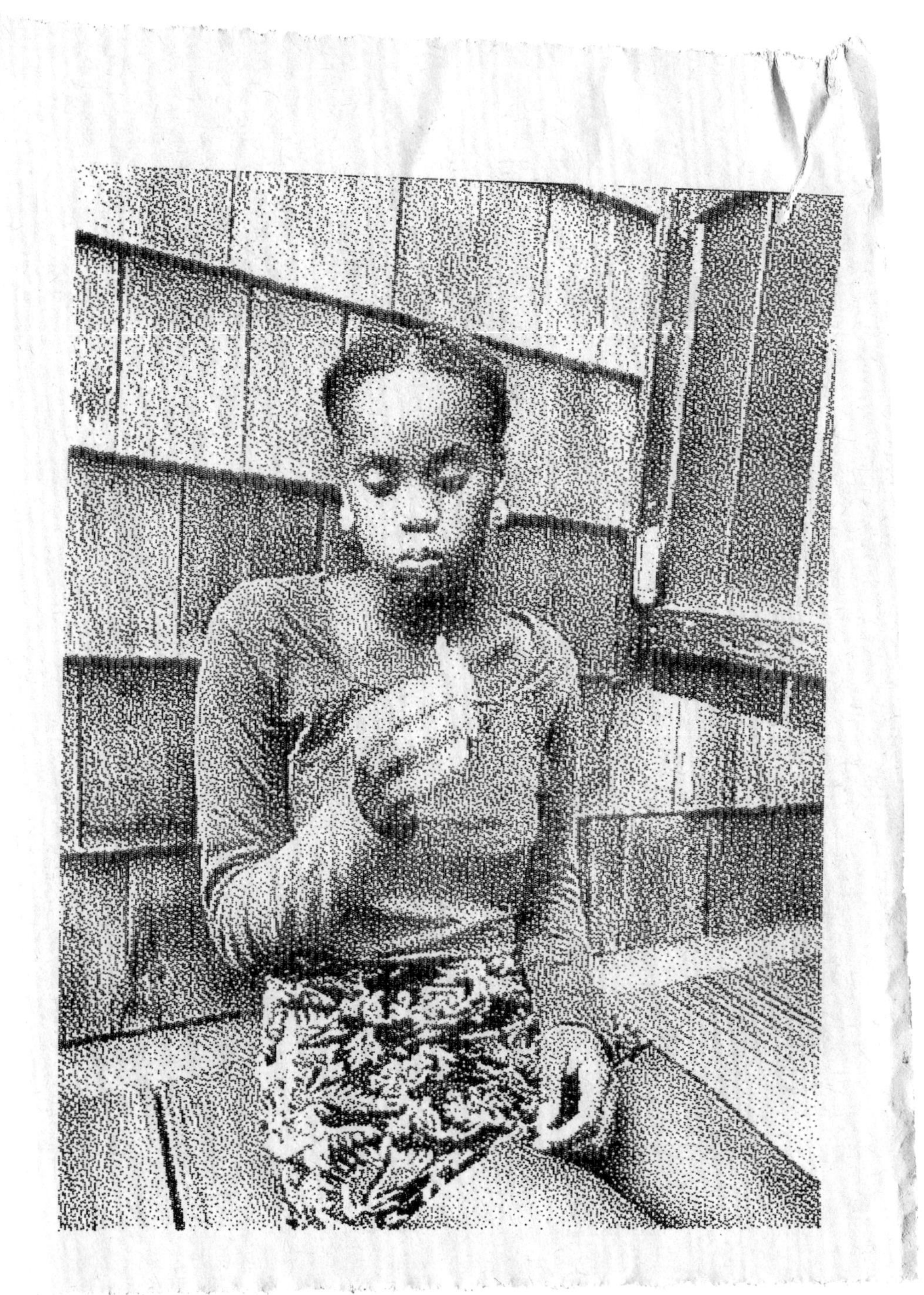

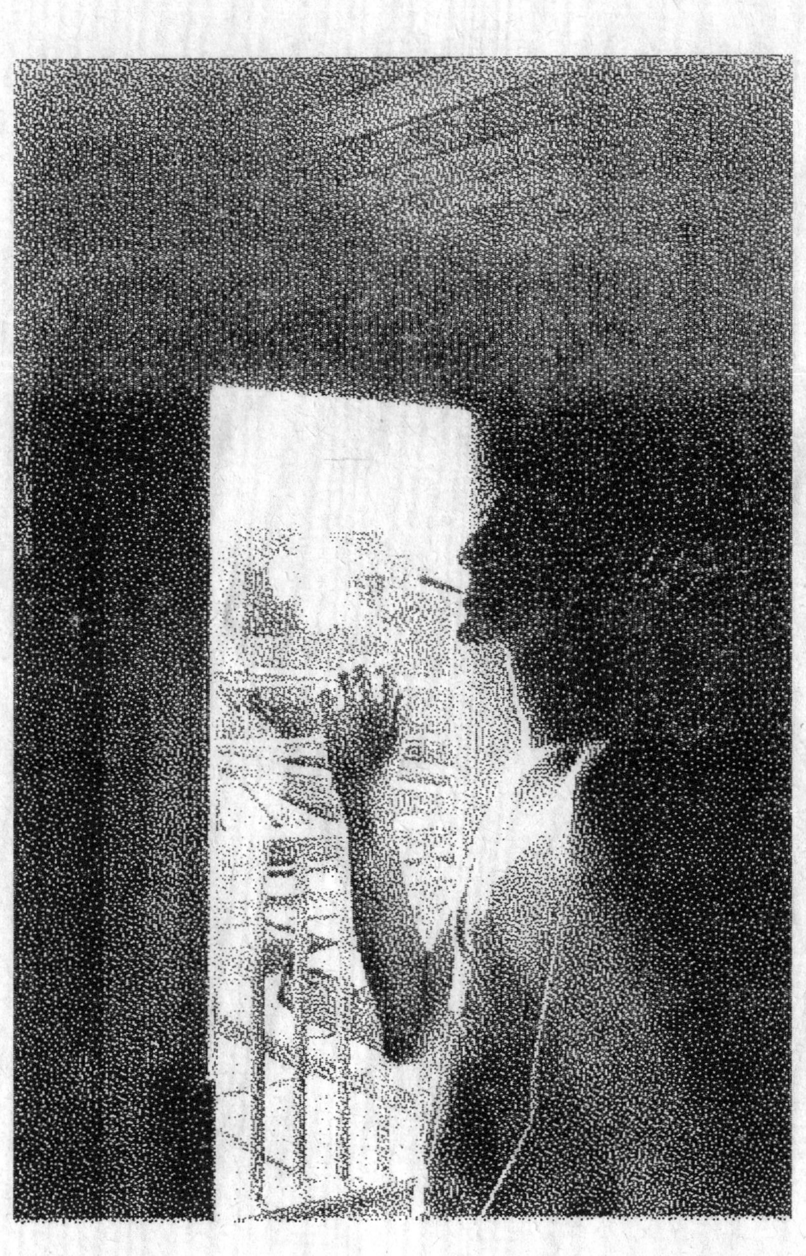

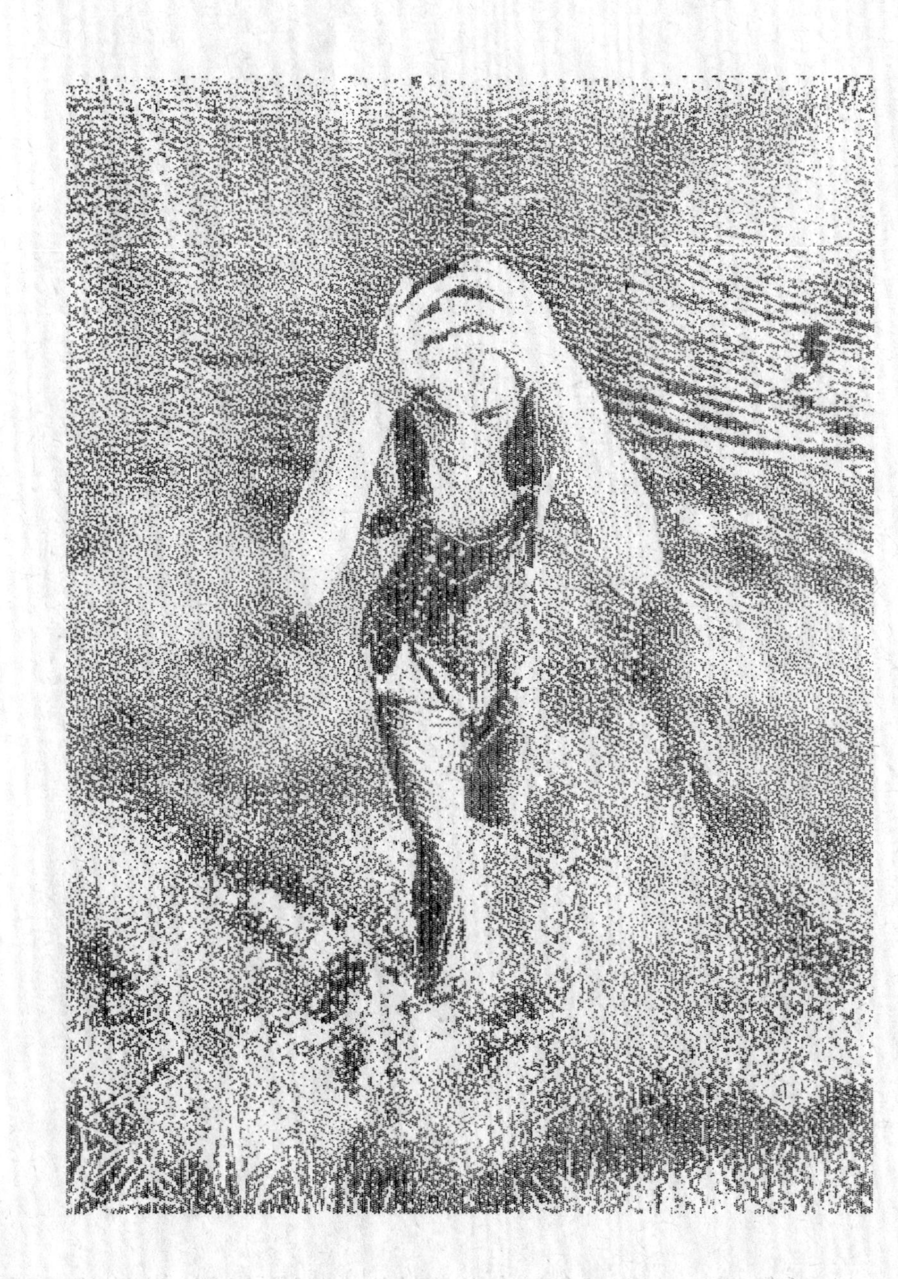

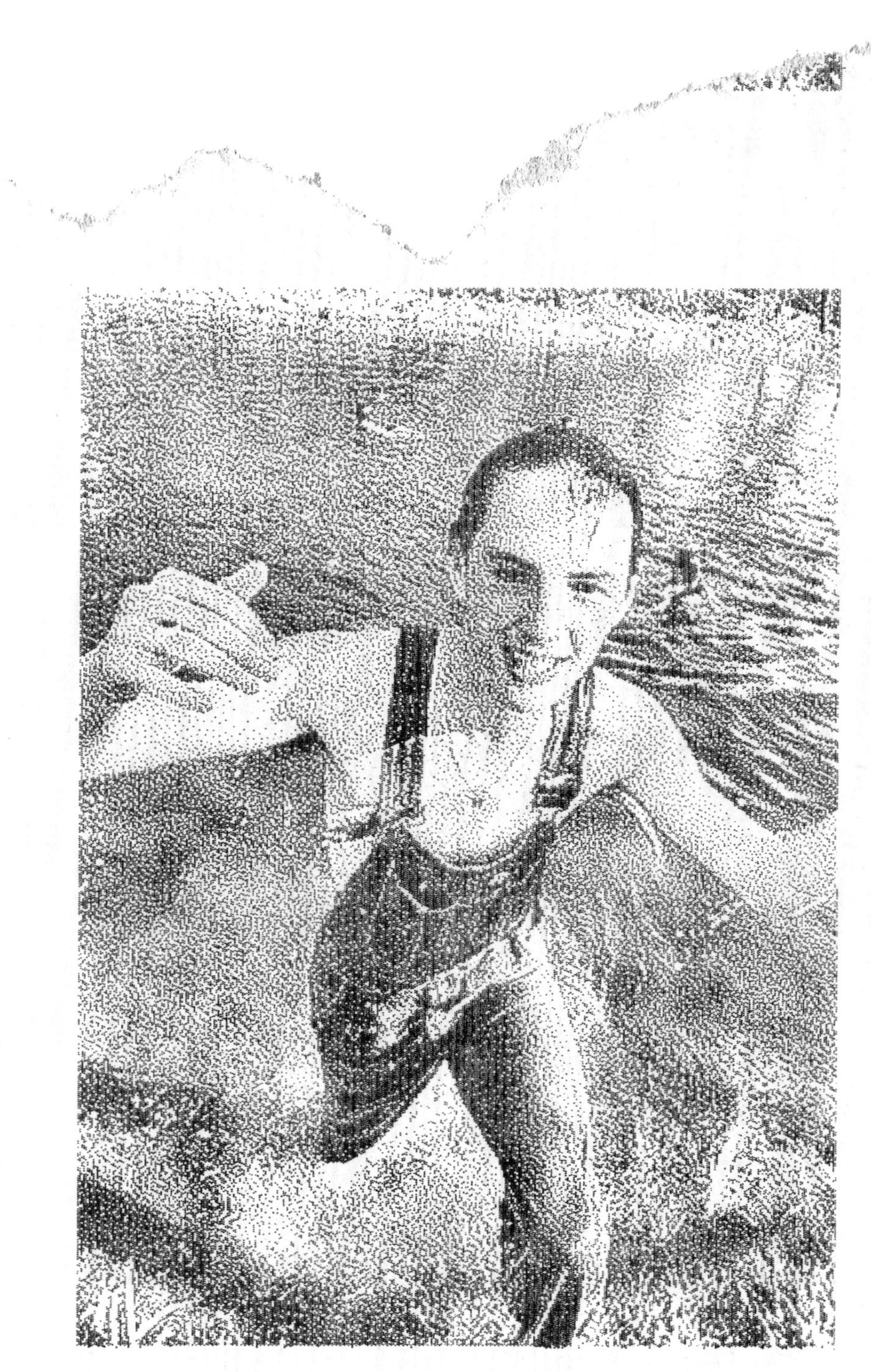

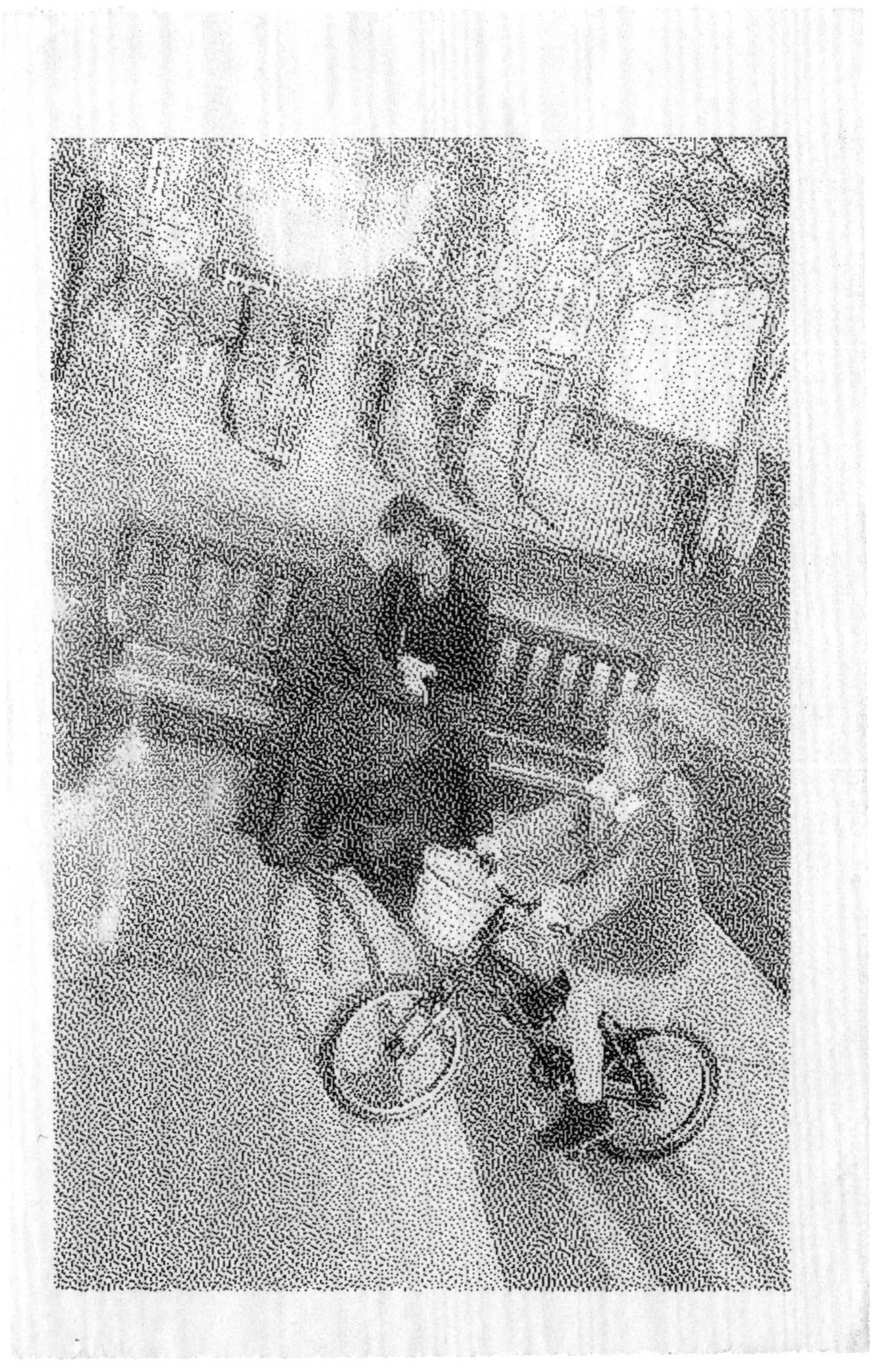

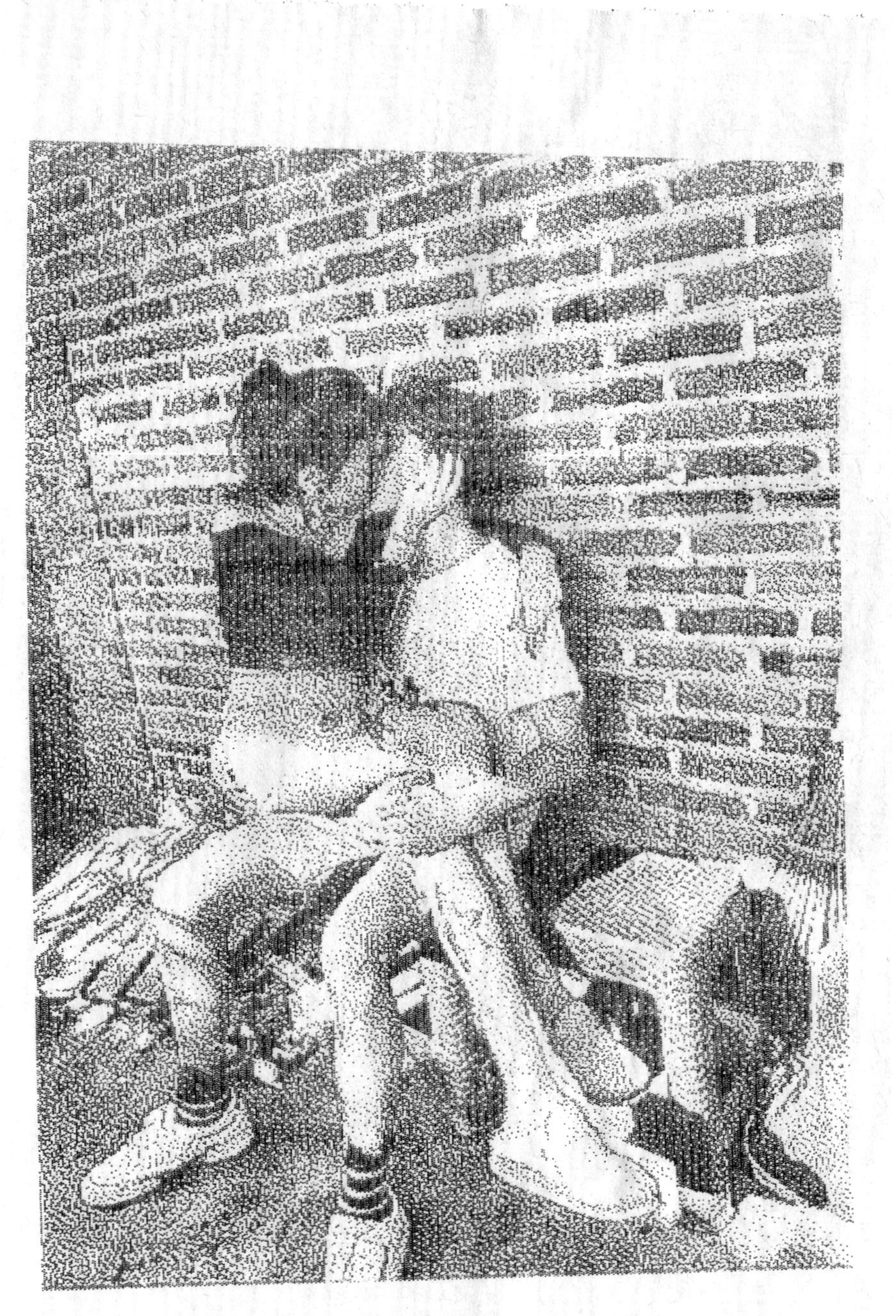

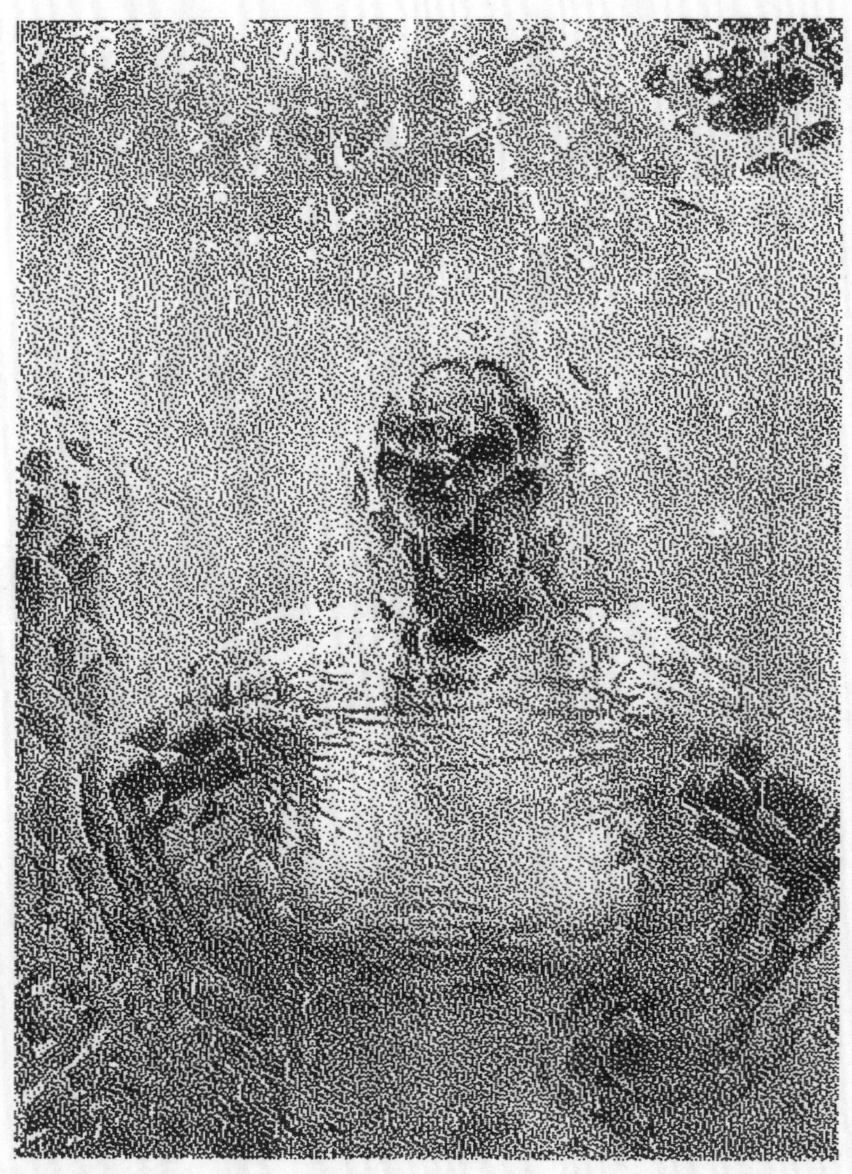

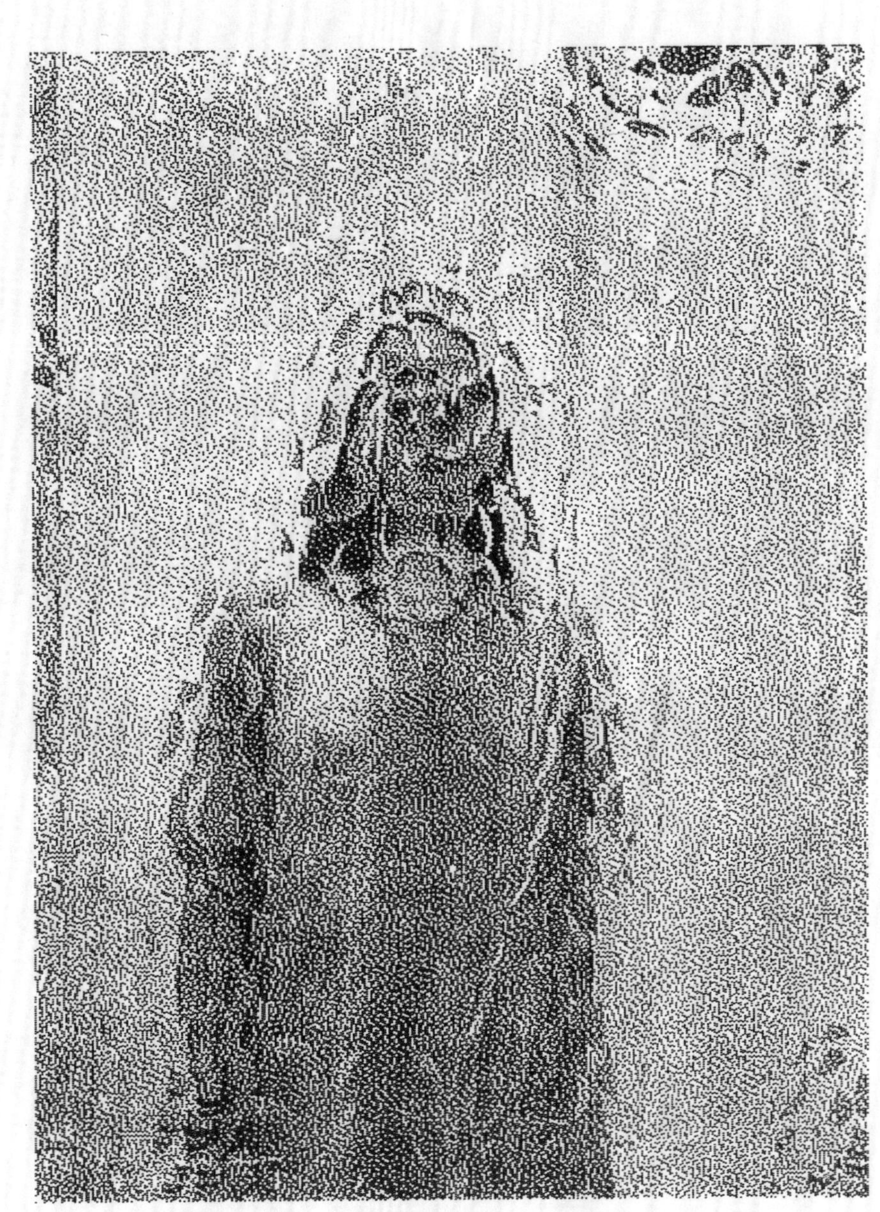

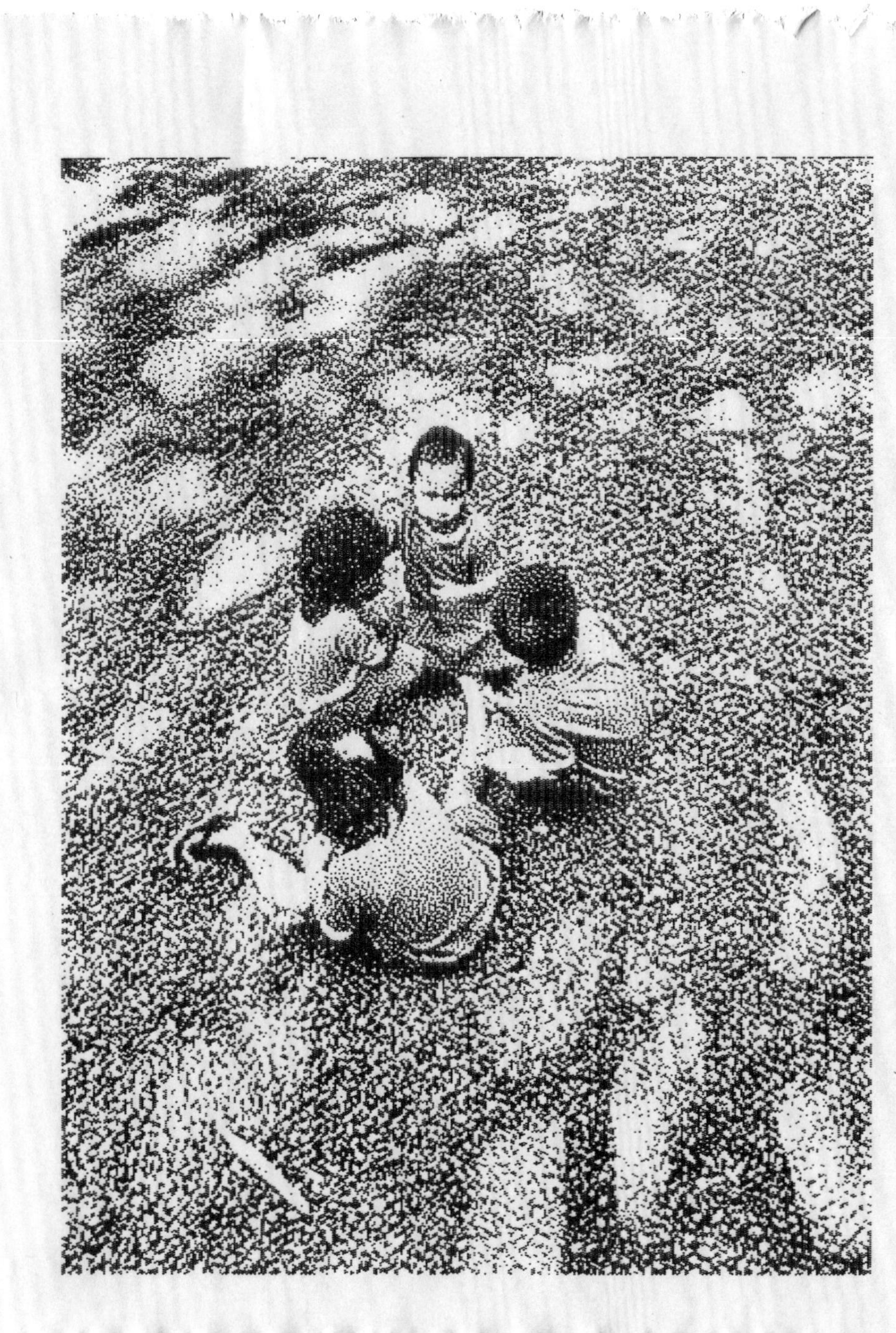

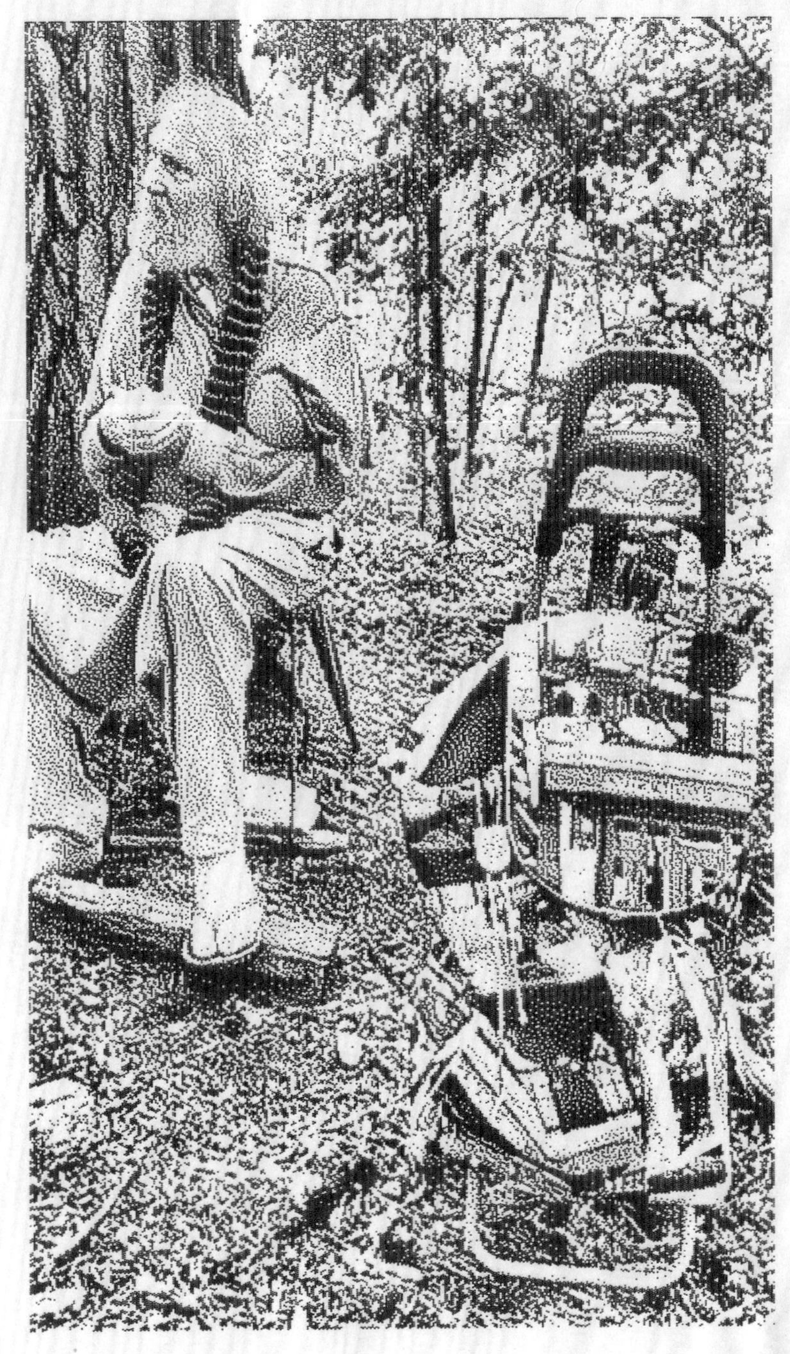

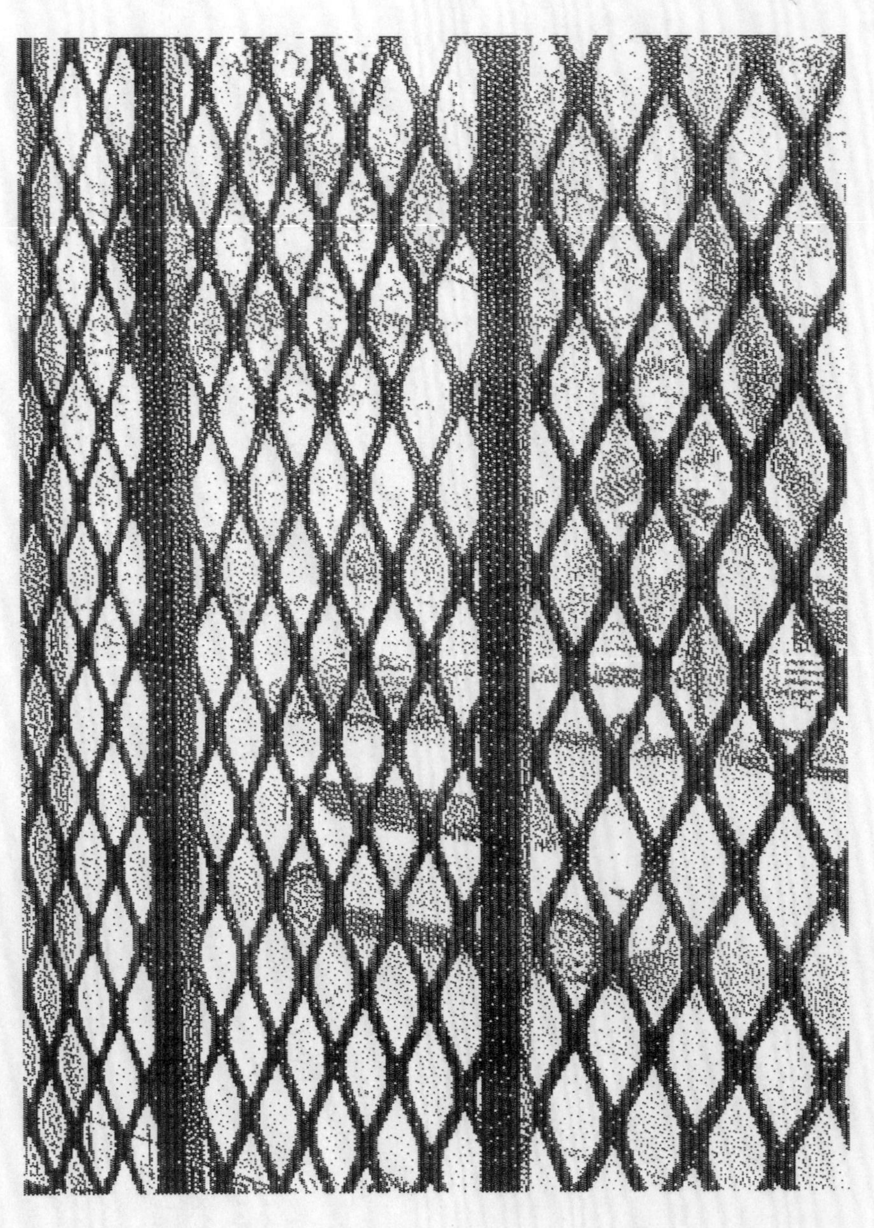

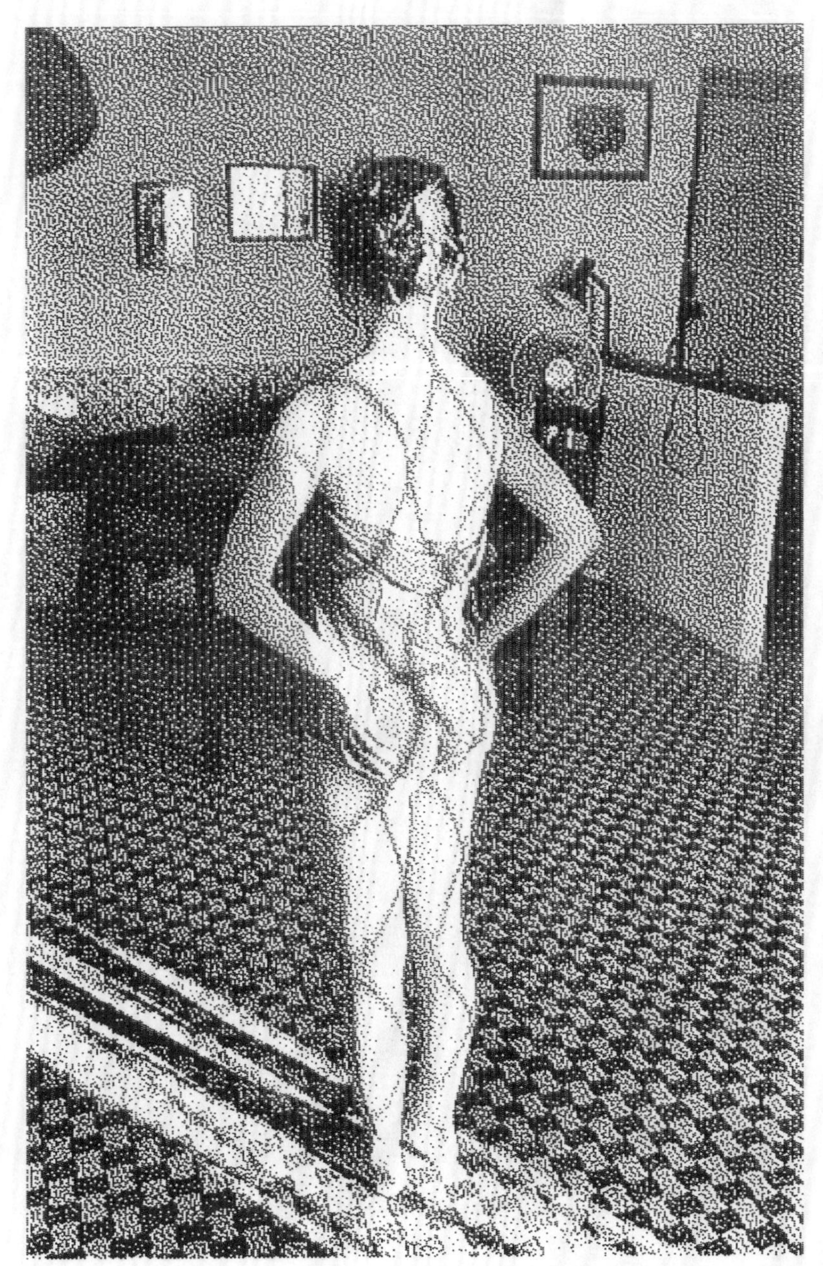

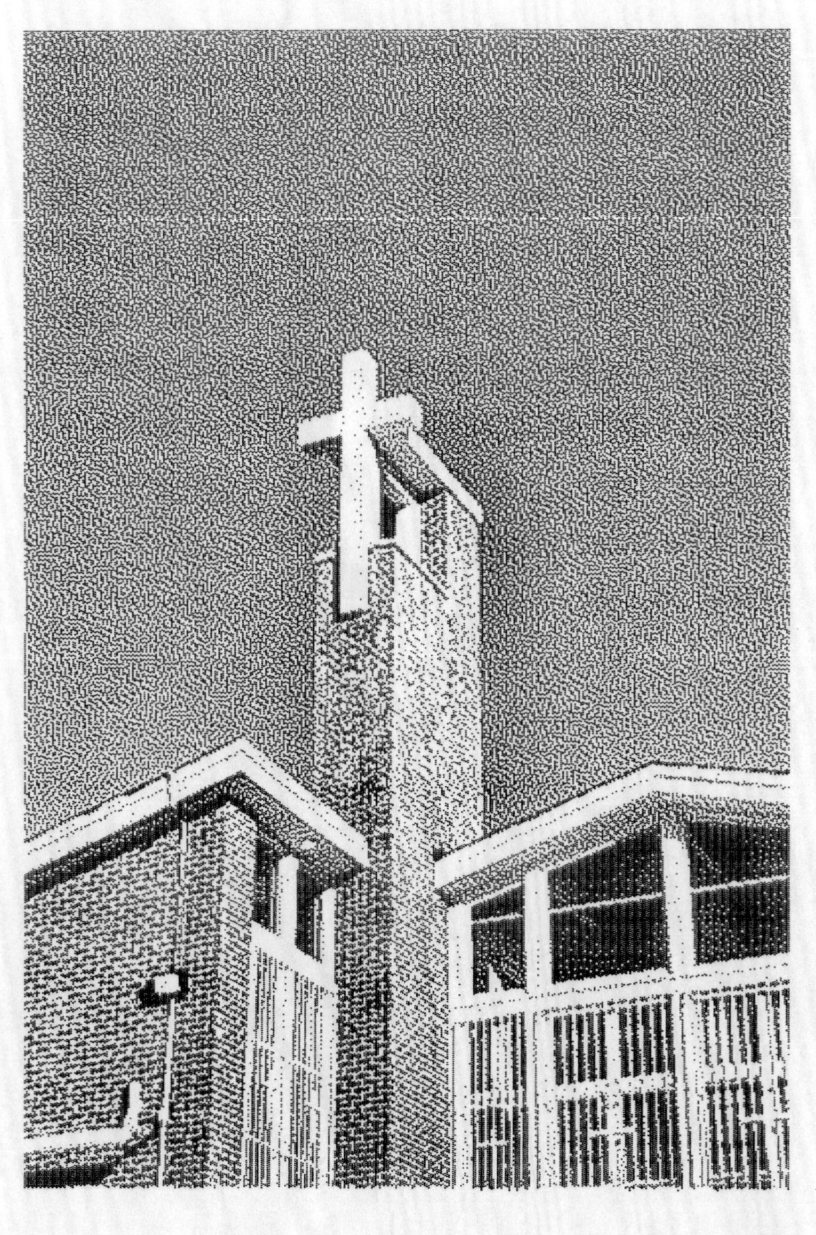

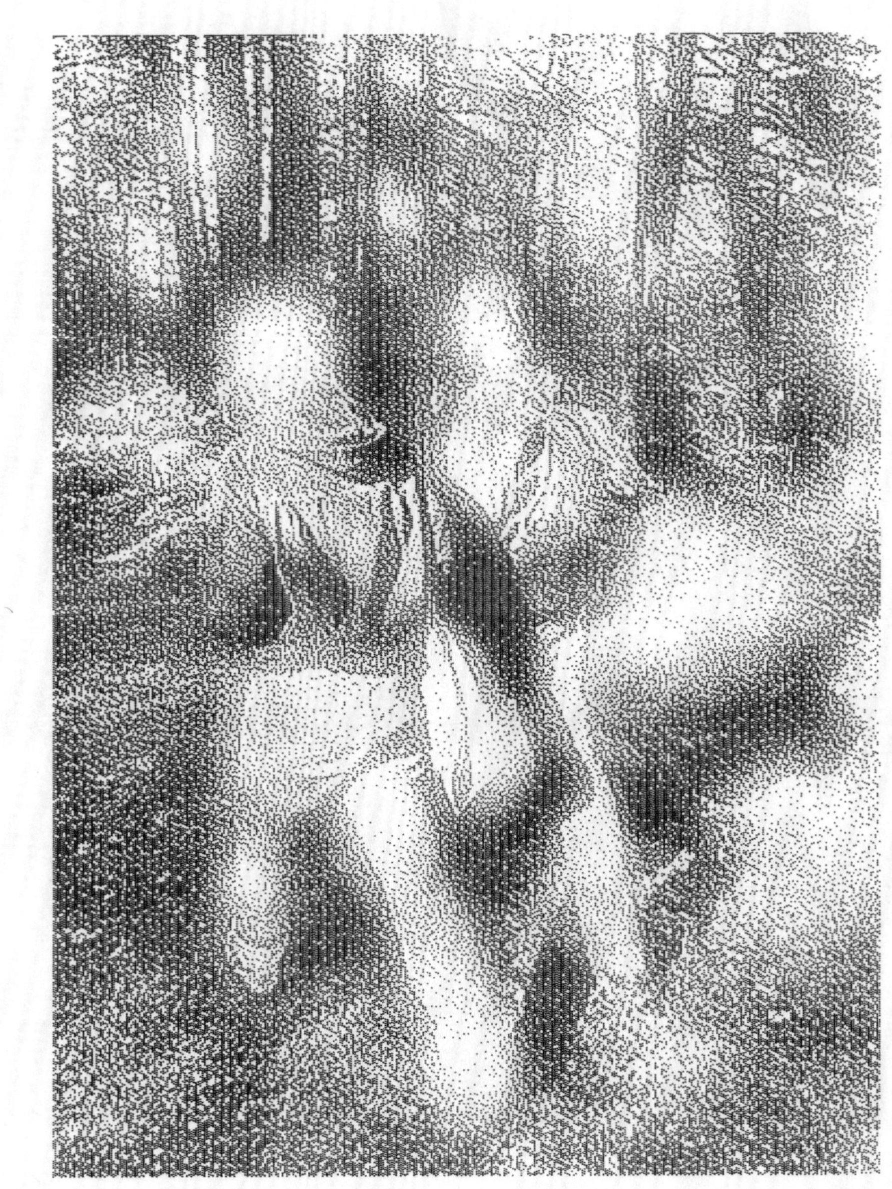

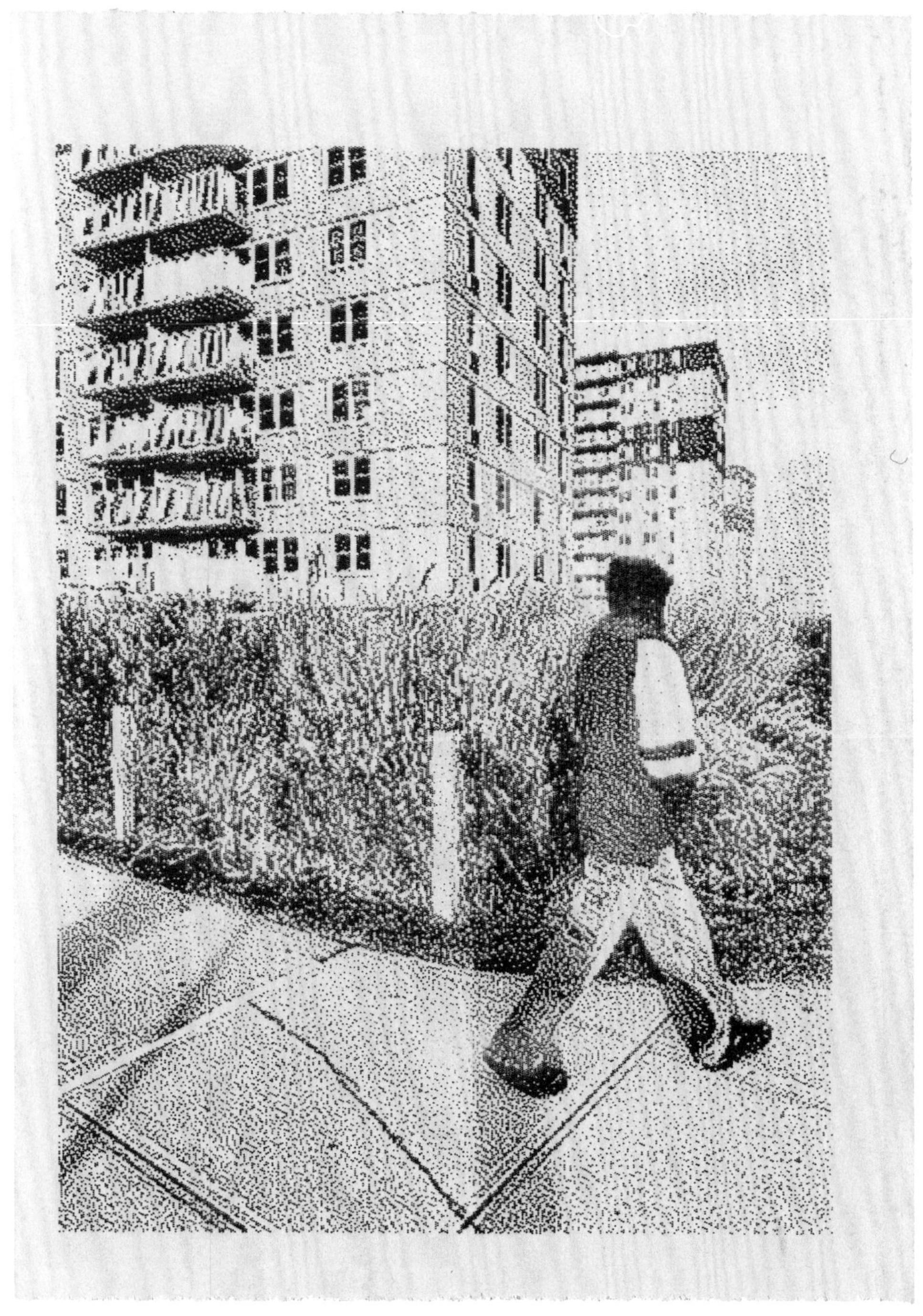

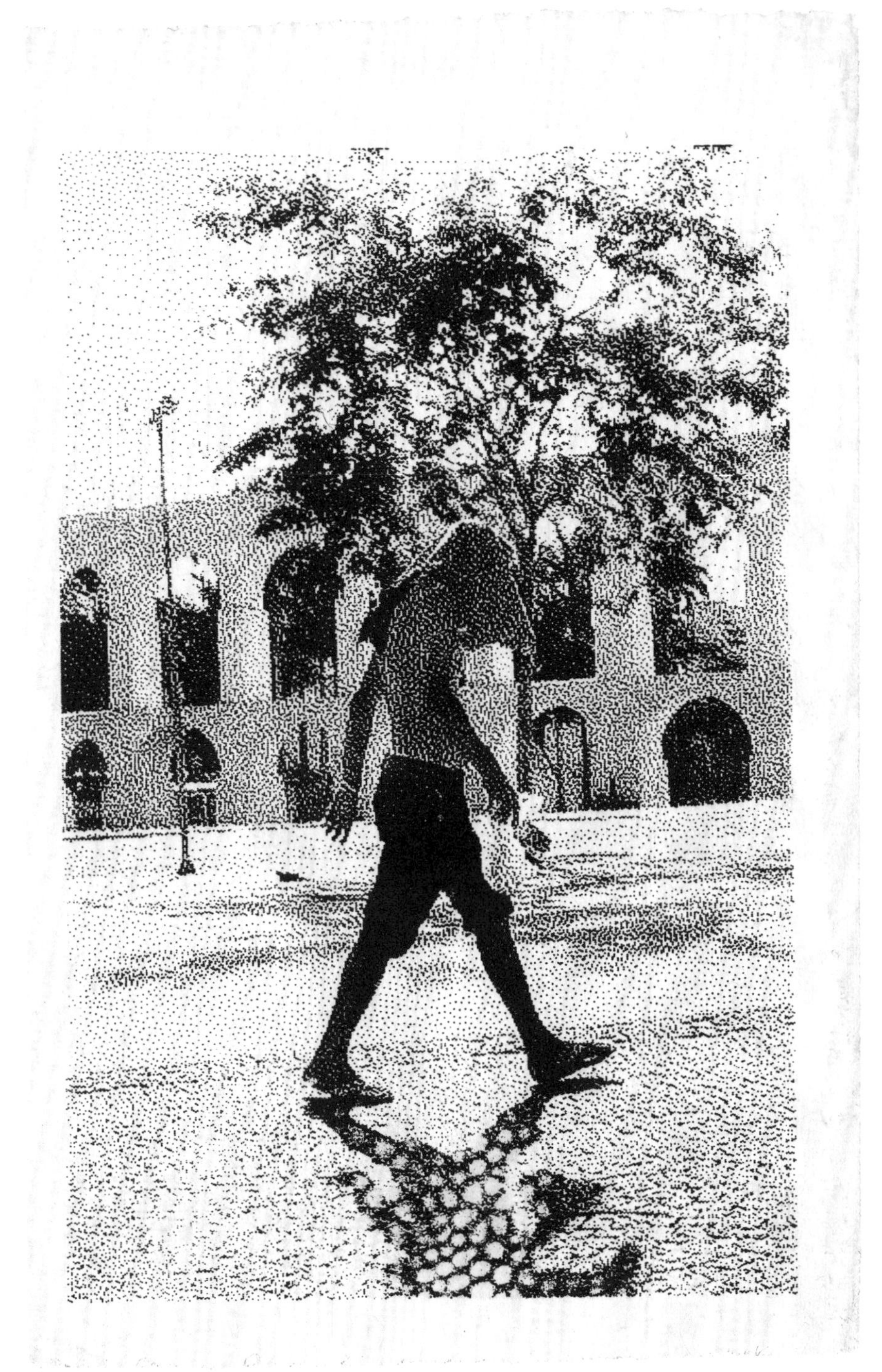

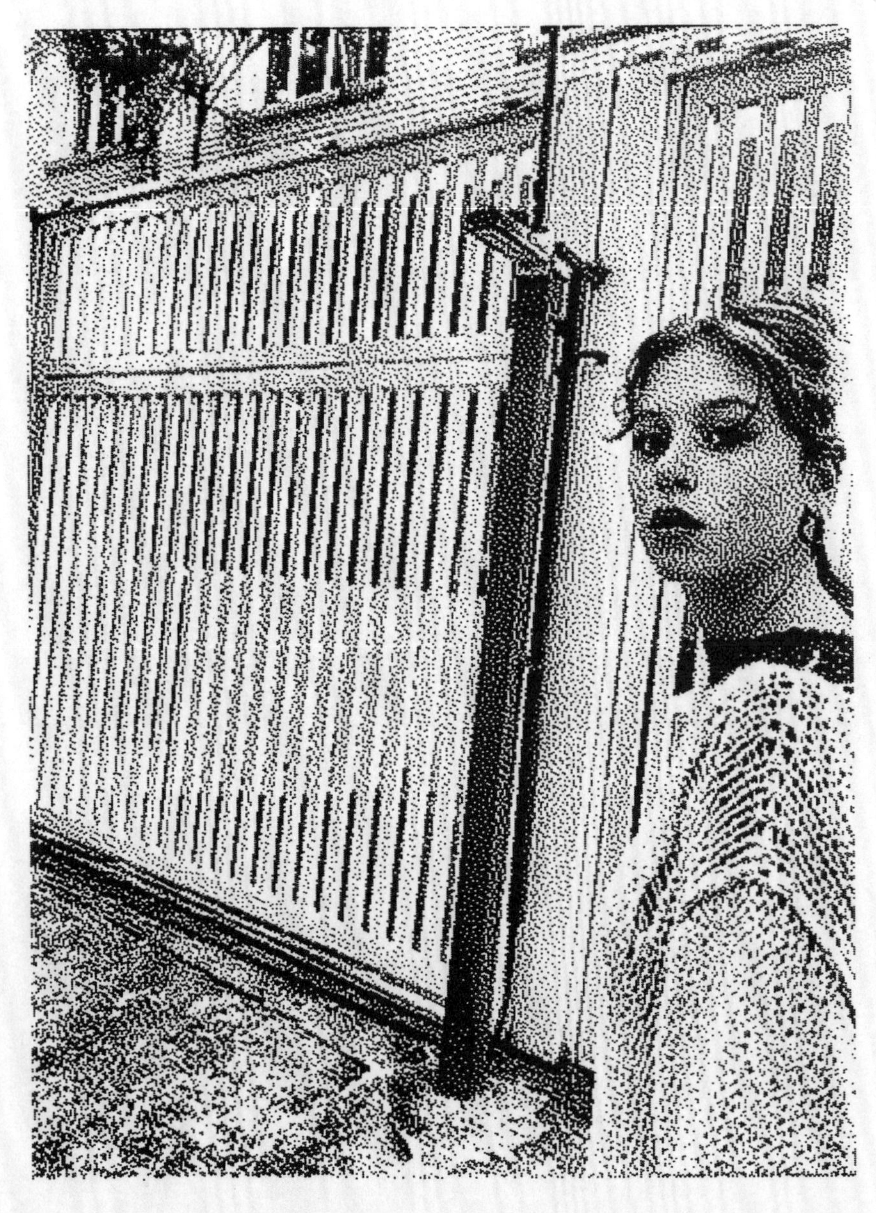

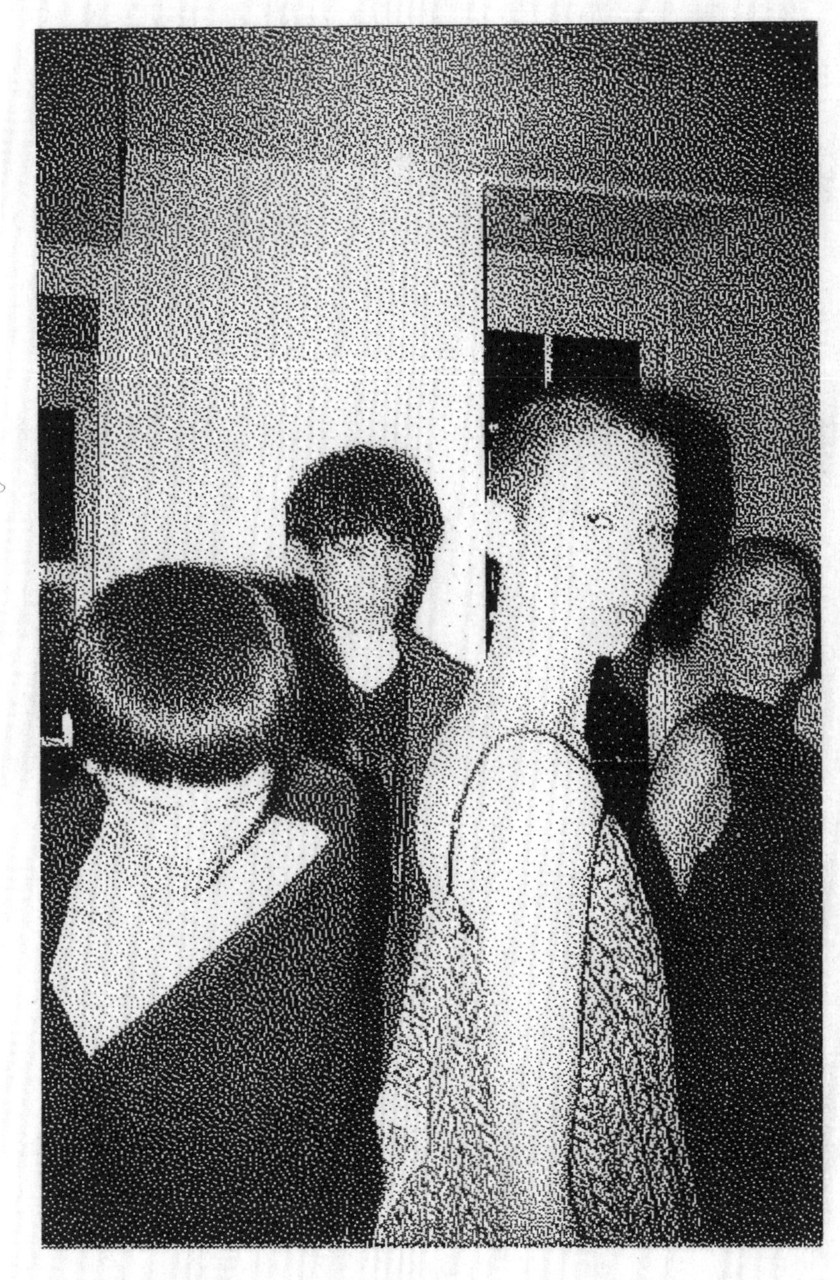

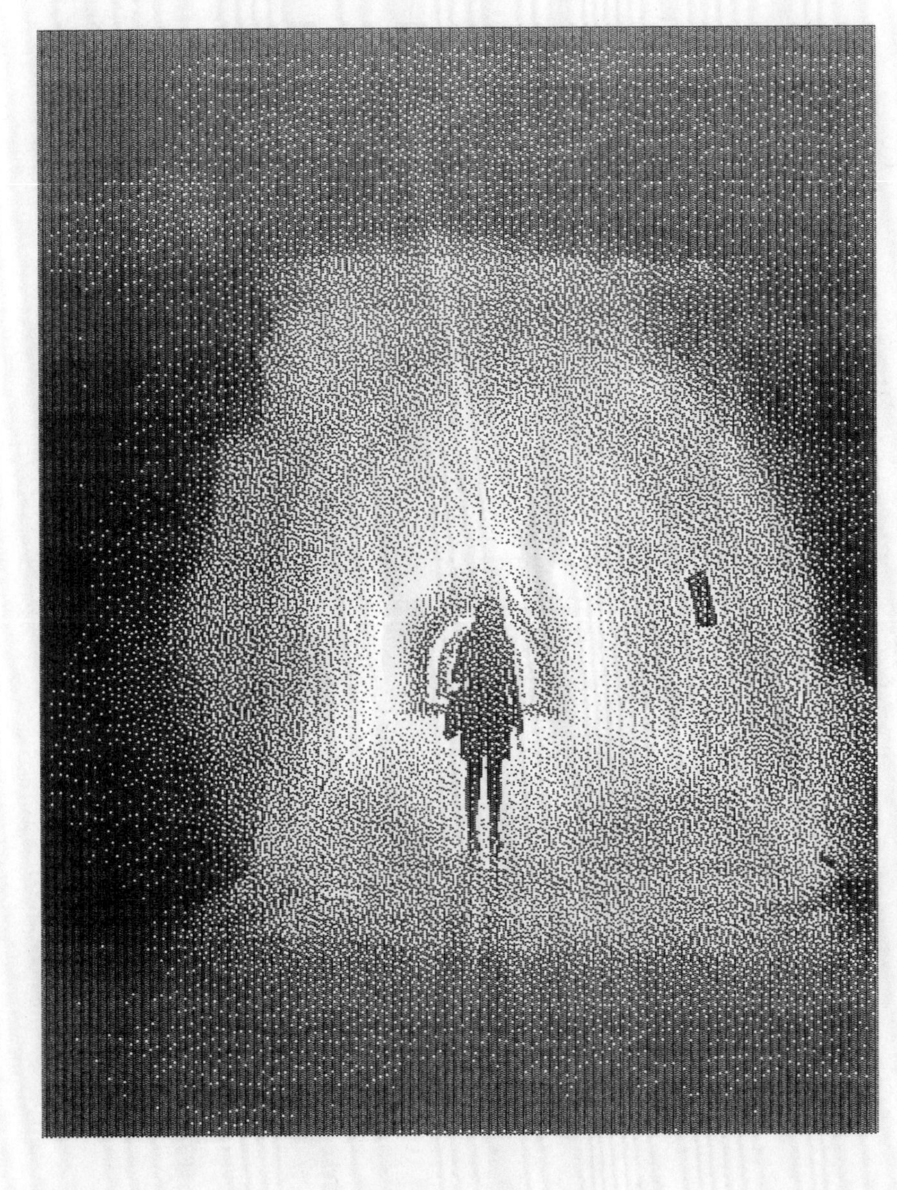

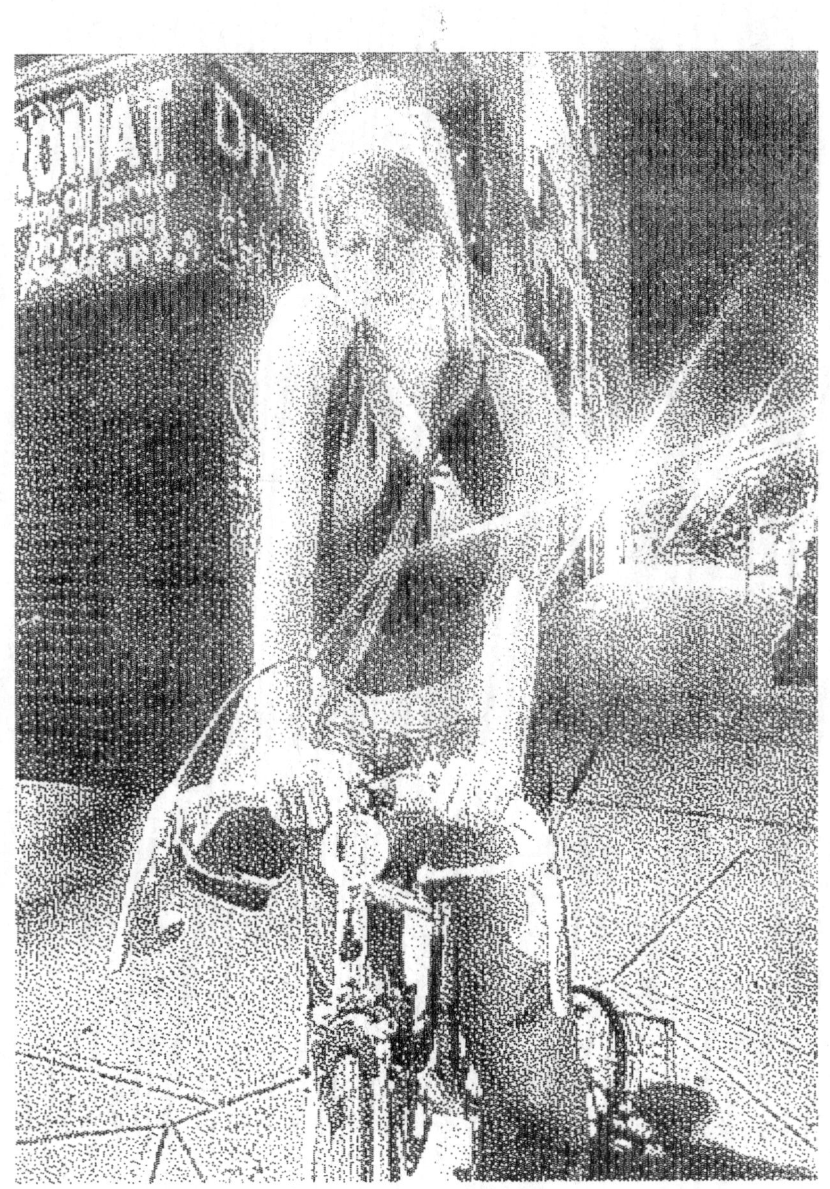
Off Service
Cleaning

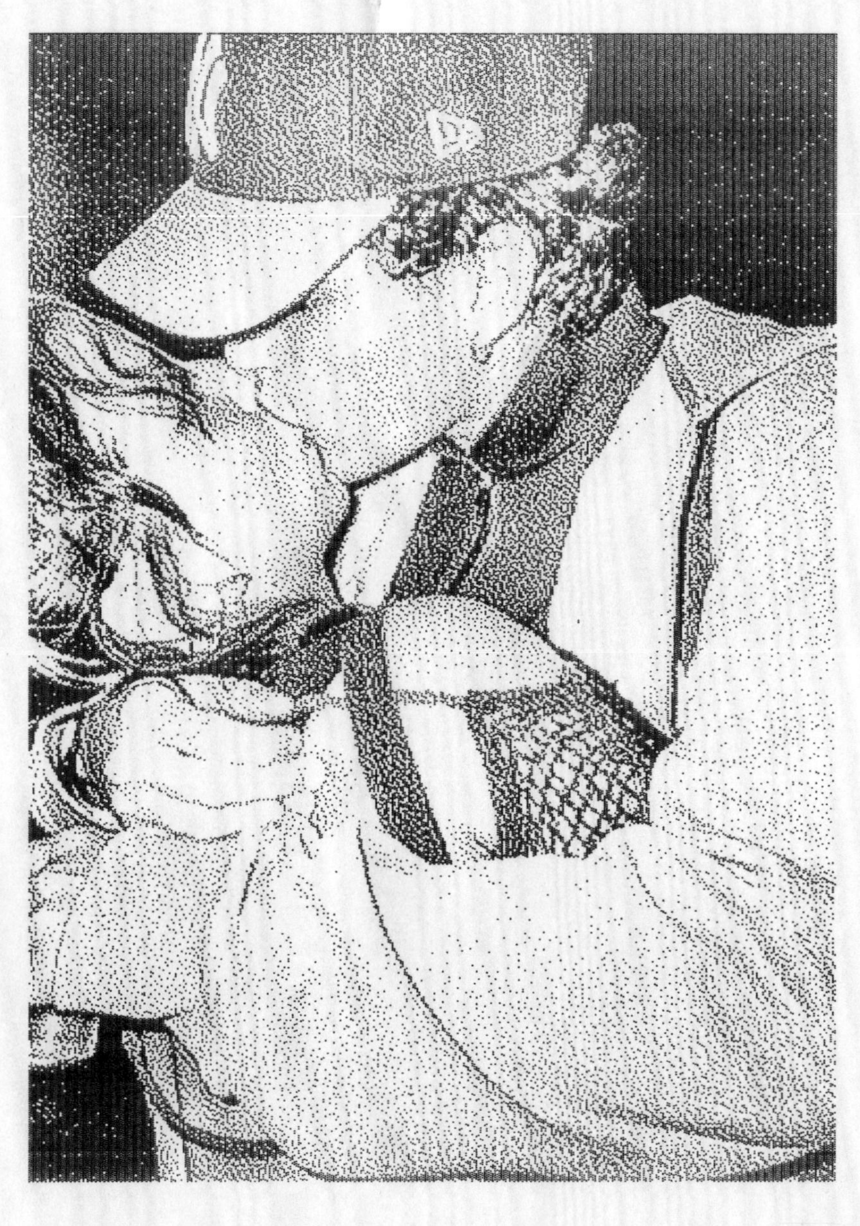

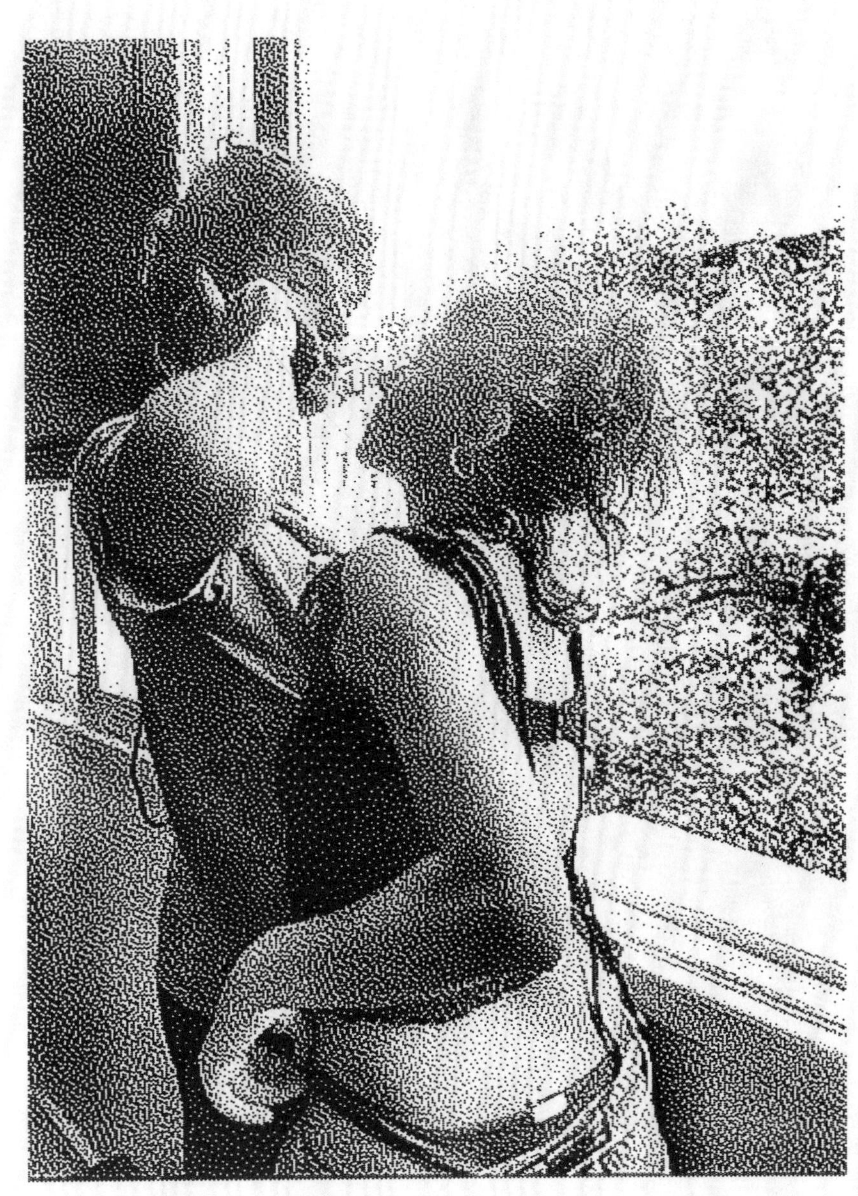

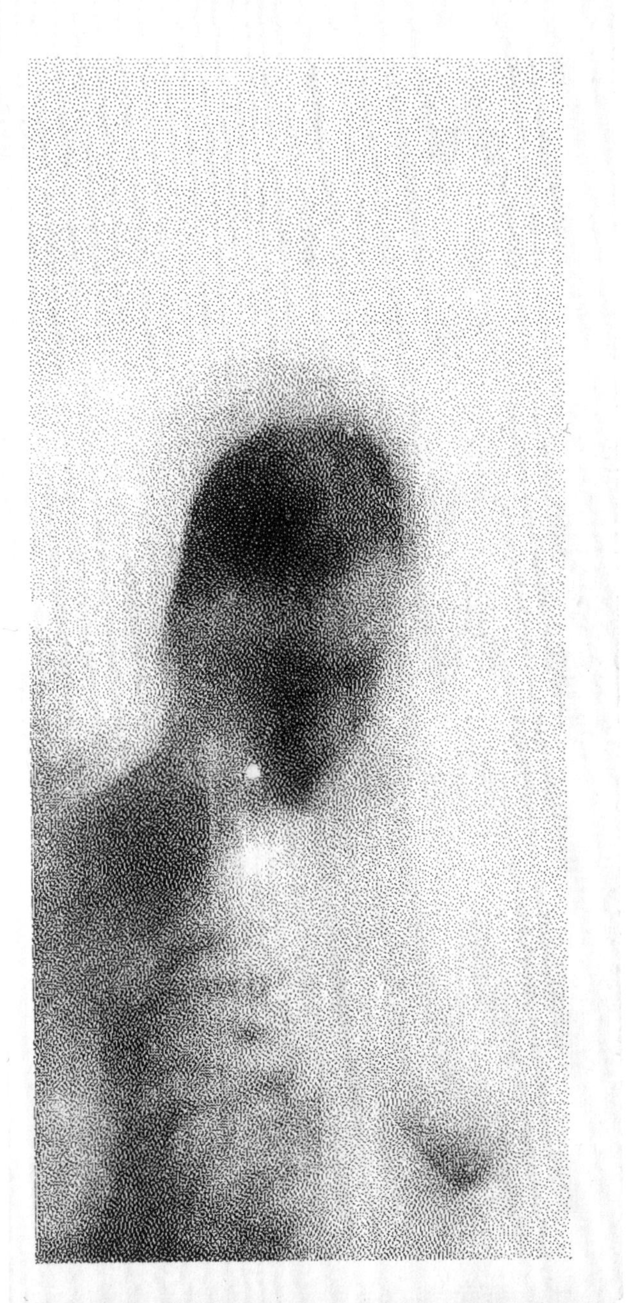

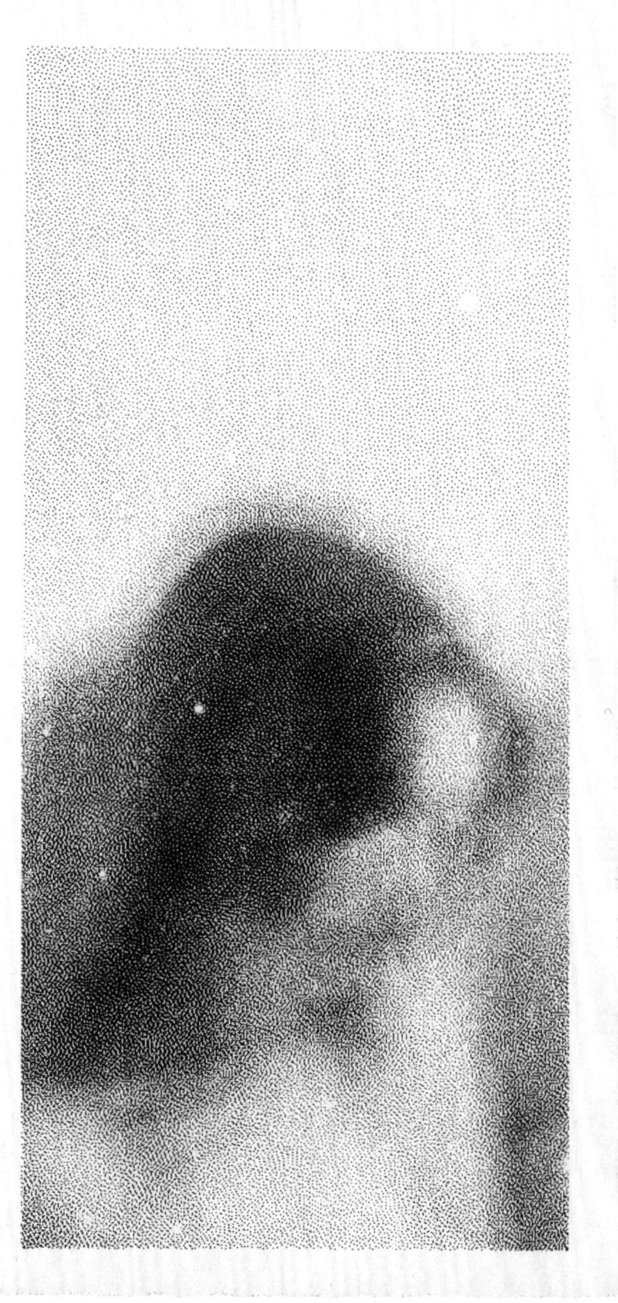

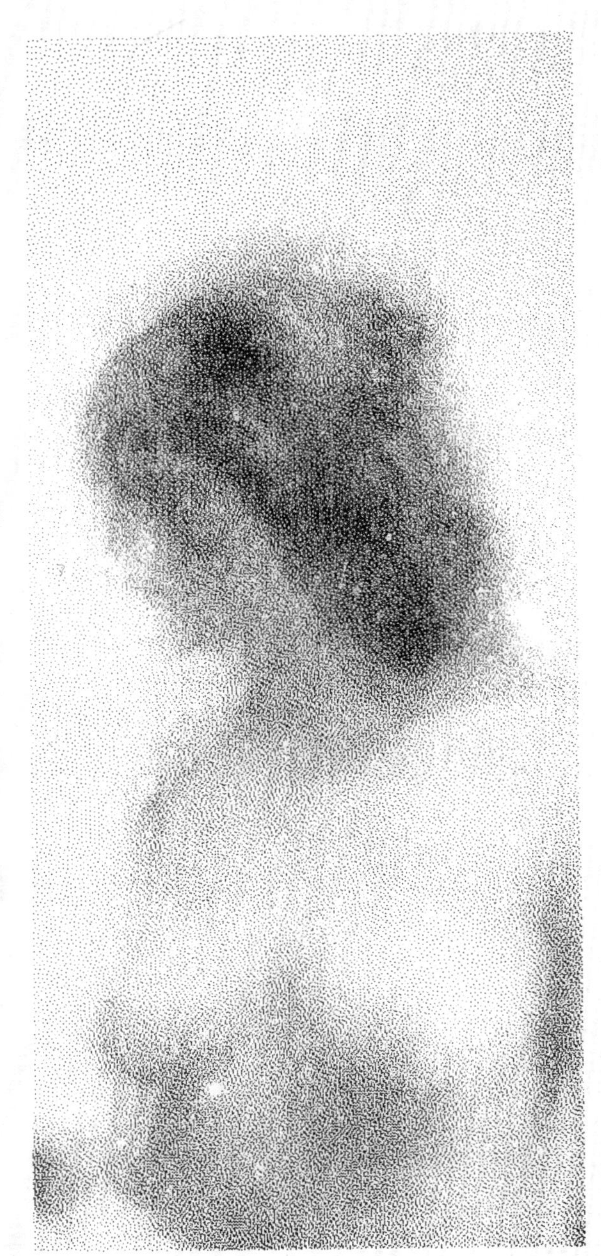

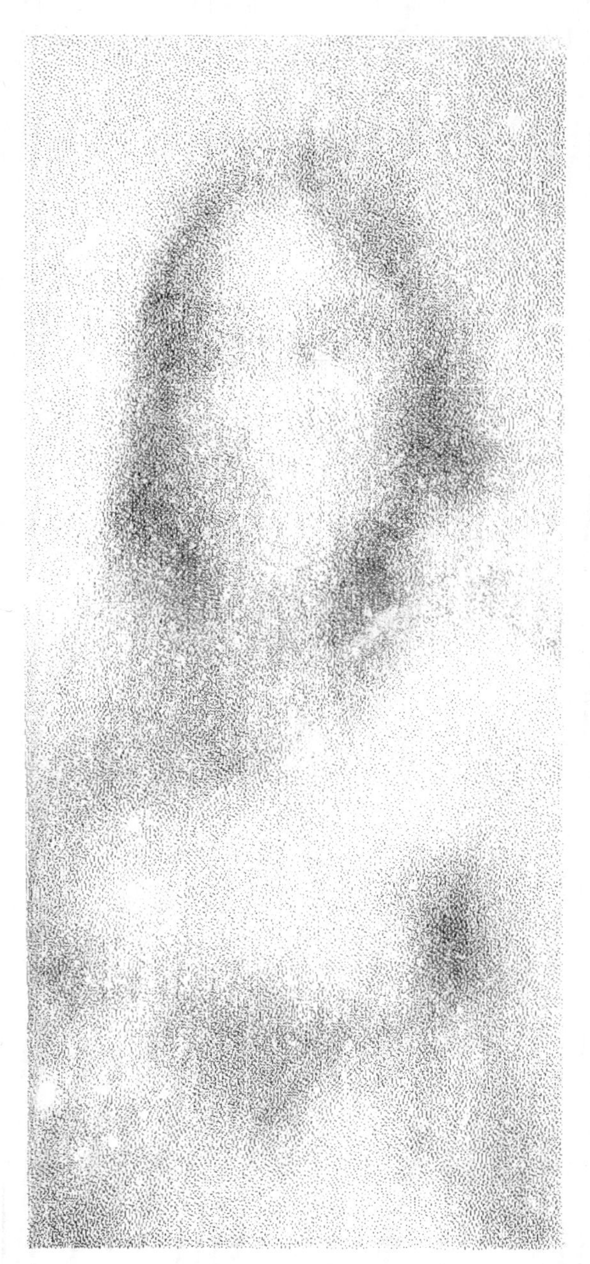

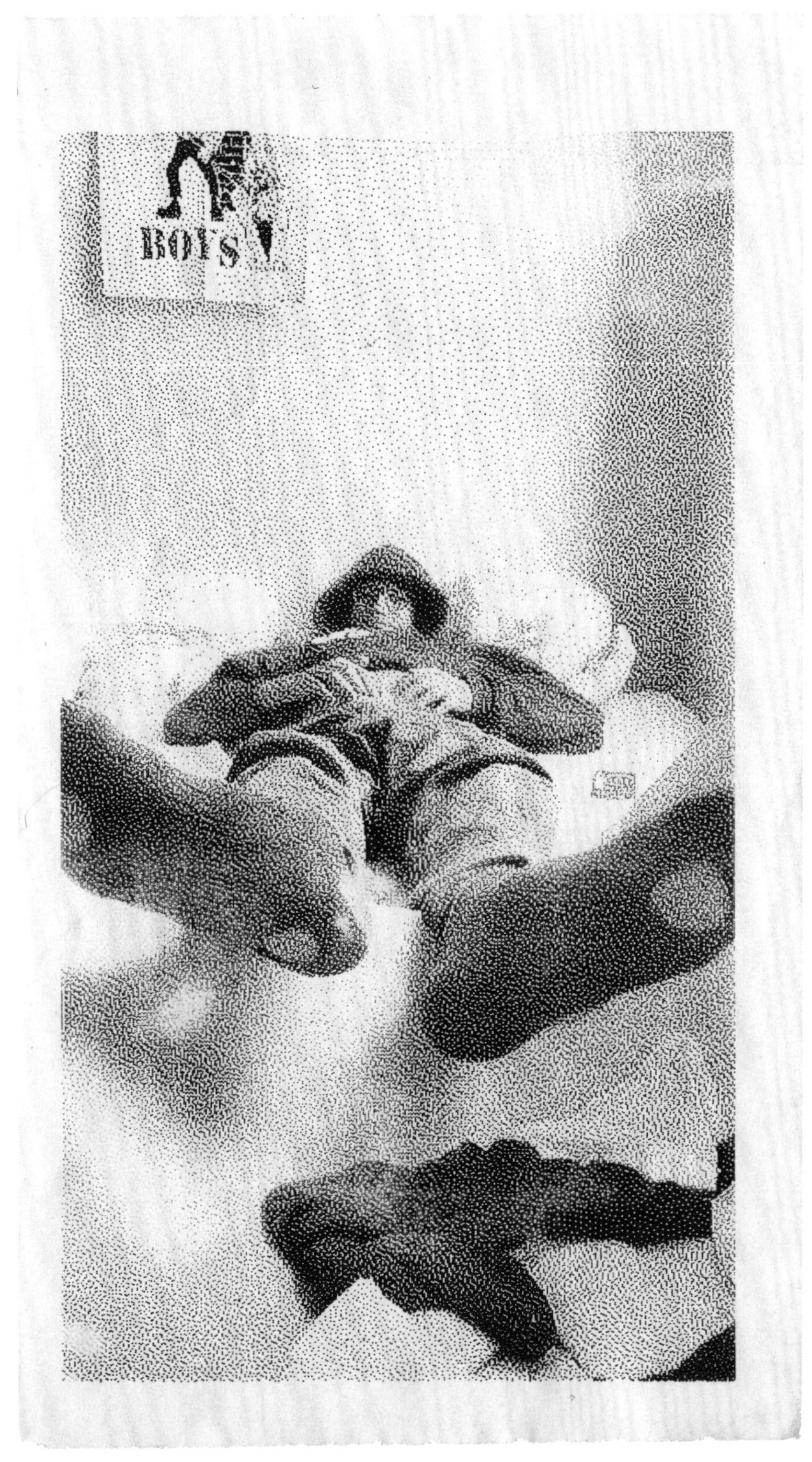
BOYS

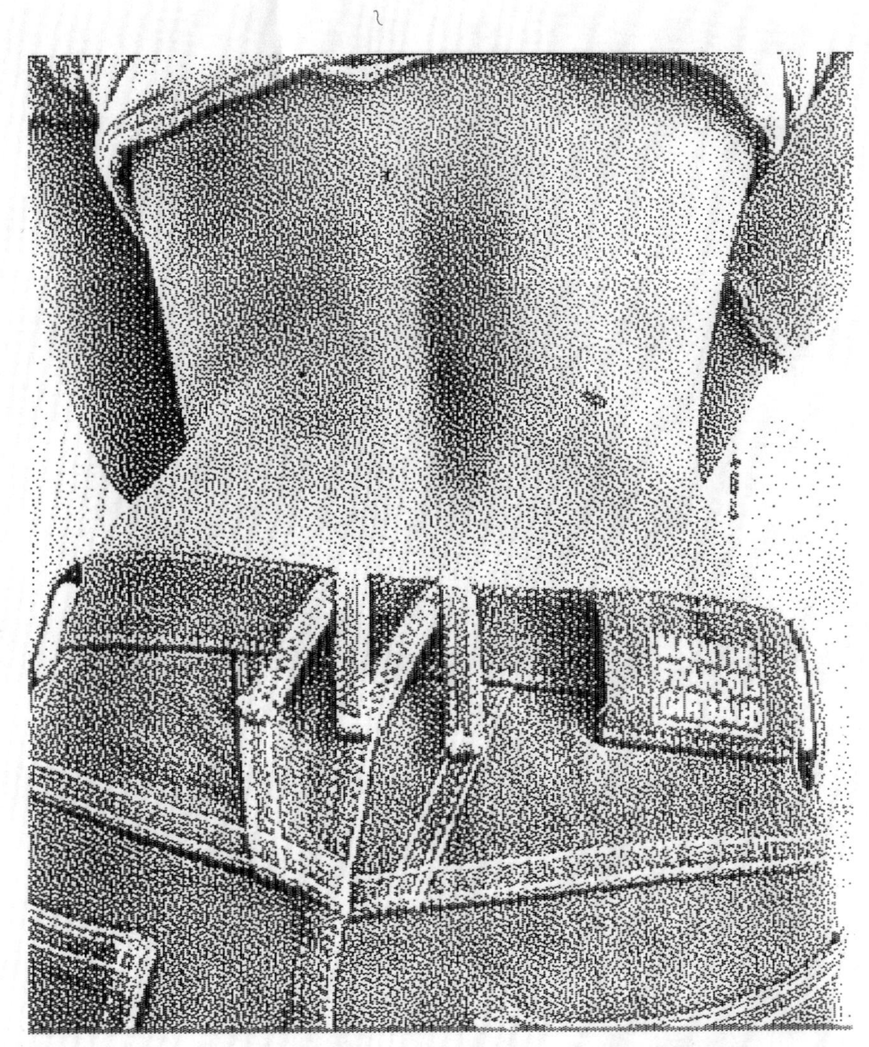

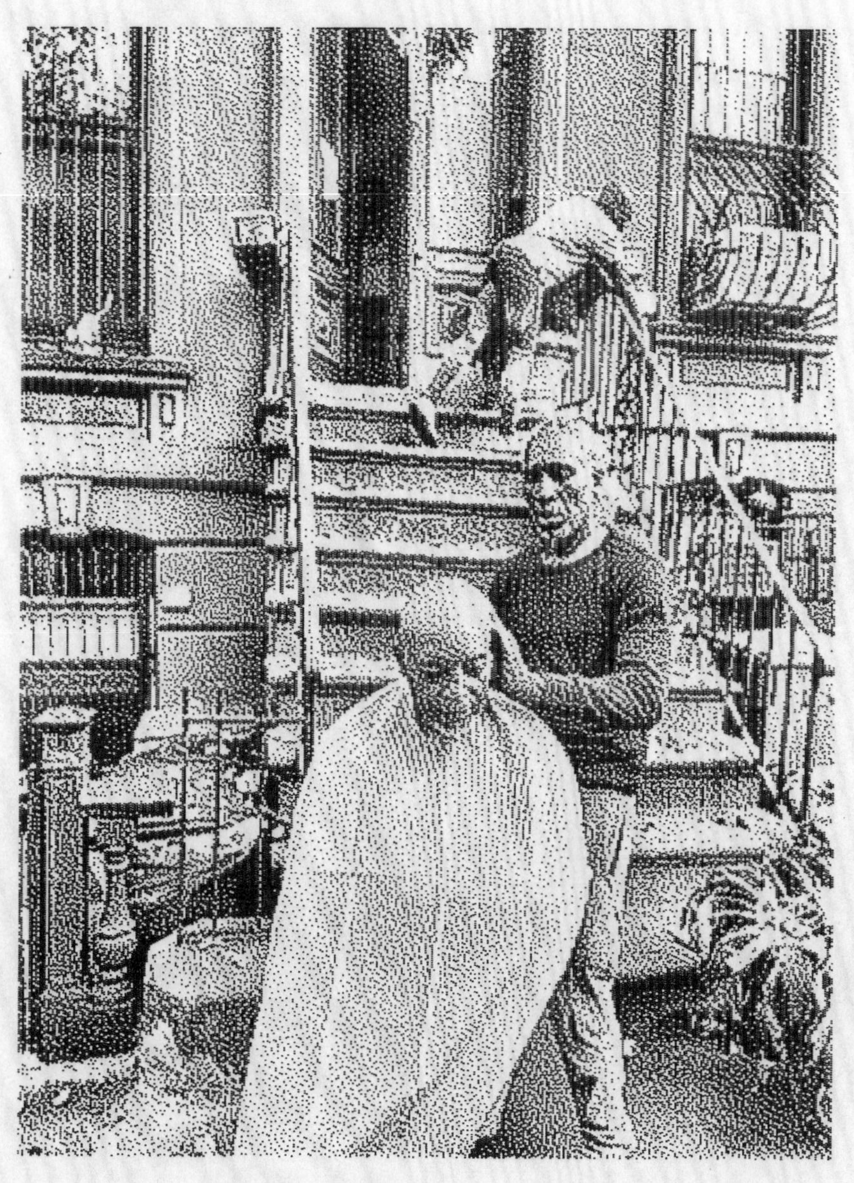

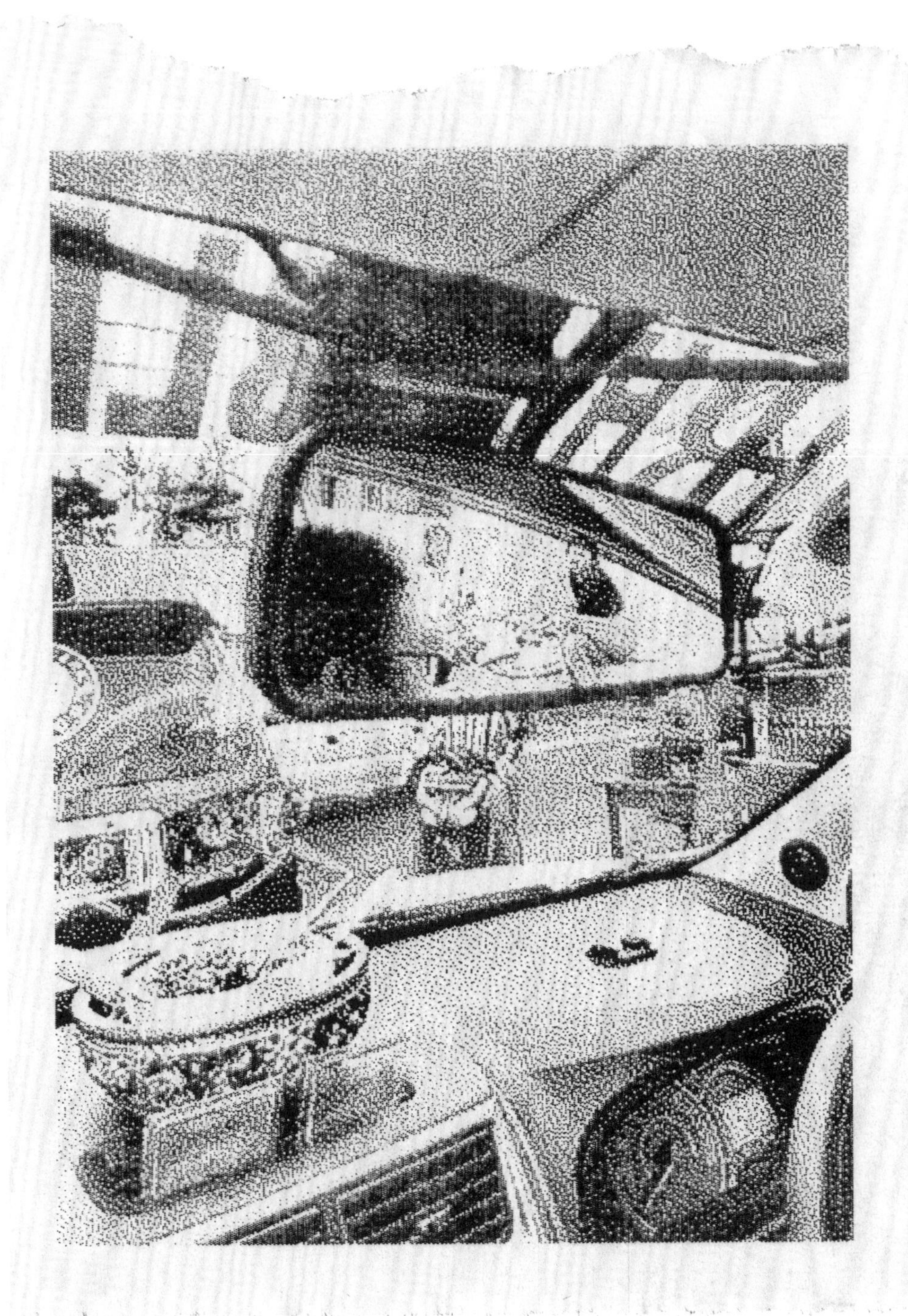

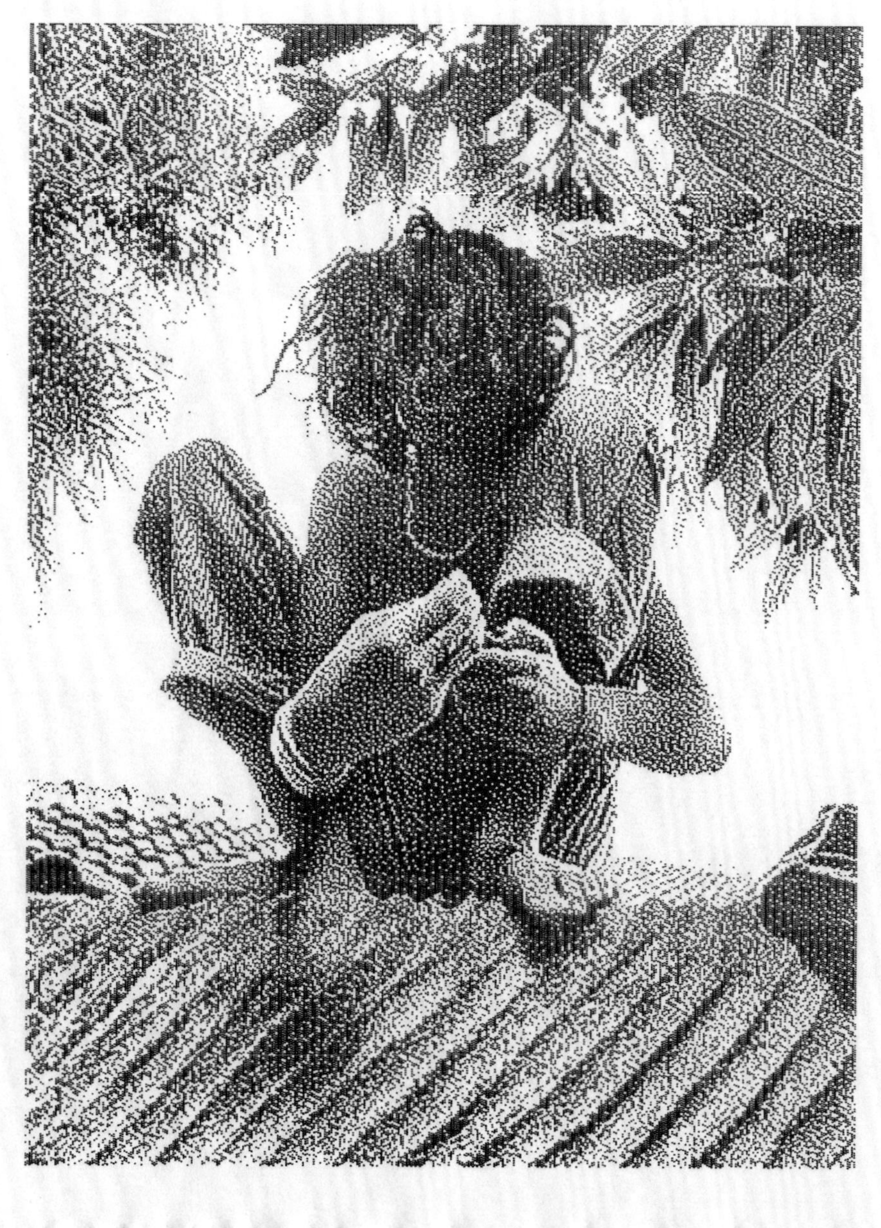

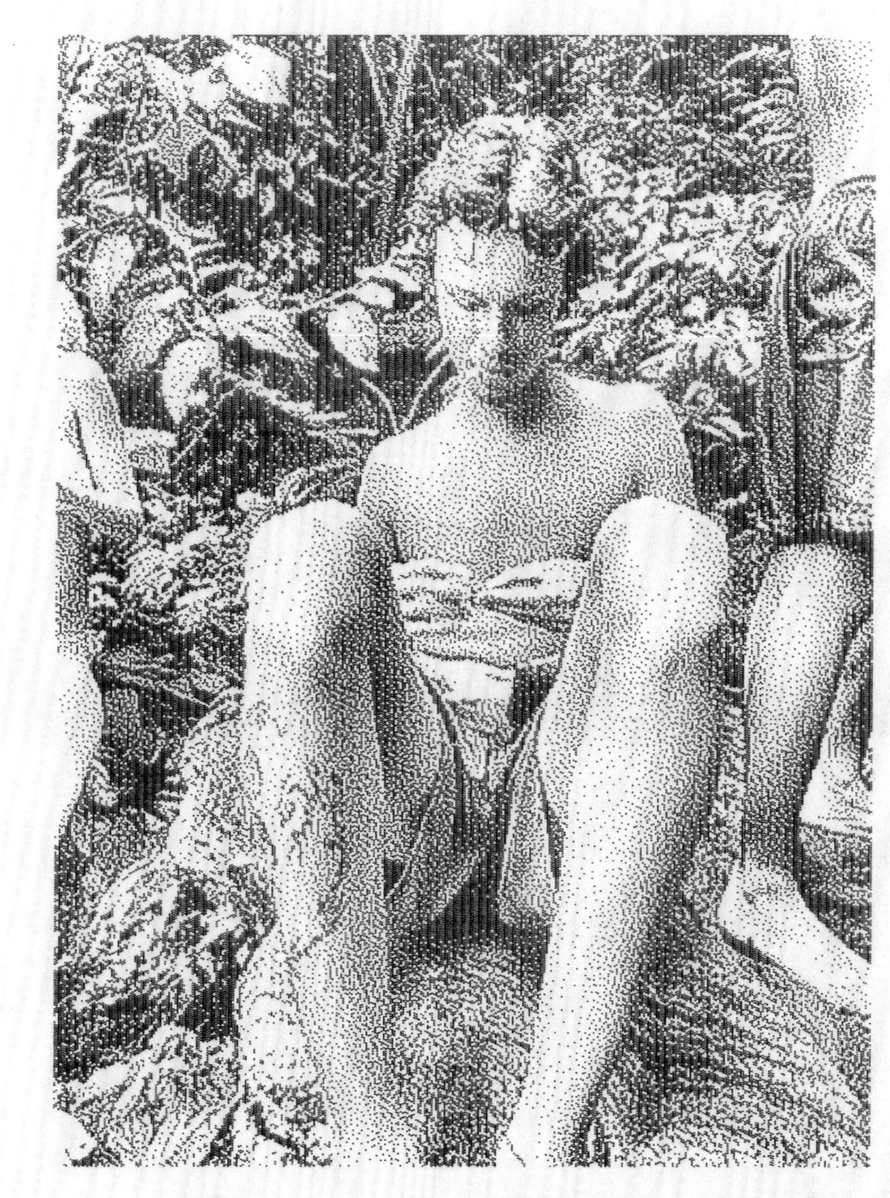

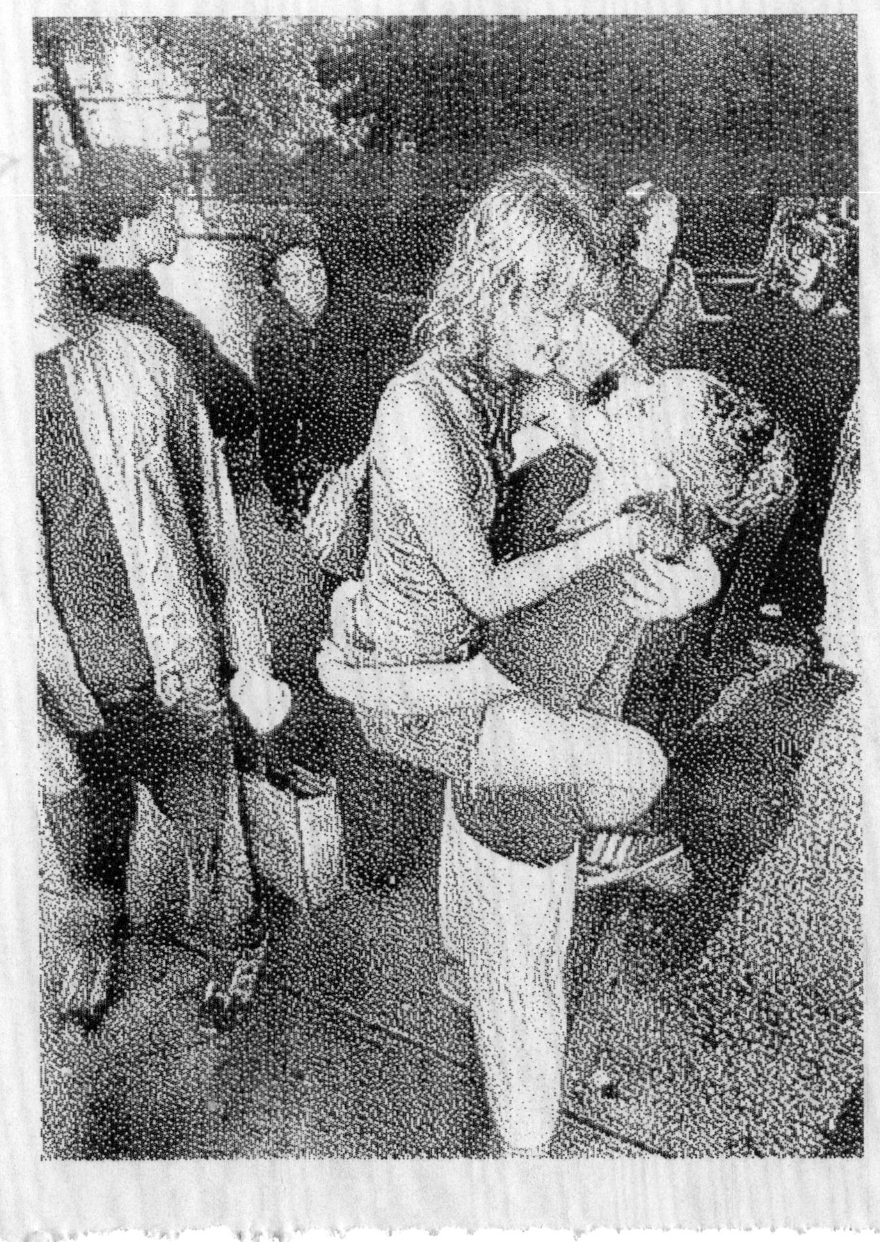

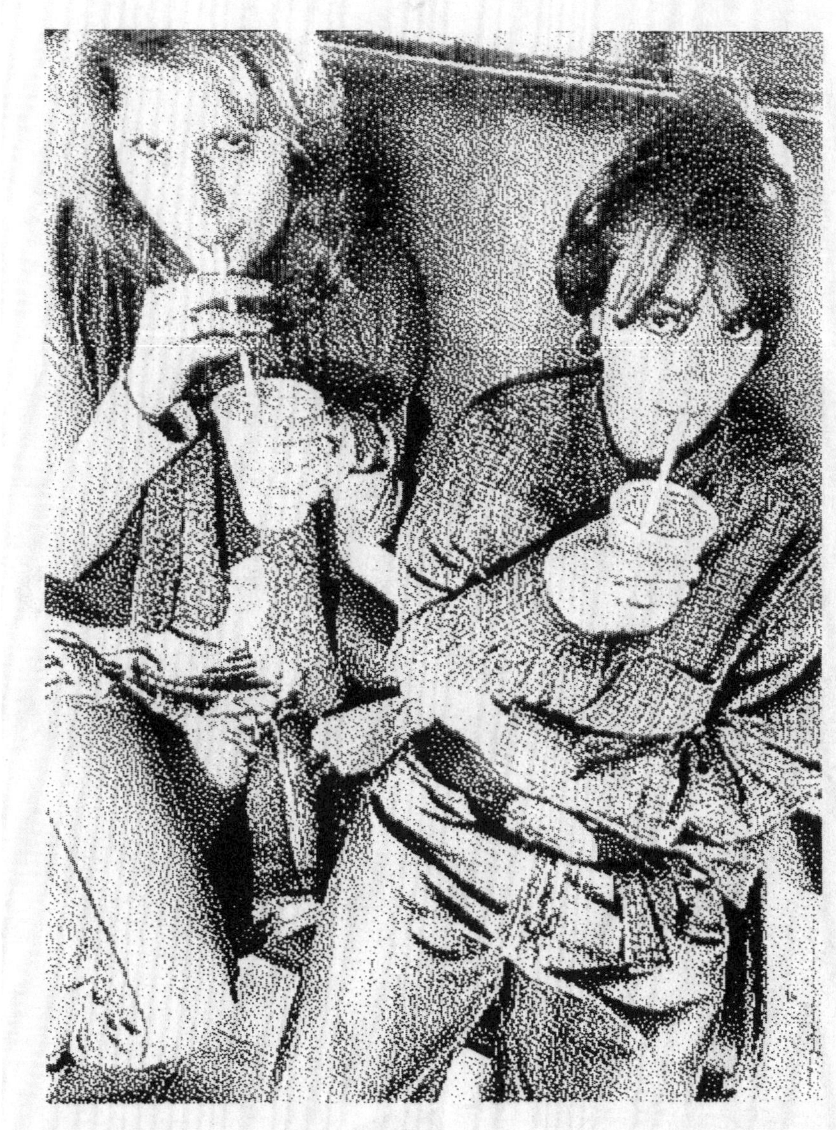

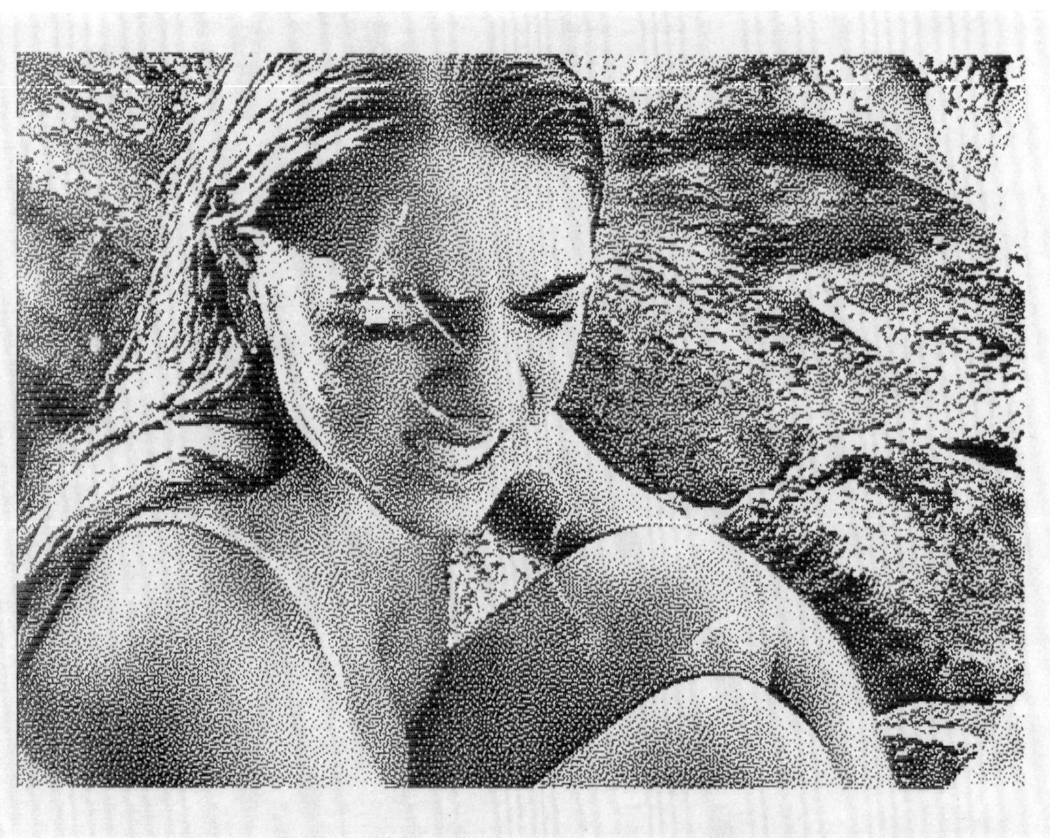

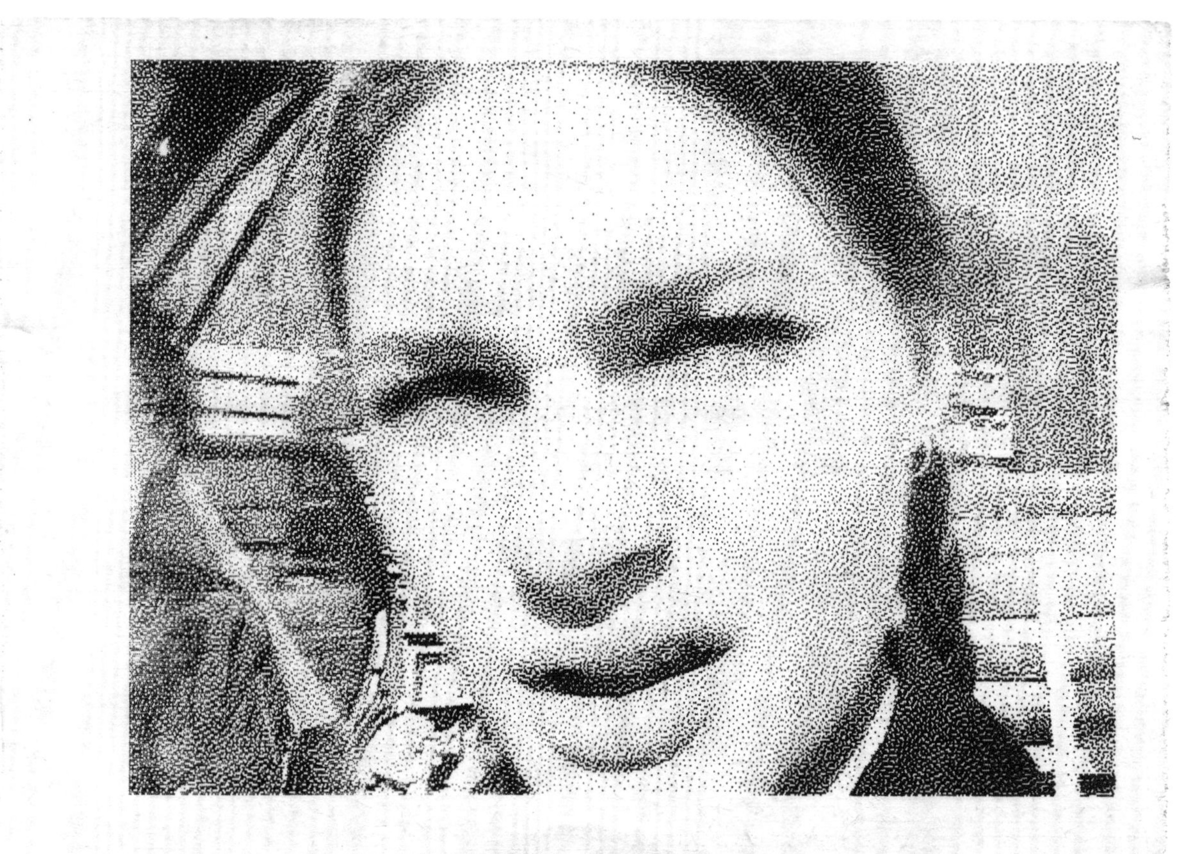

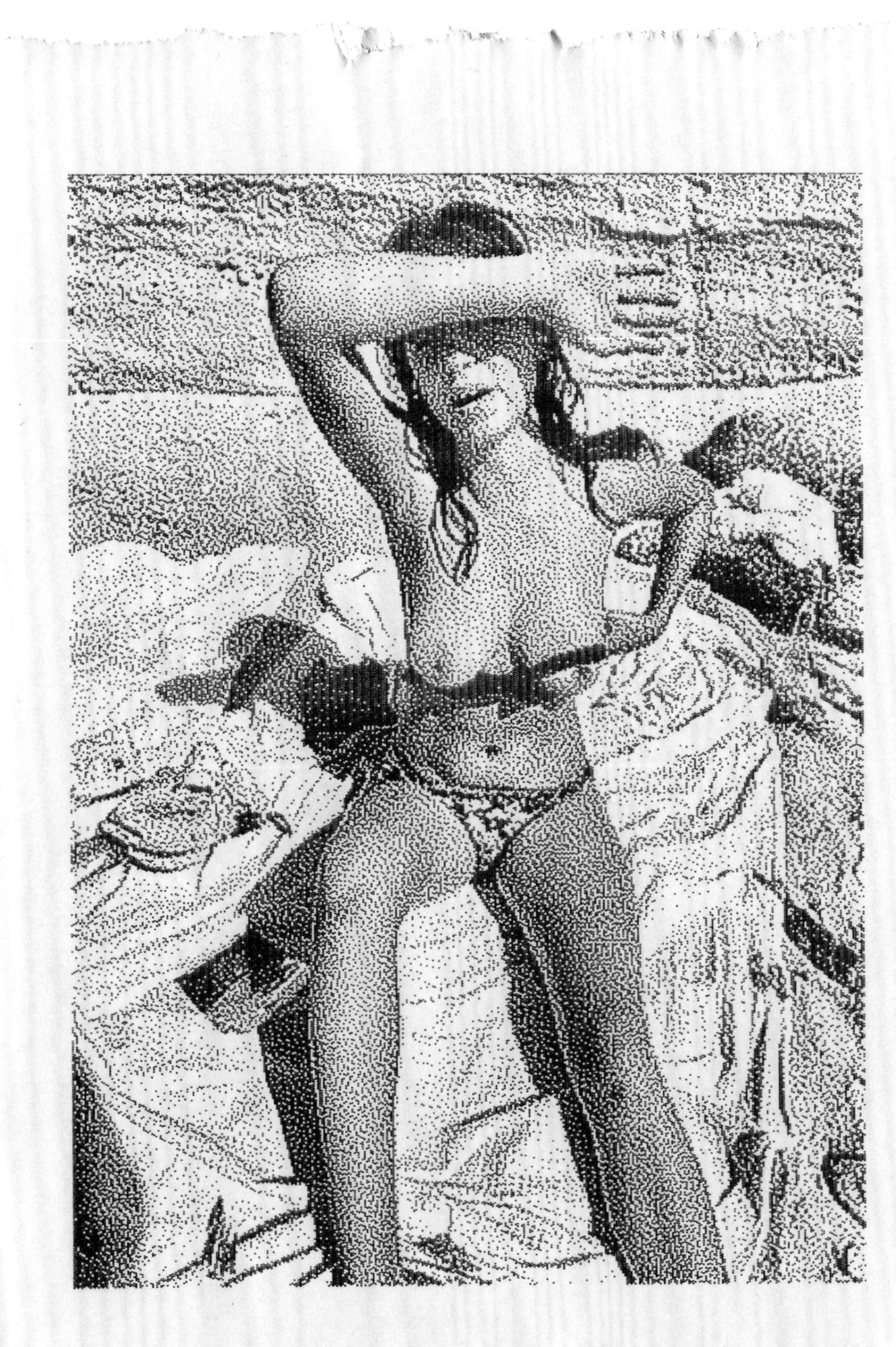

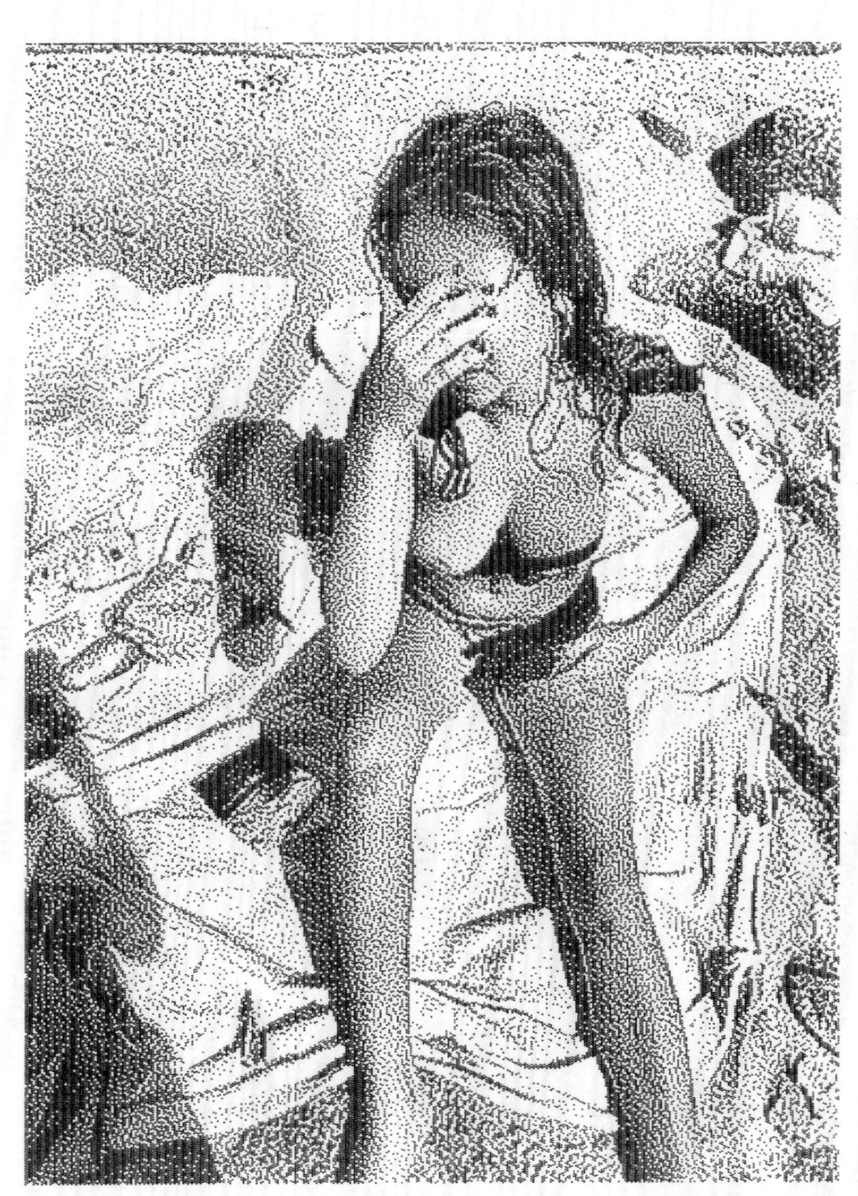

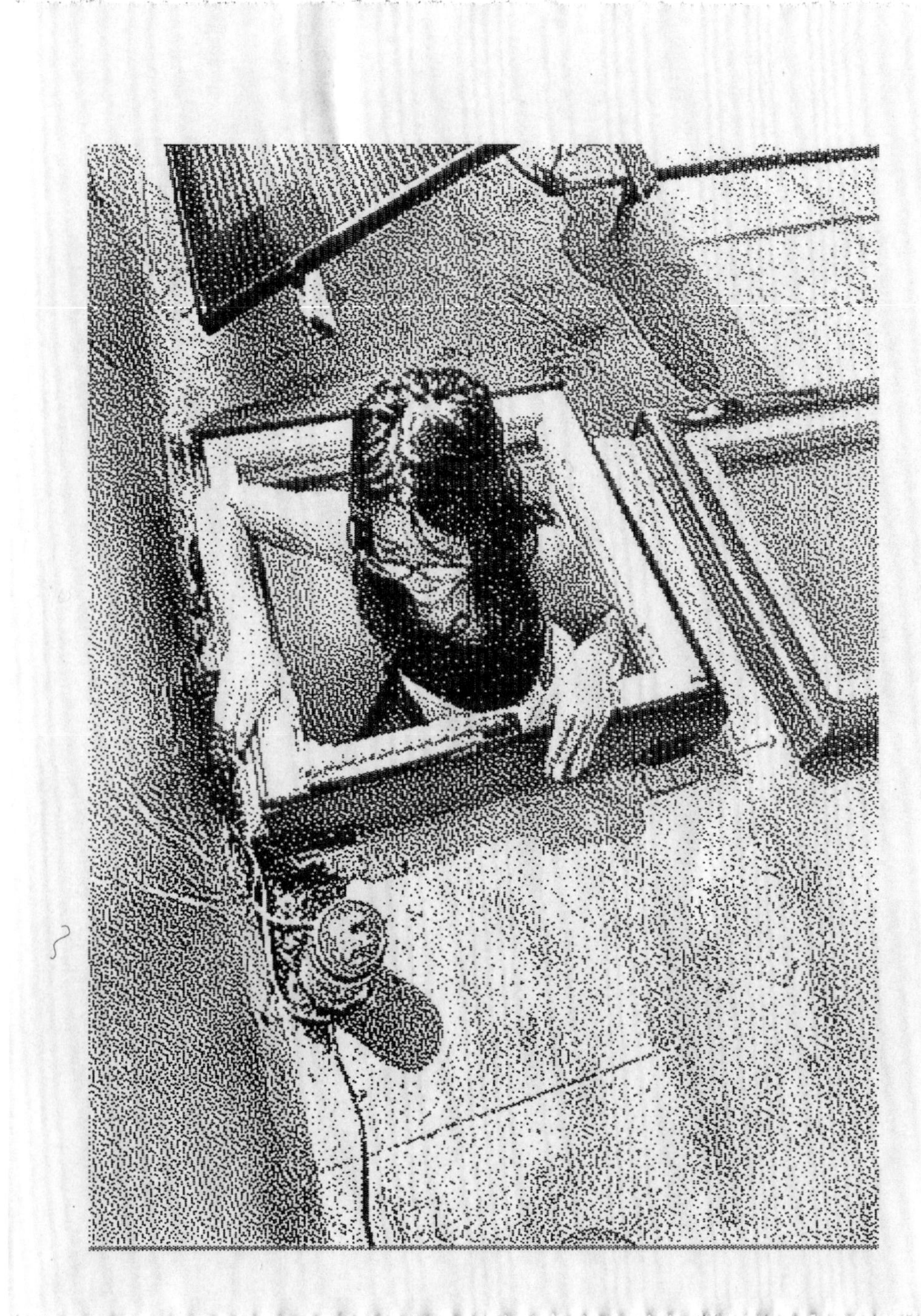

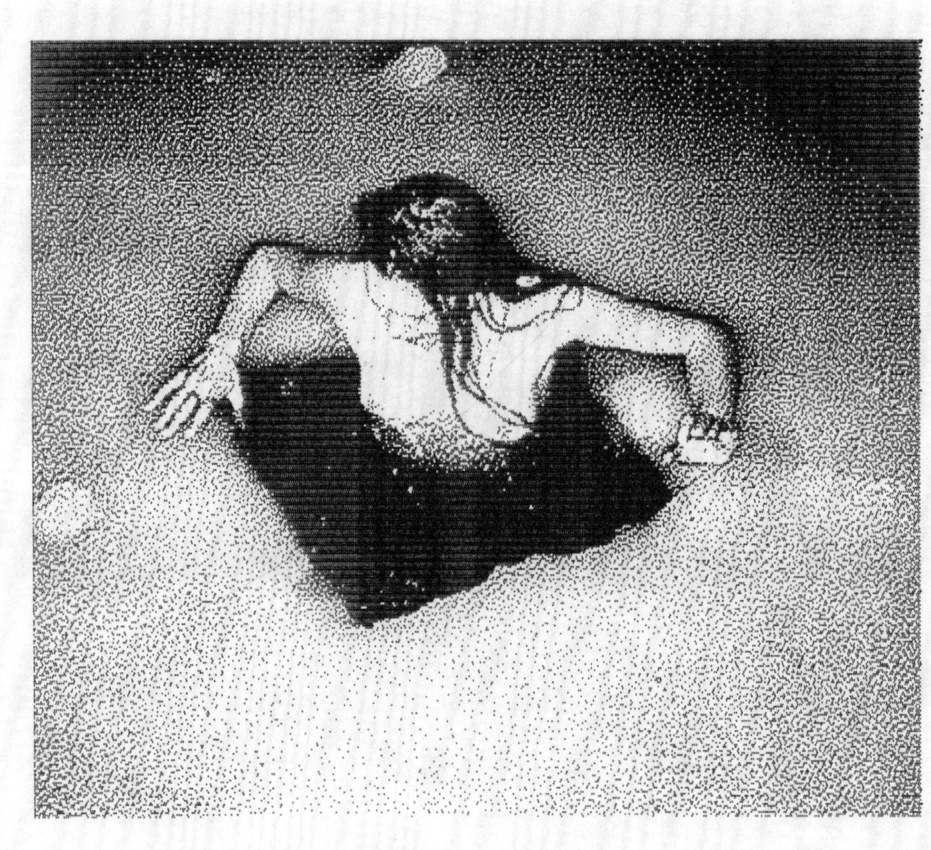

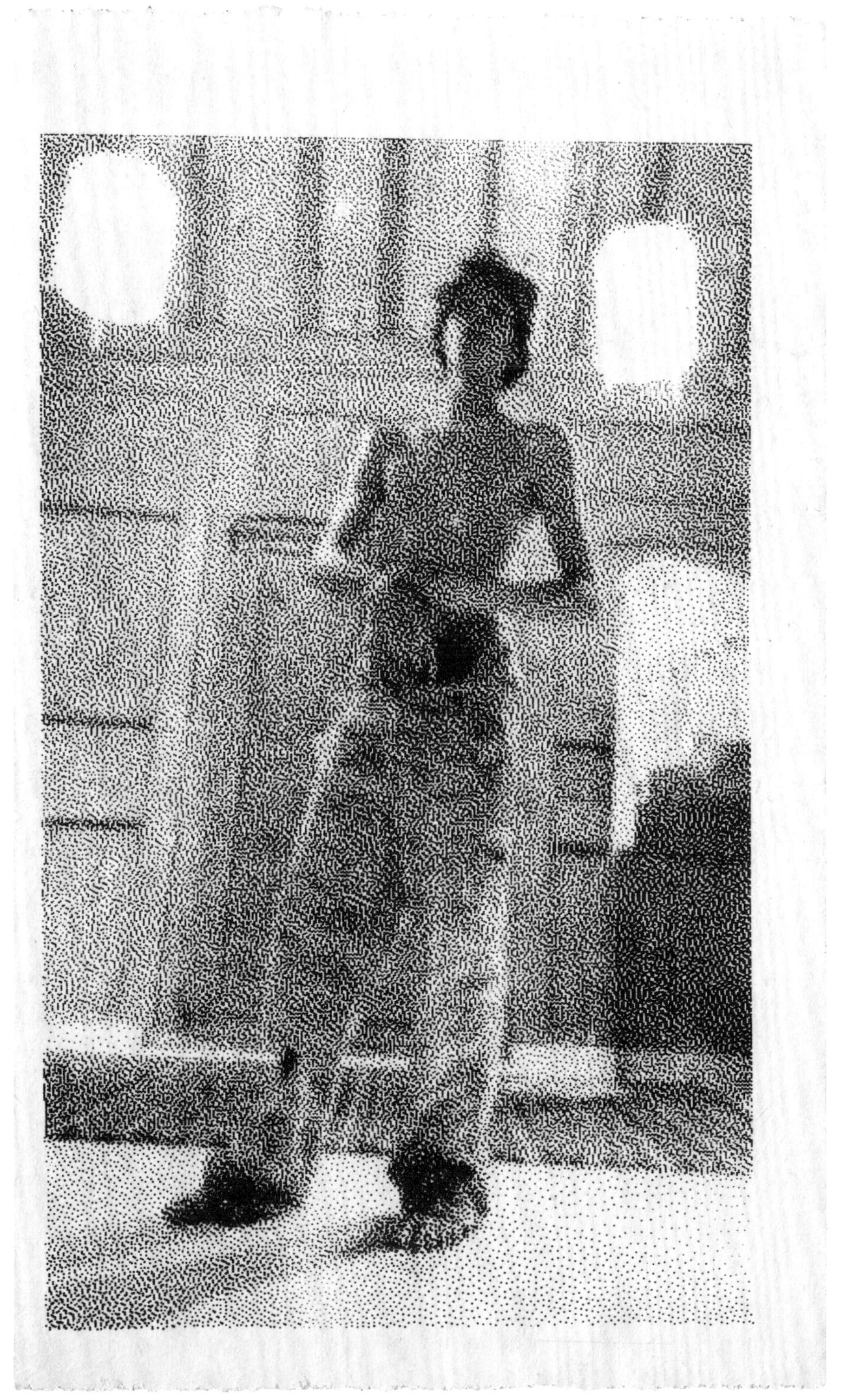

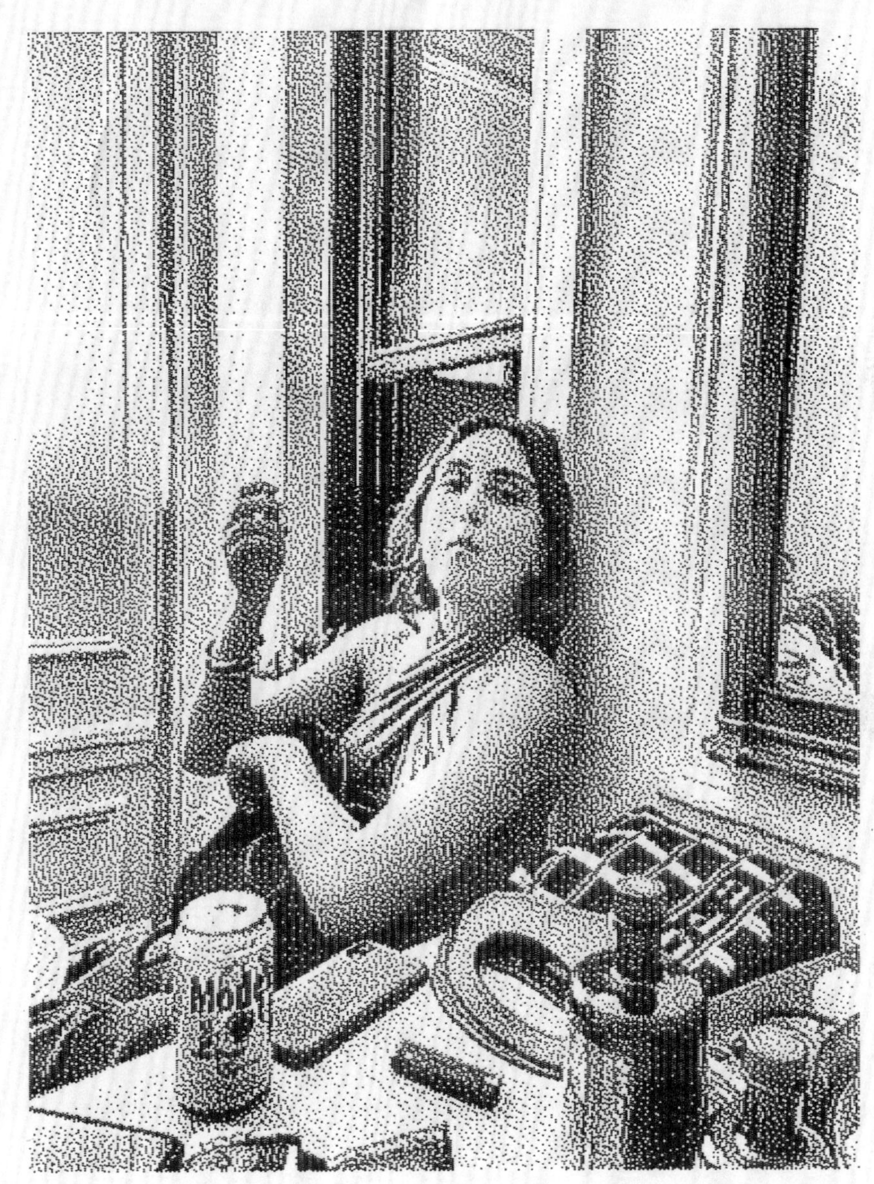

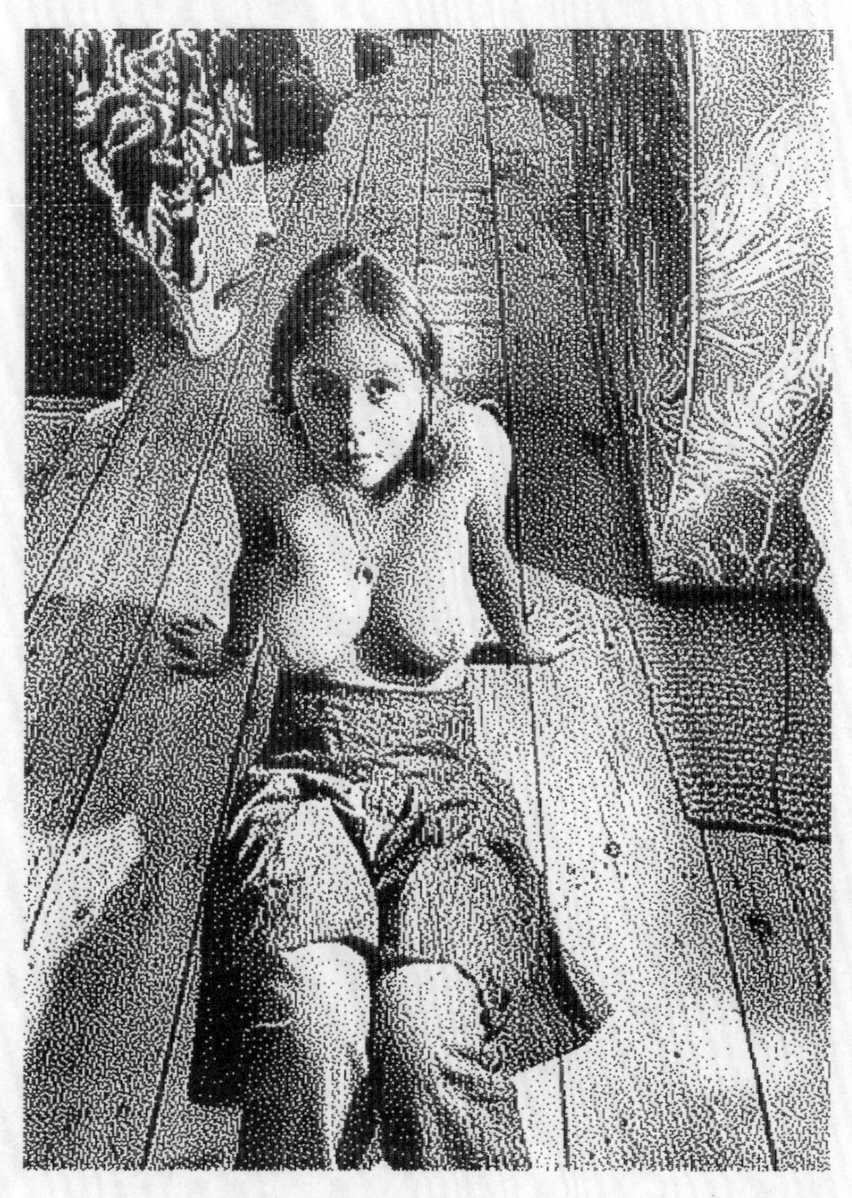

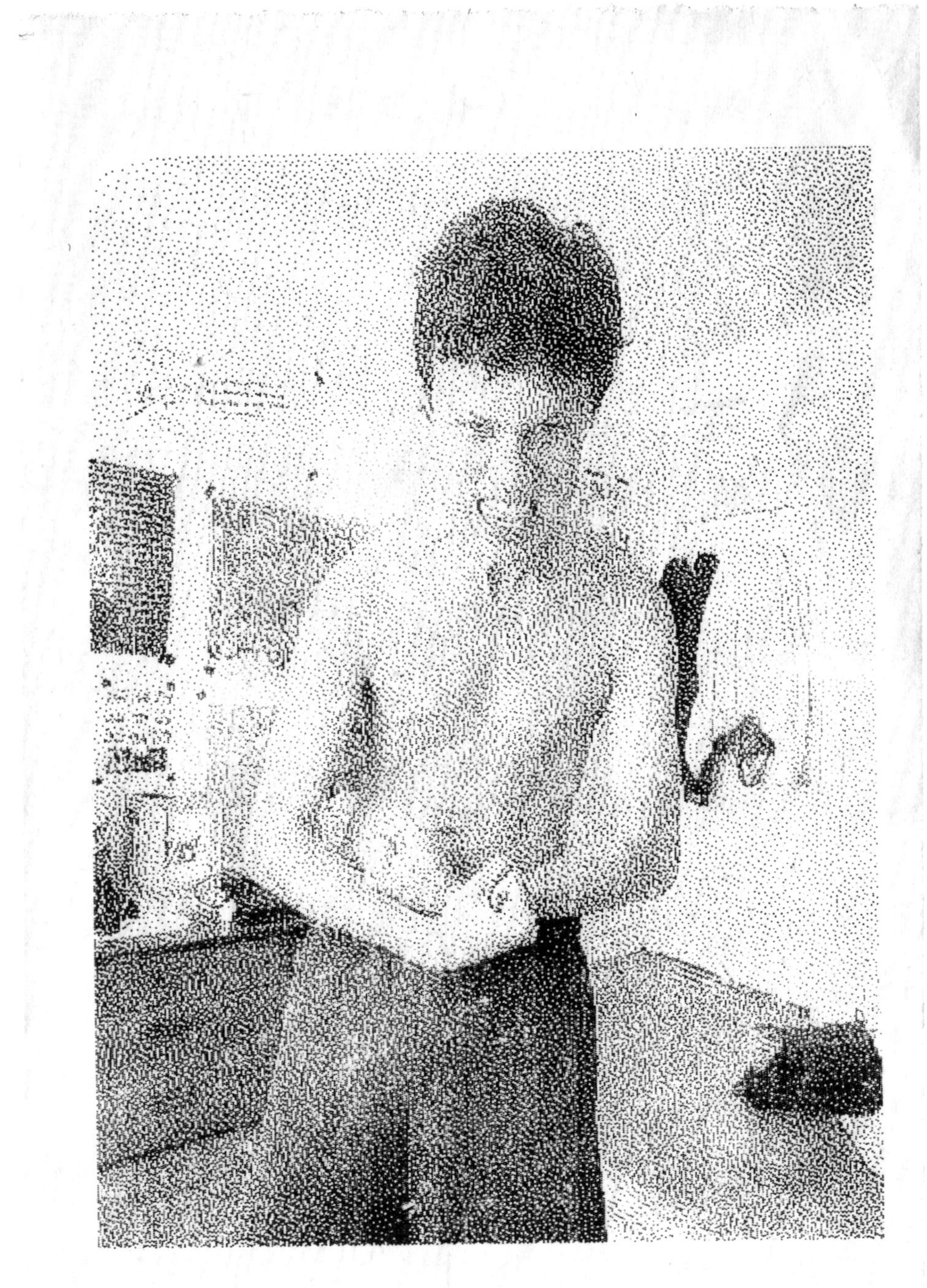

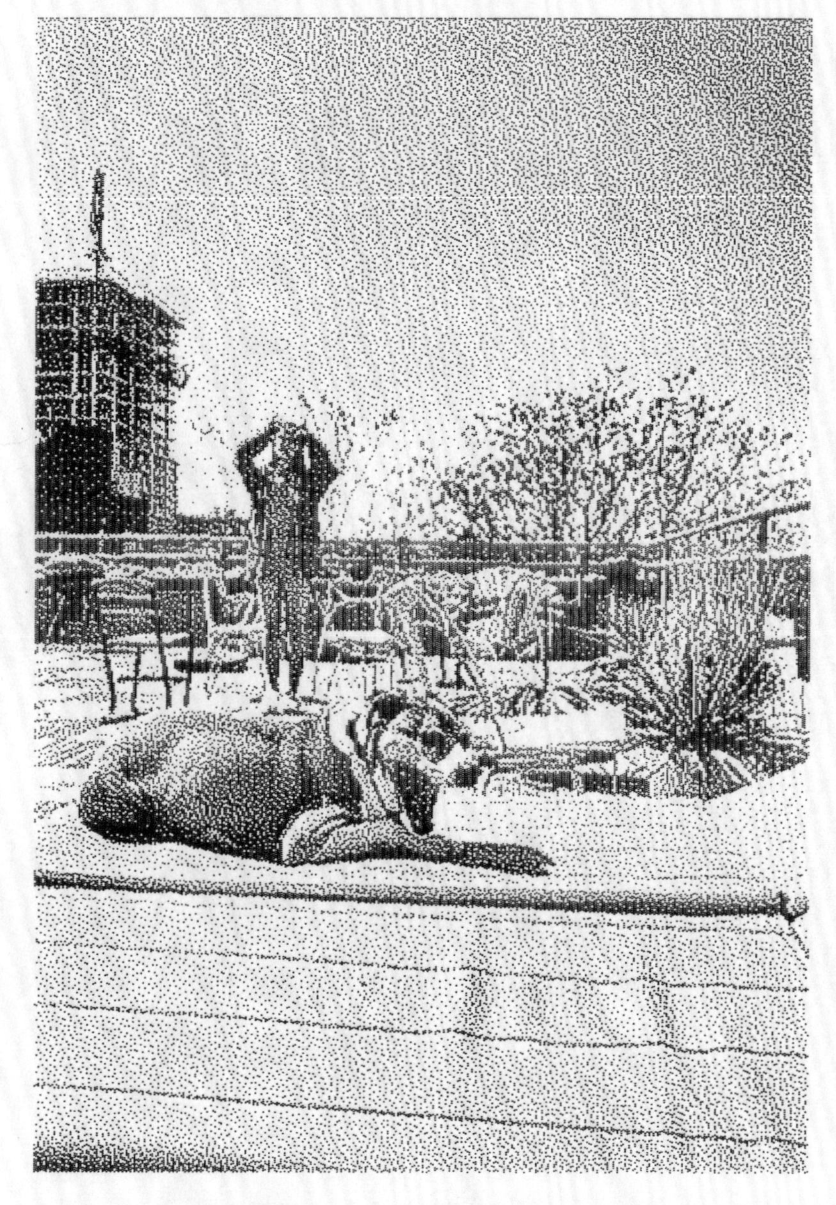

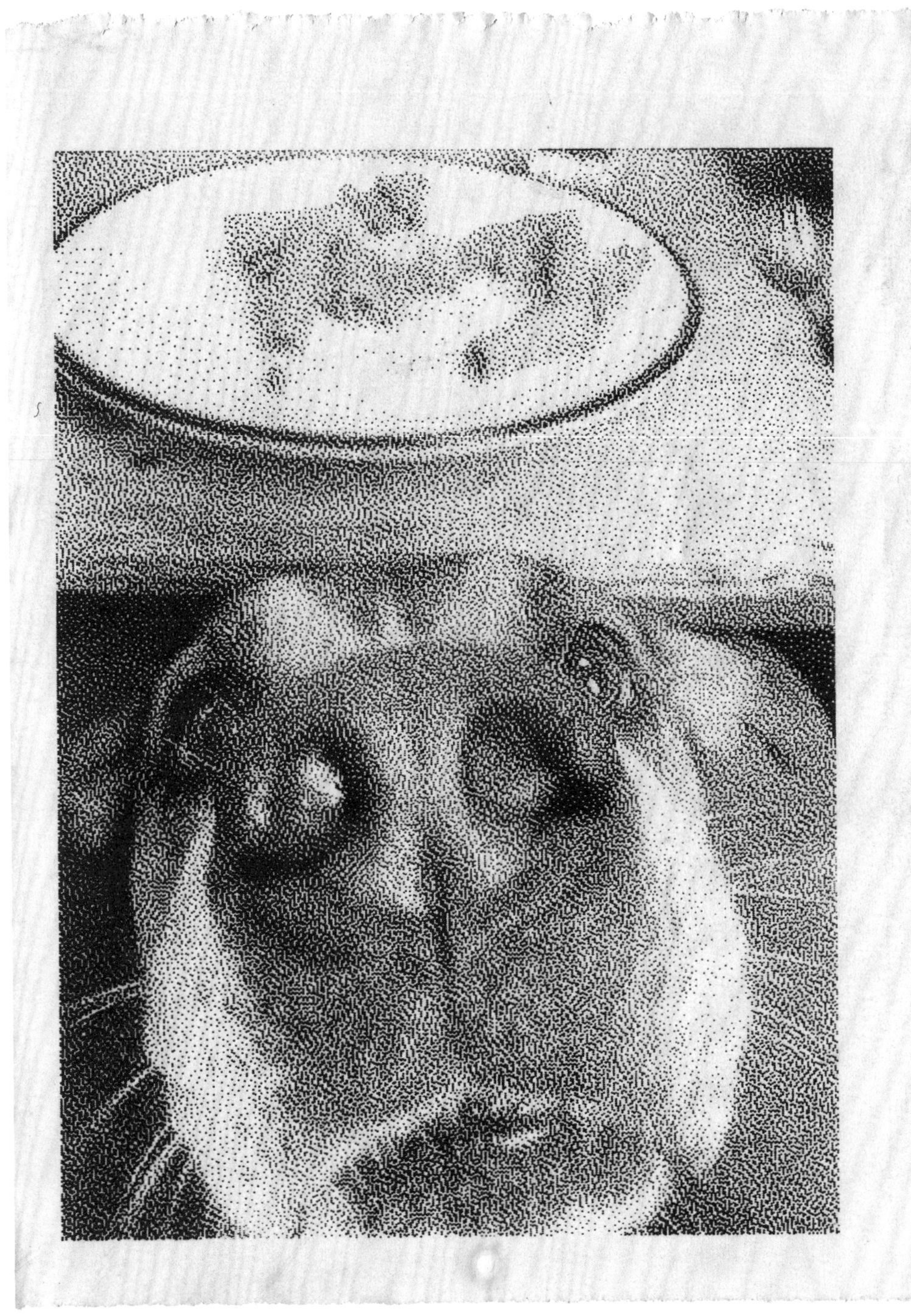

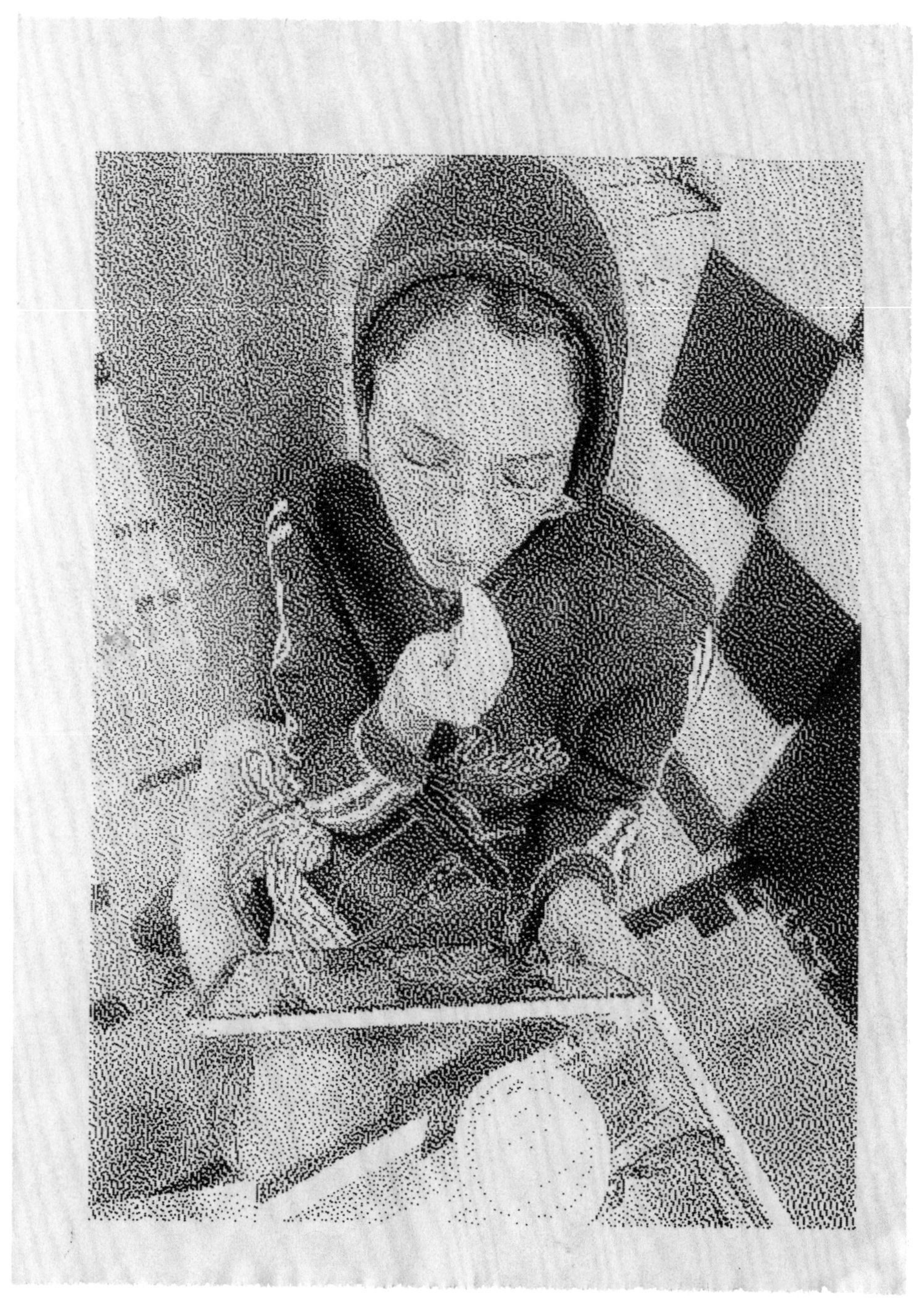

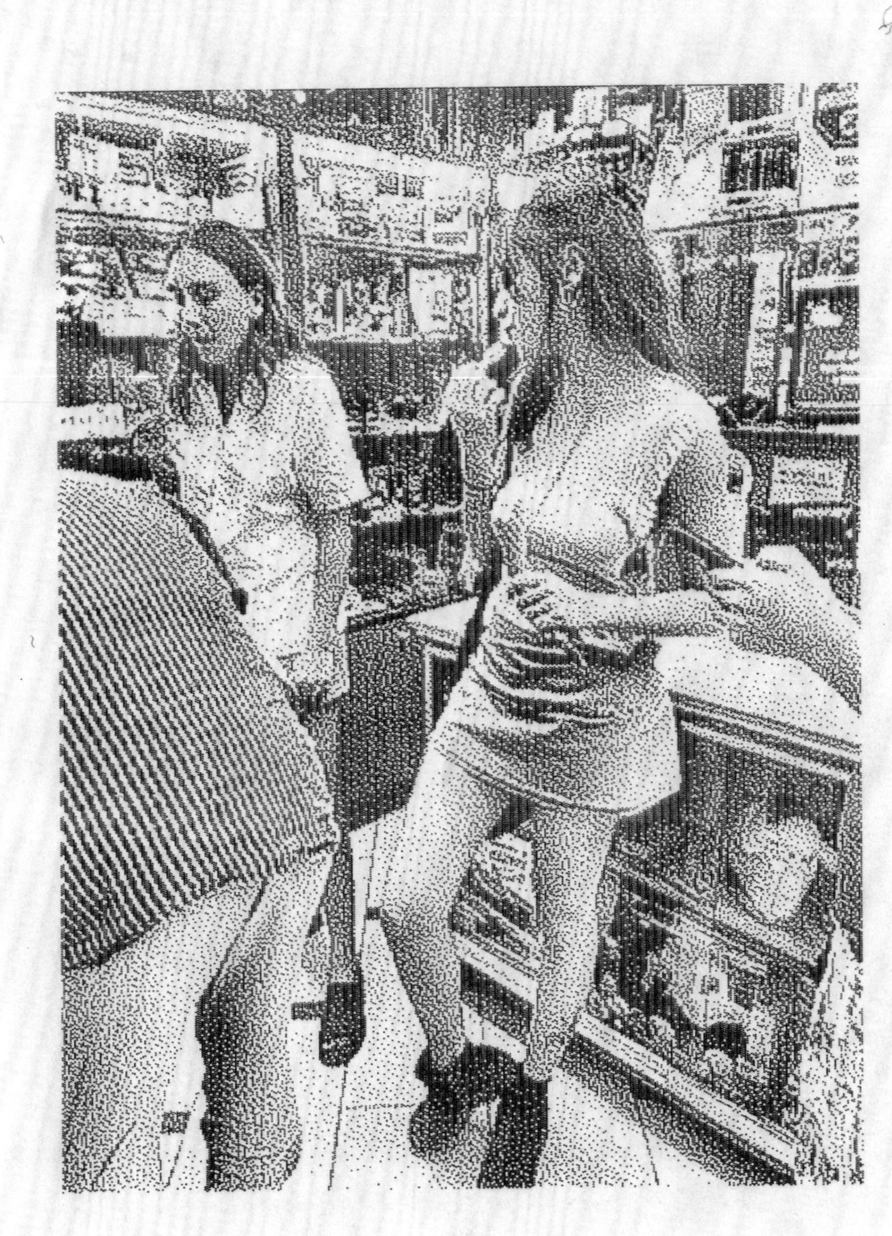

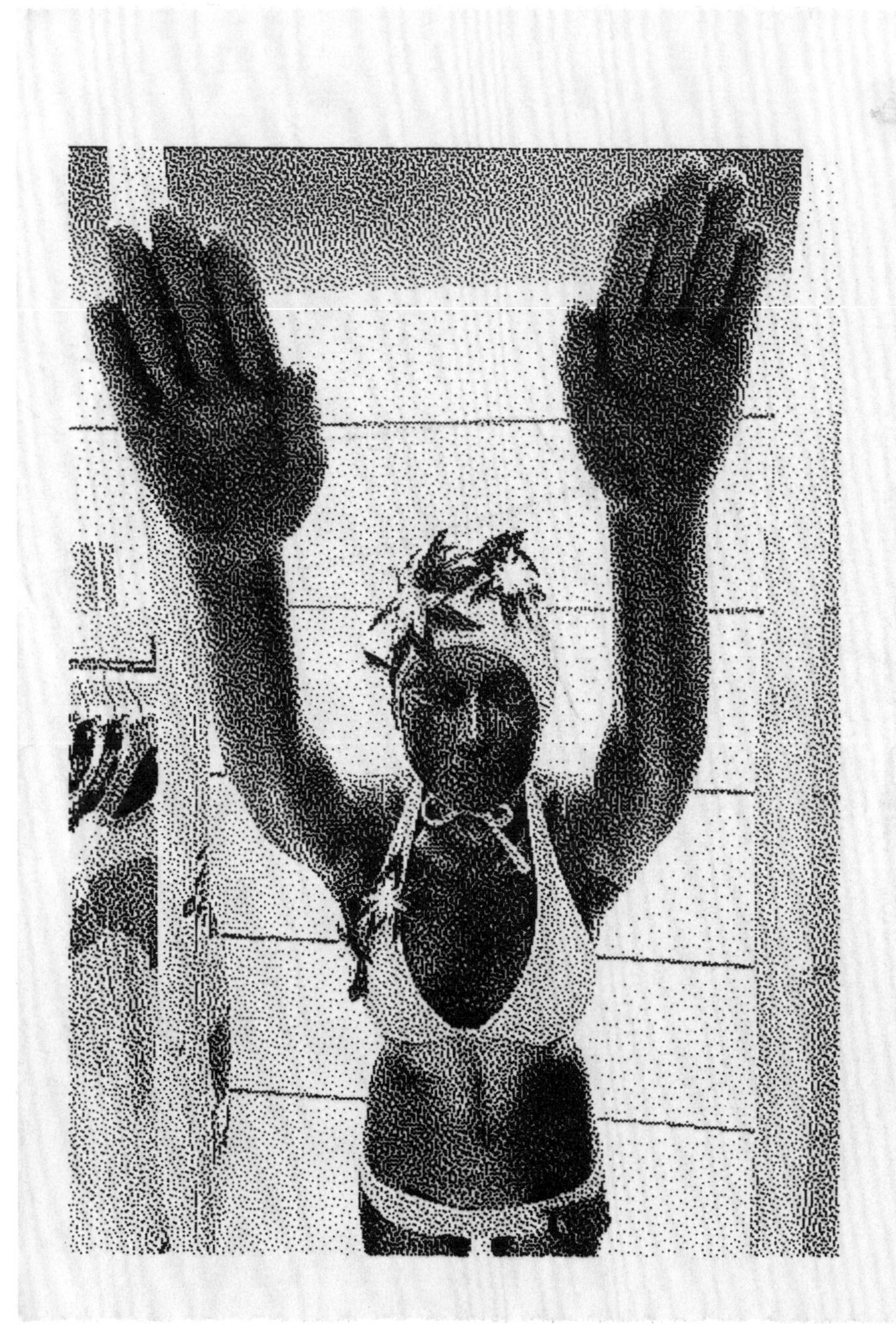

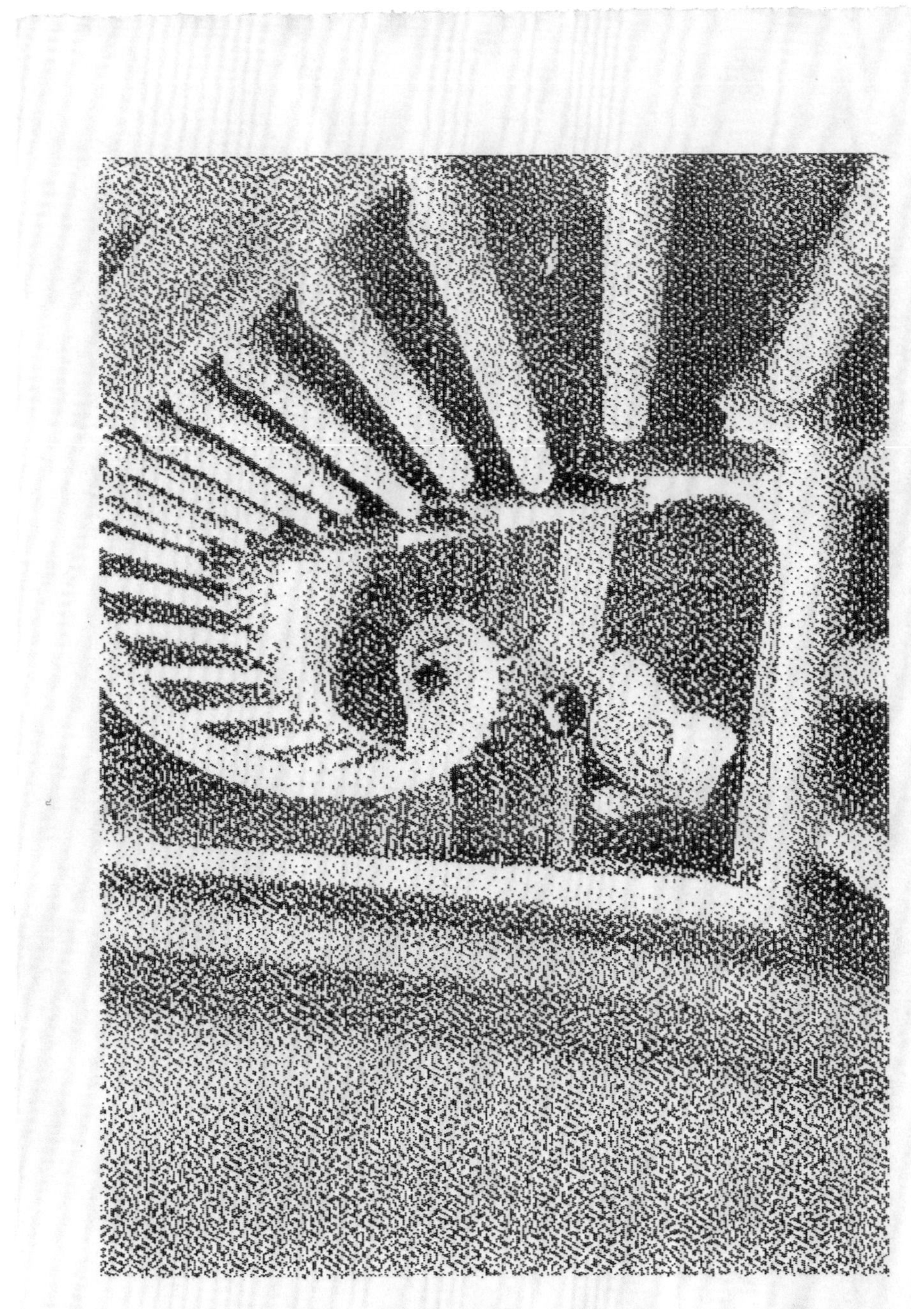

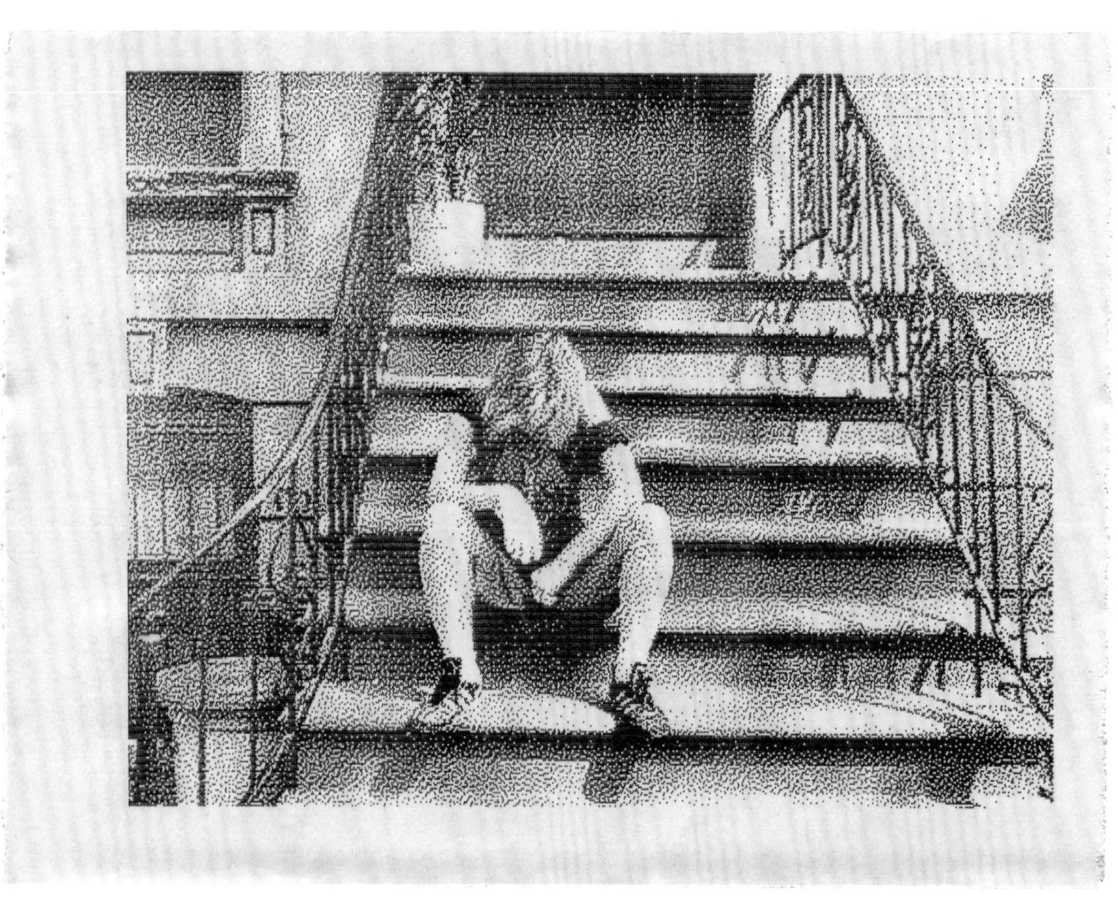

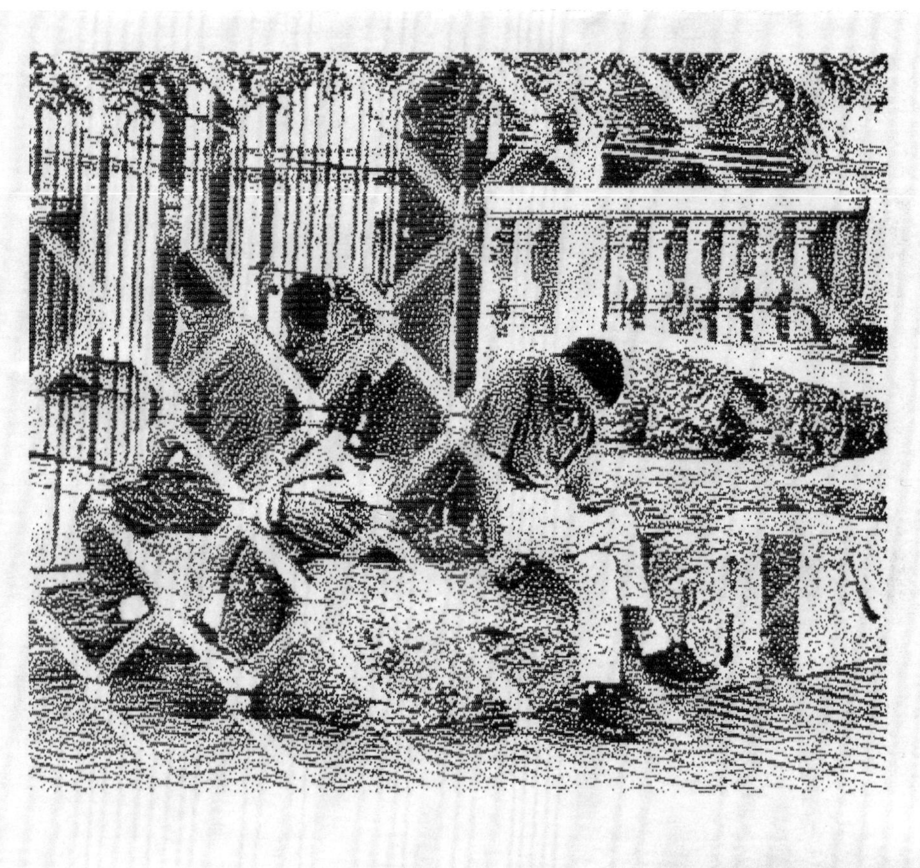

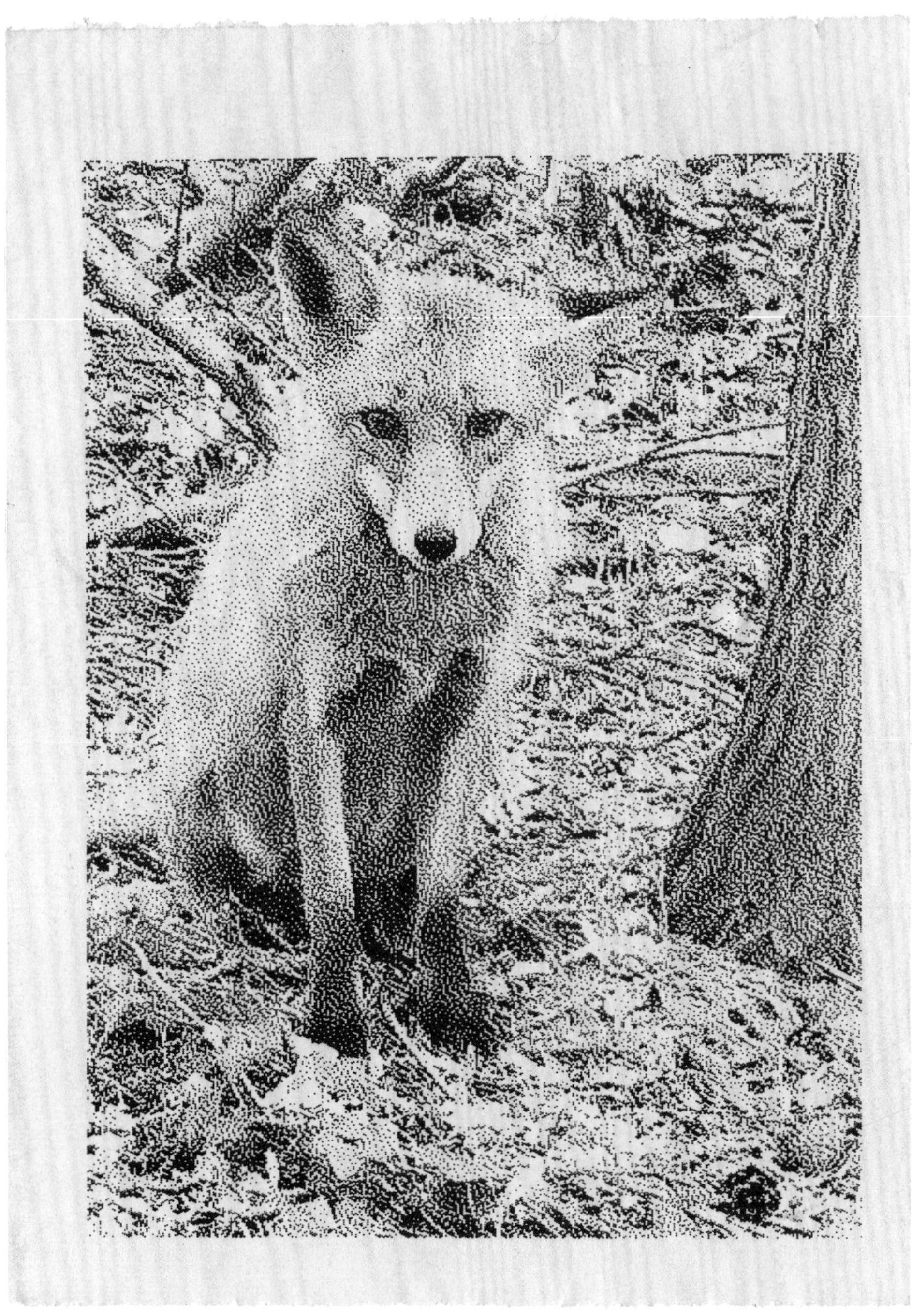

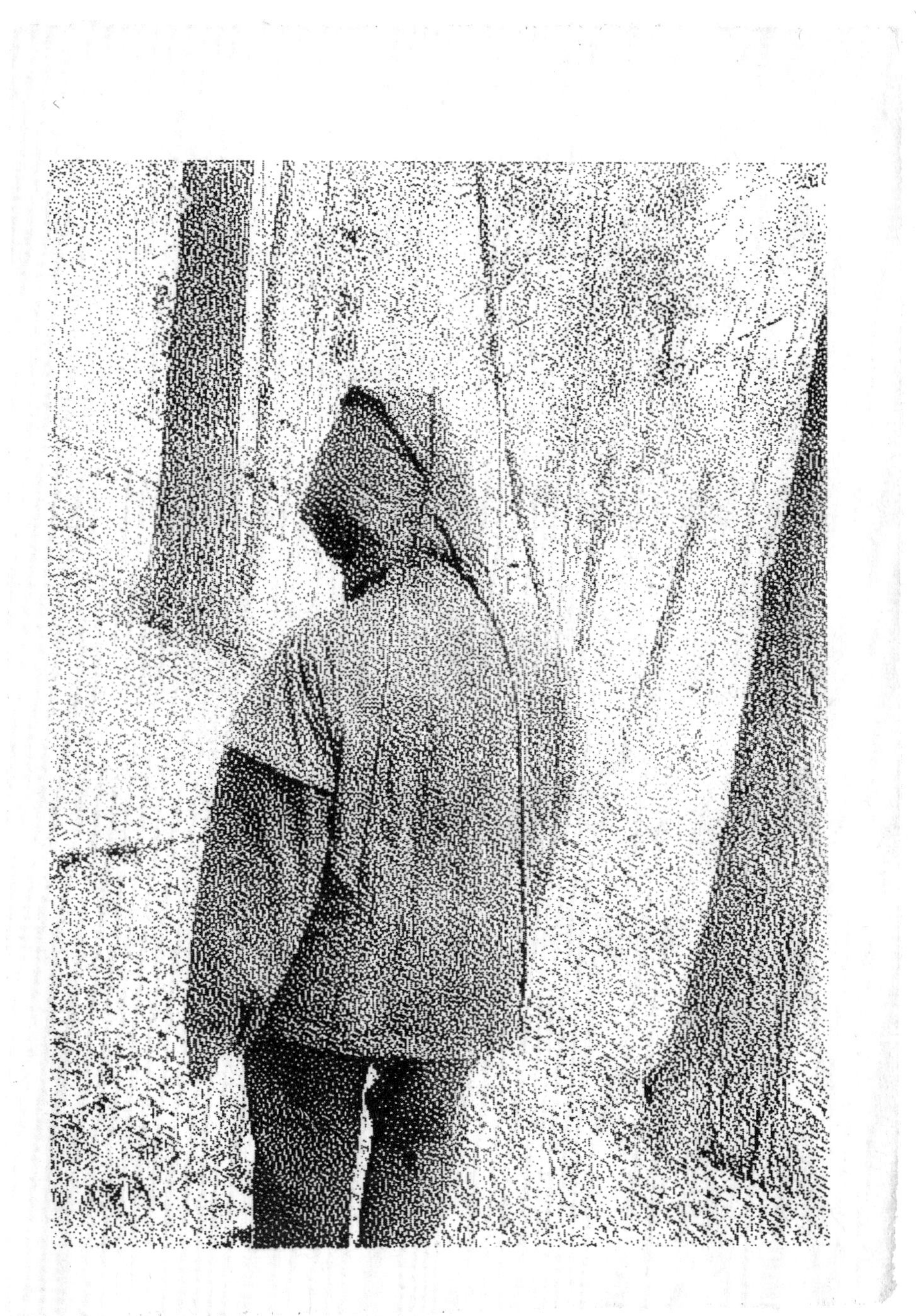

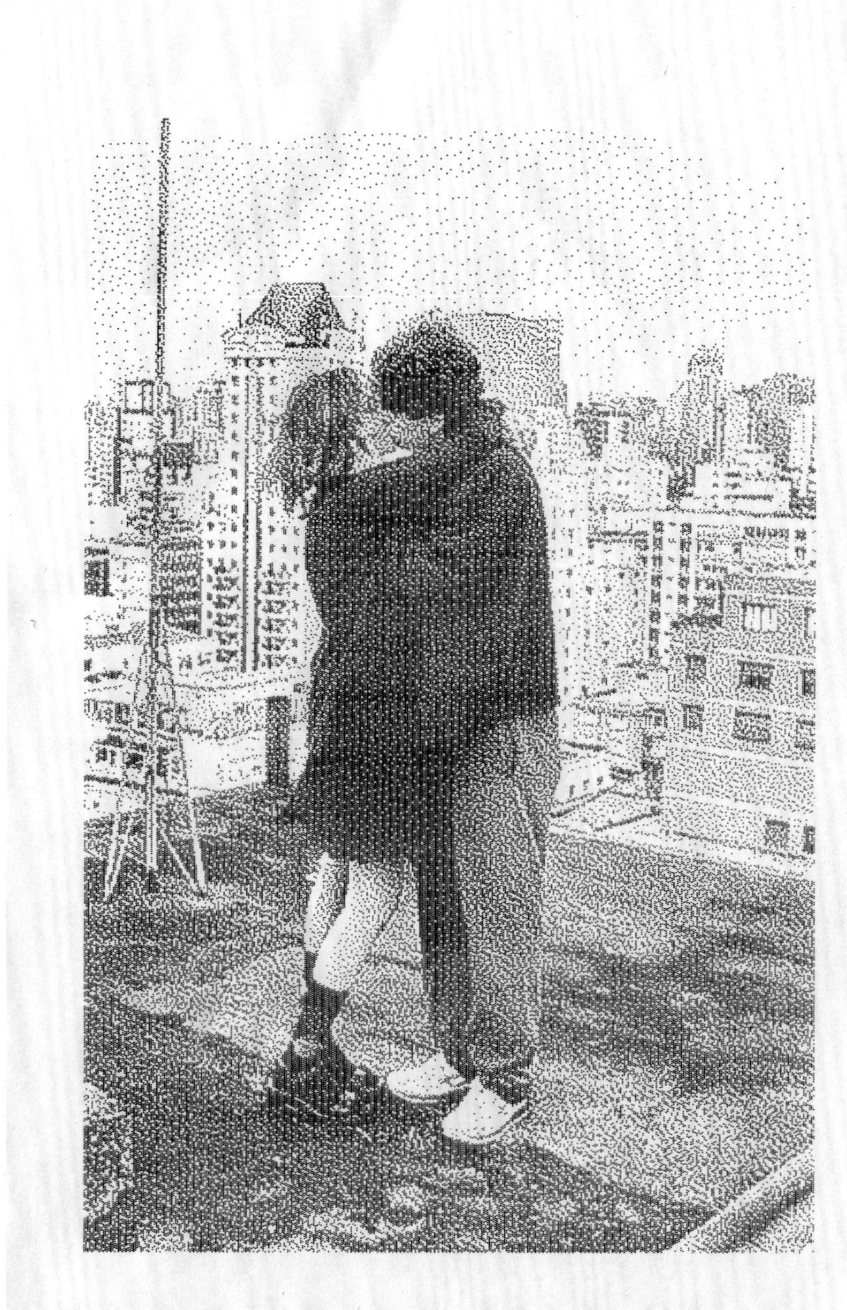

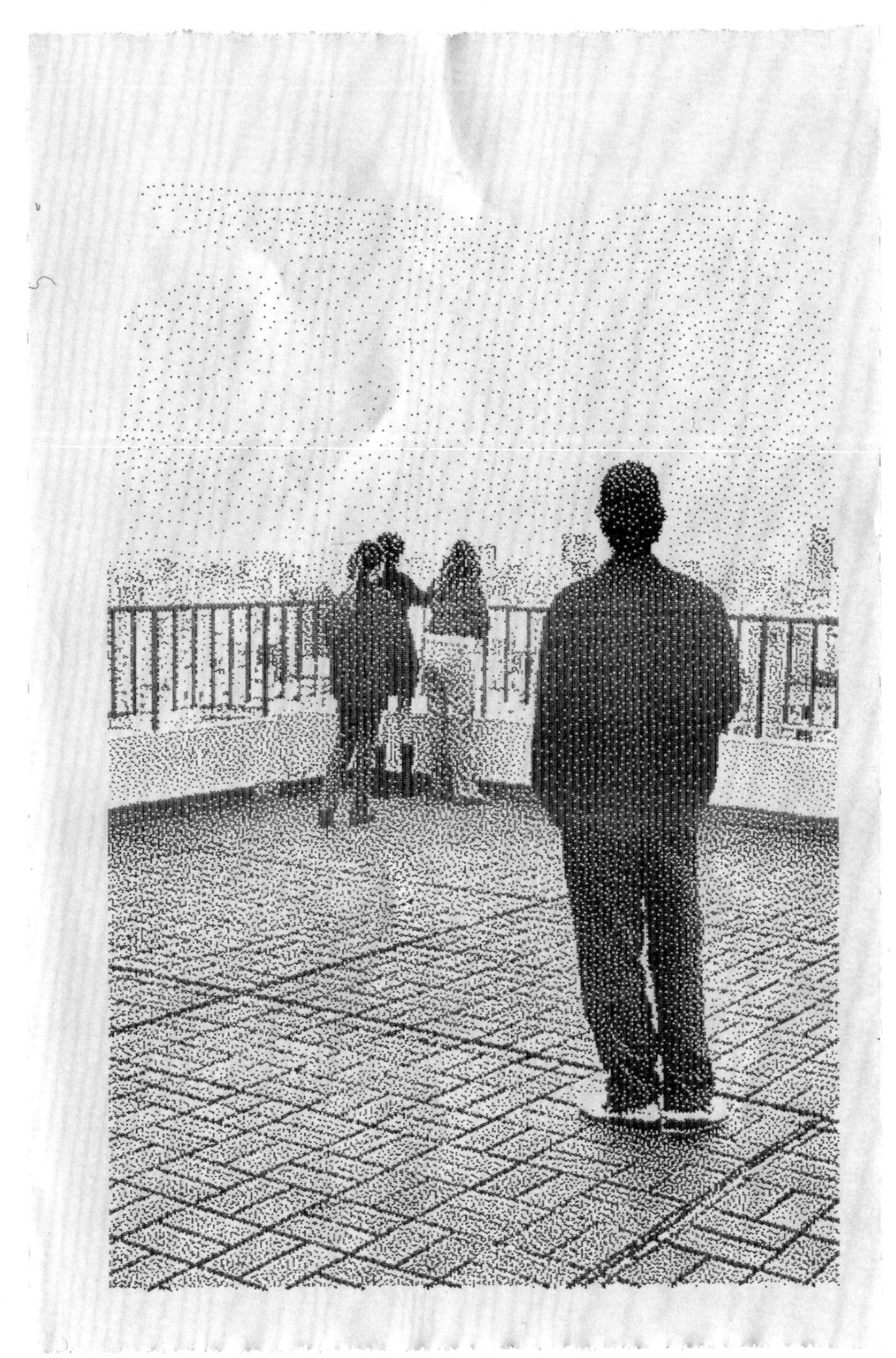

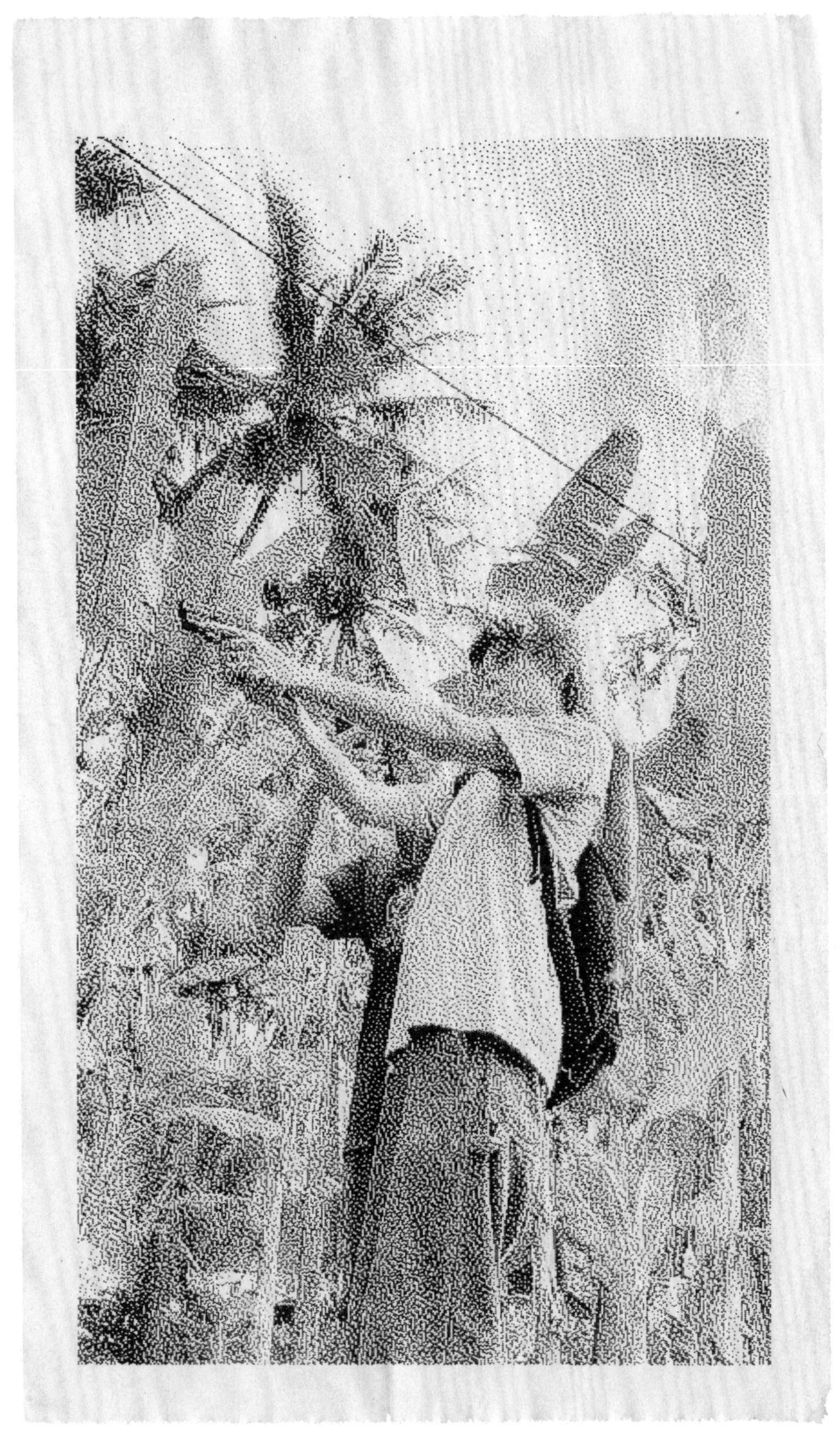

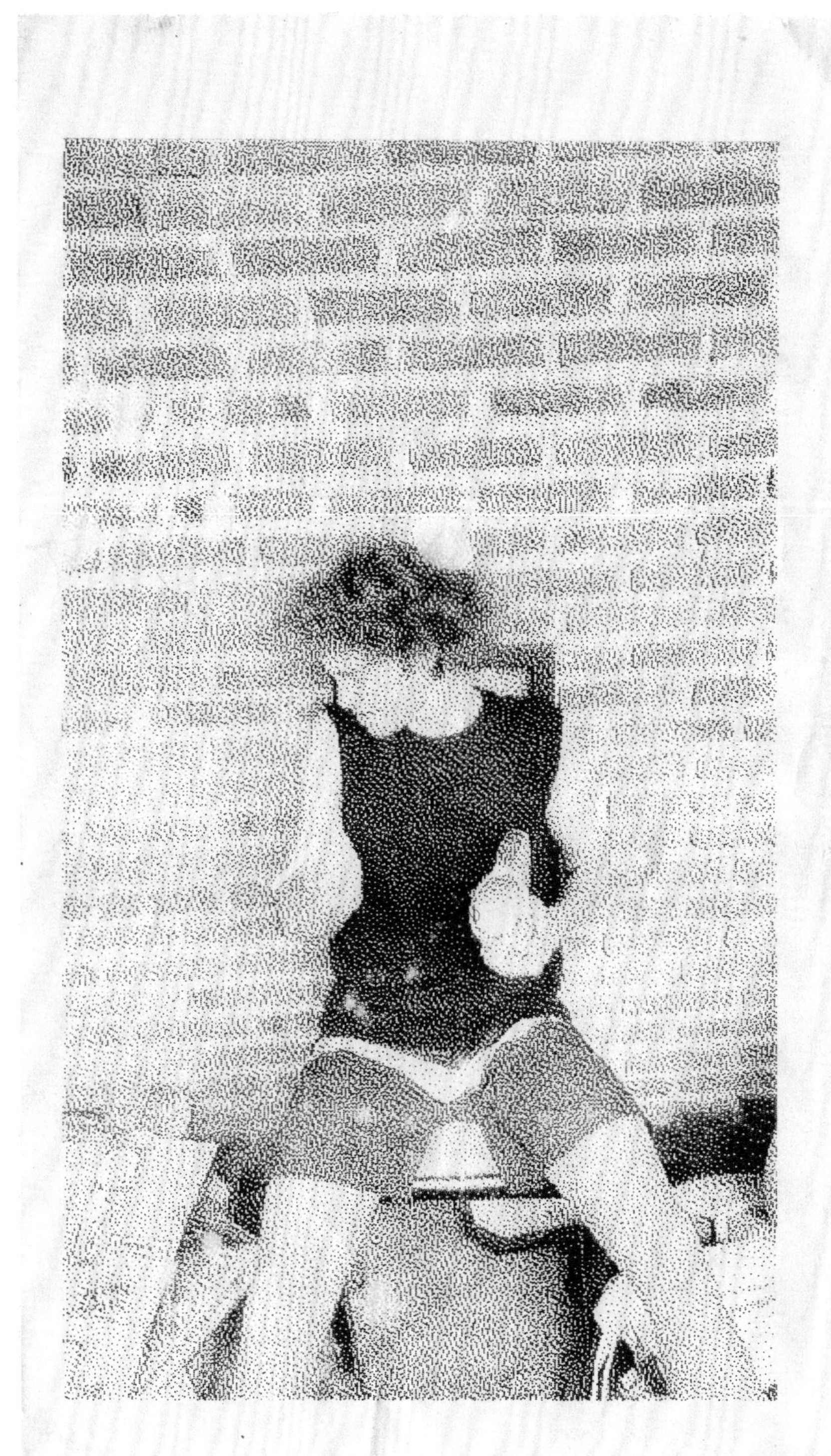

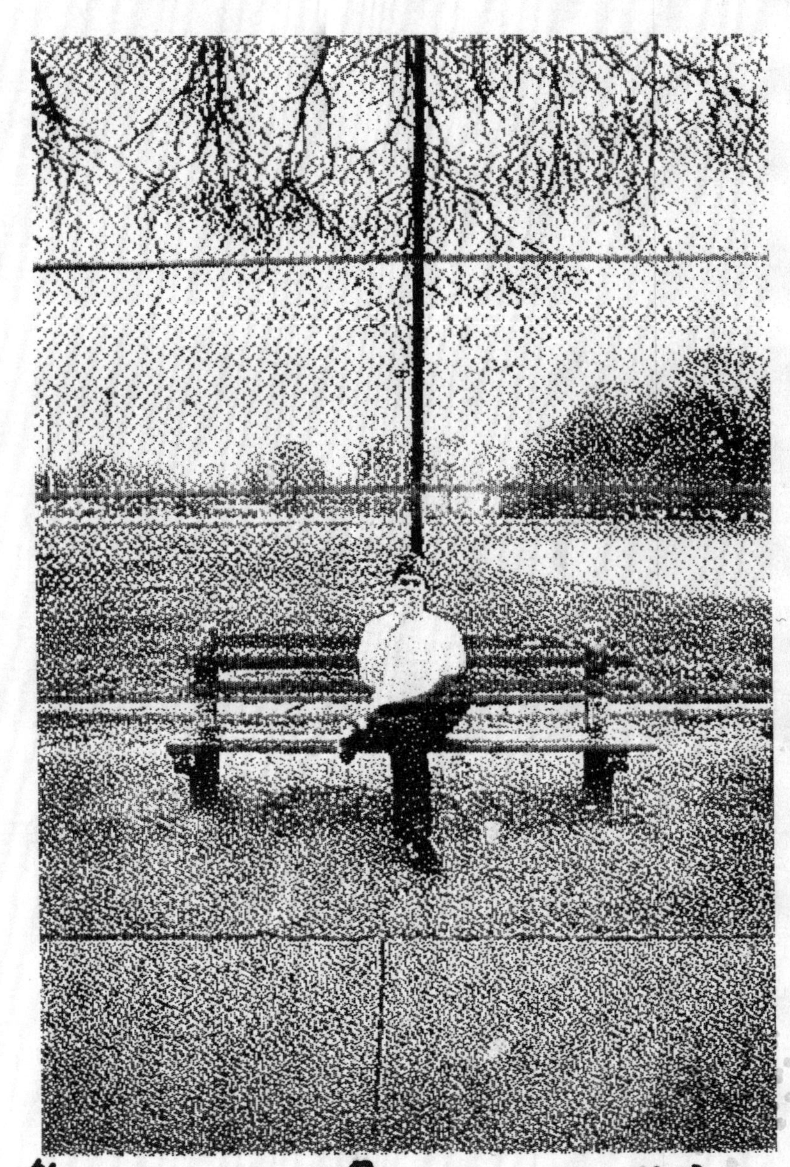
thank you for everything.

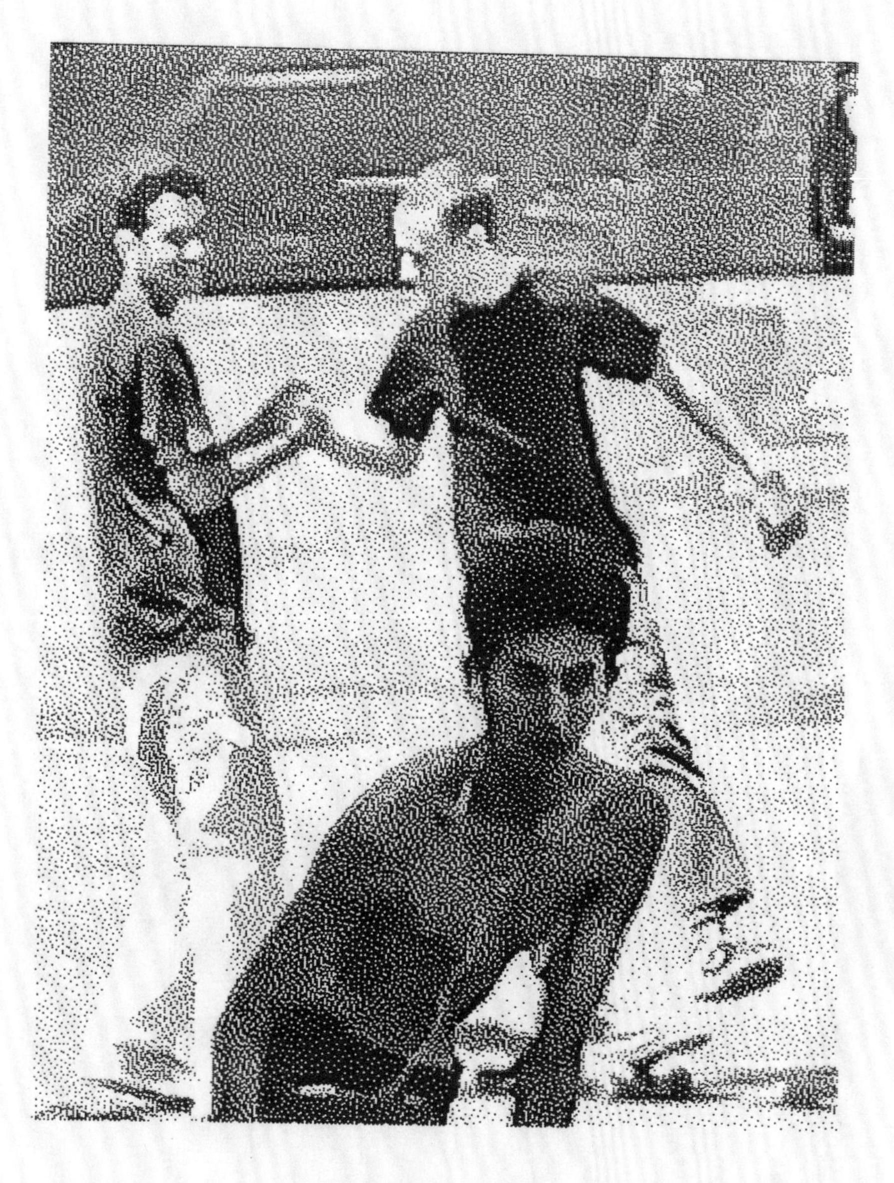

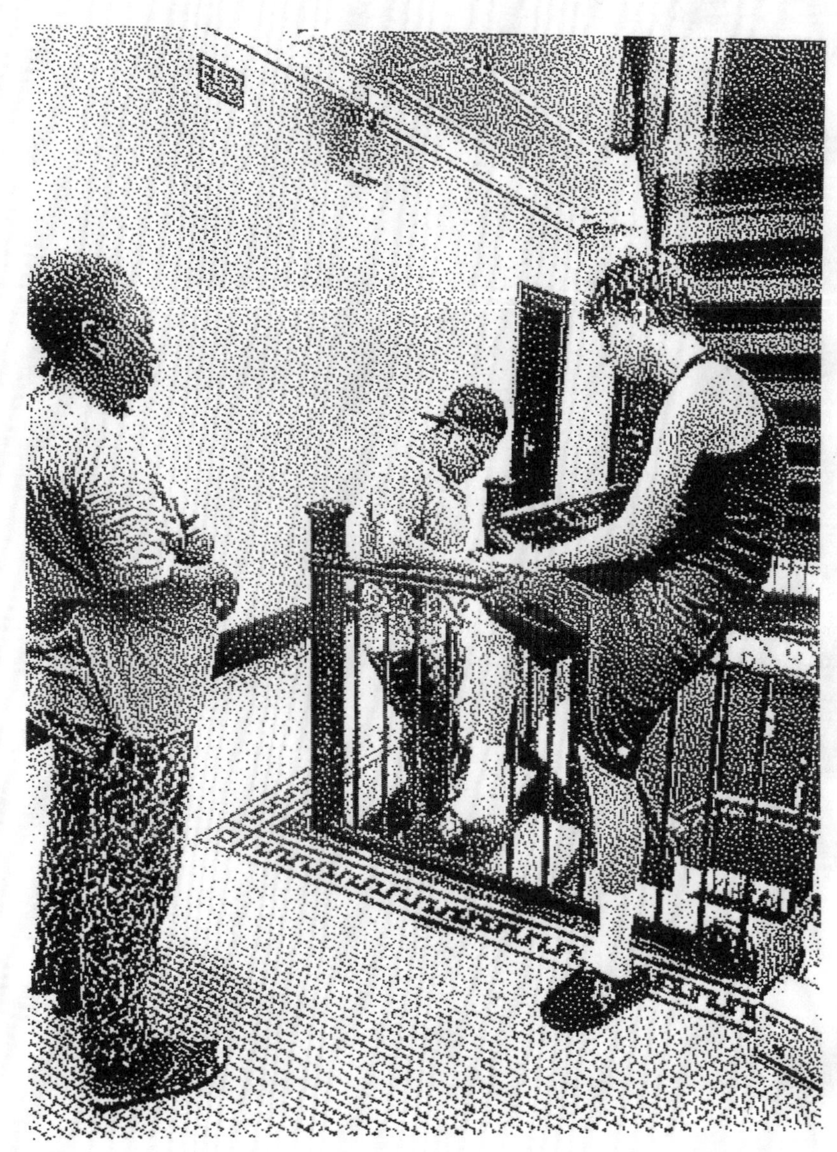

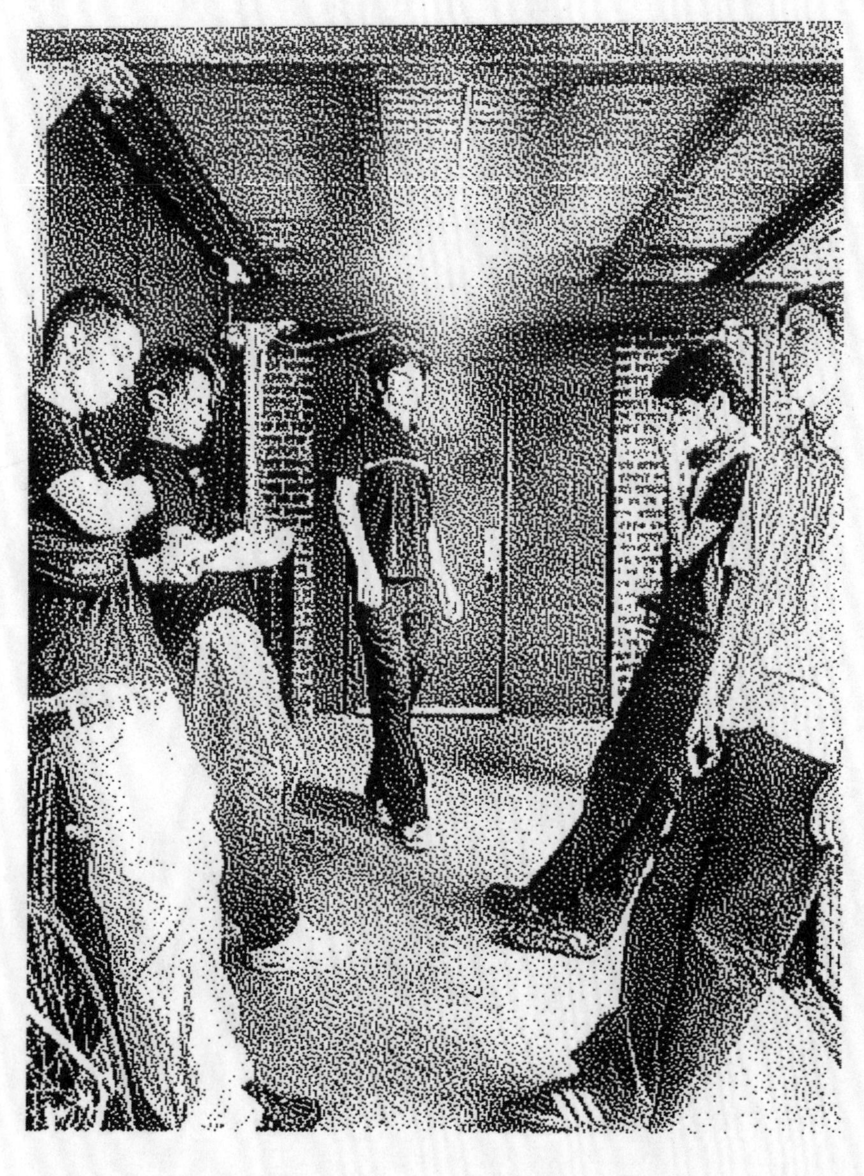

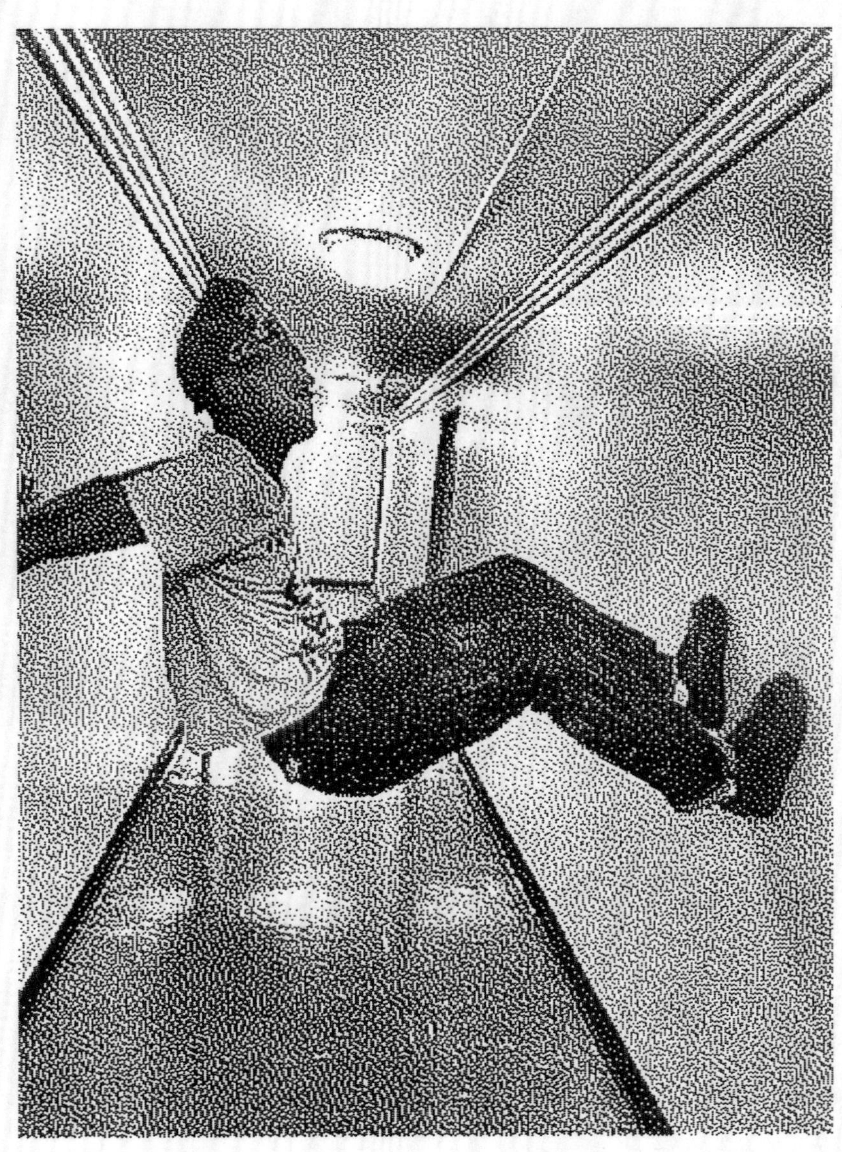

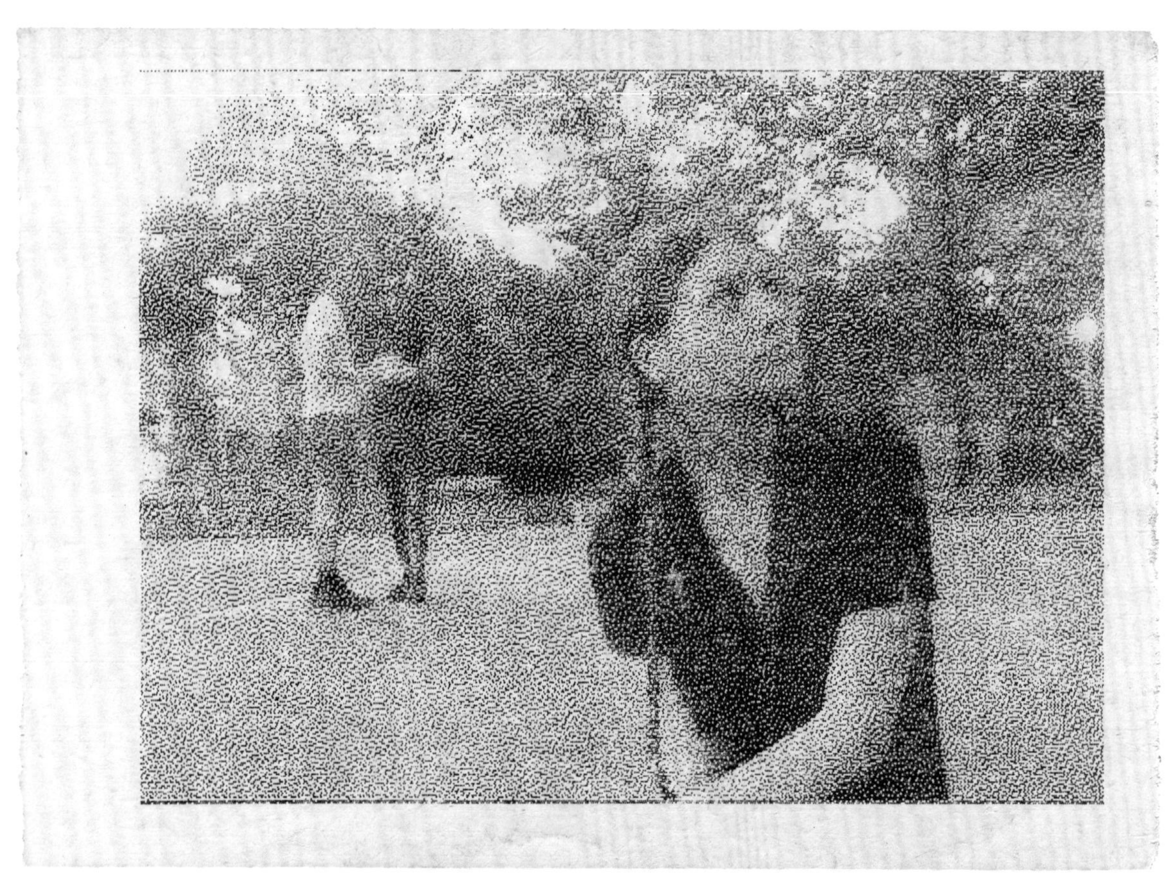

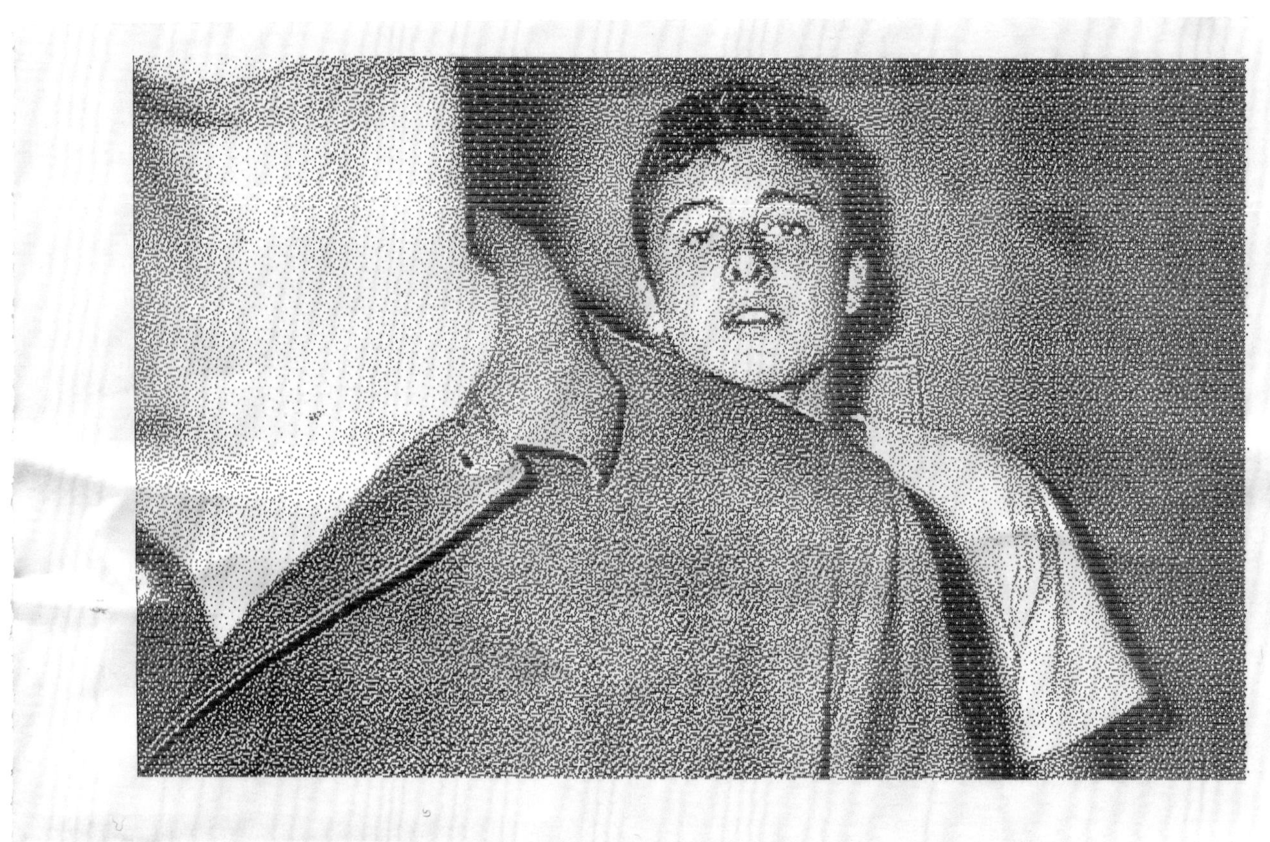

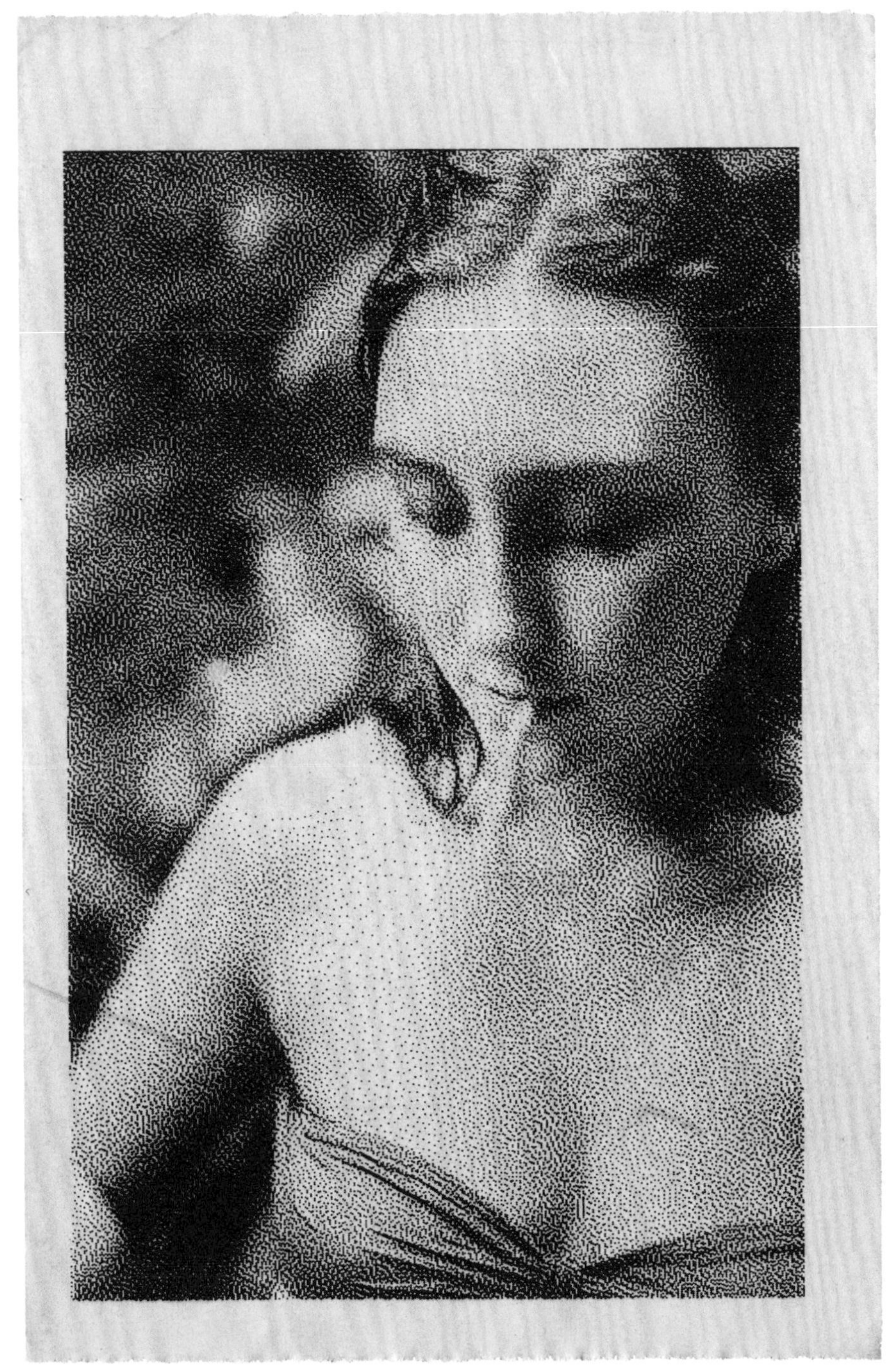

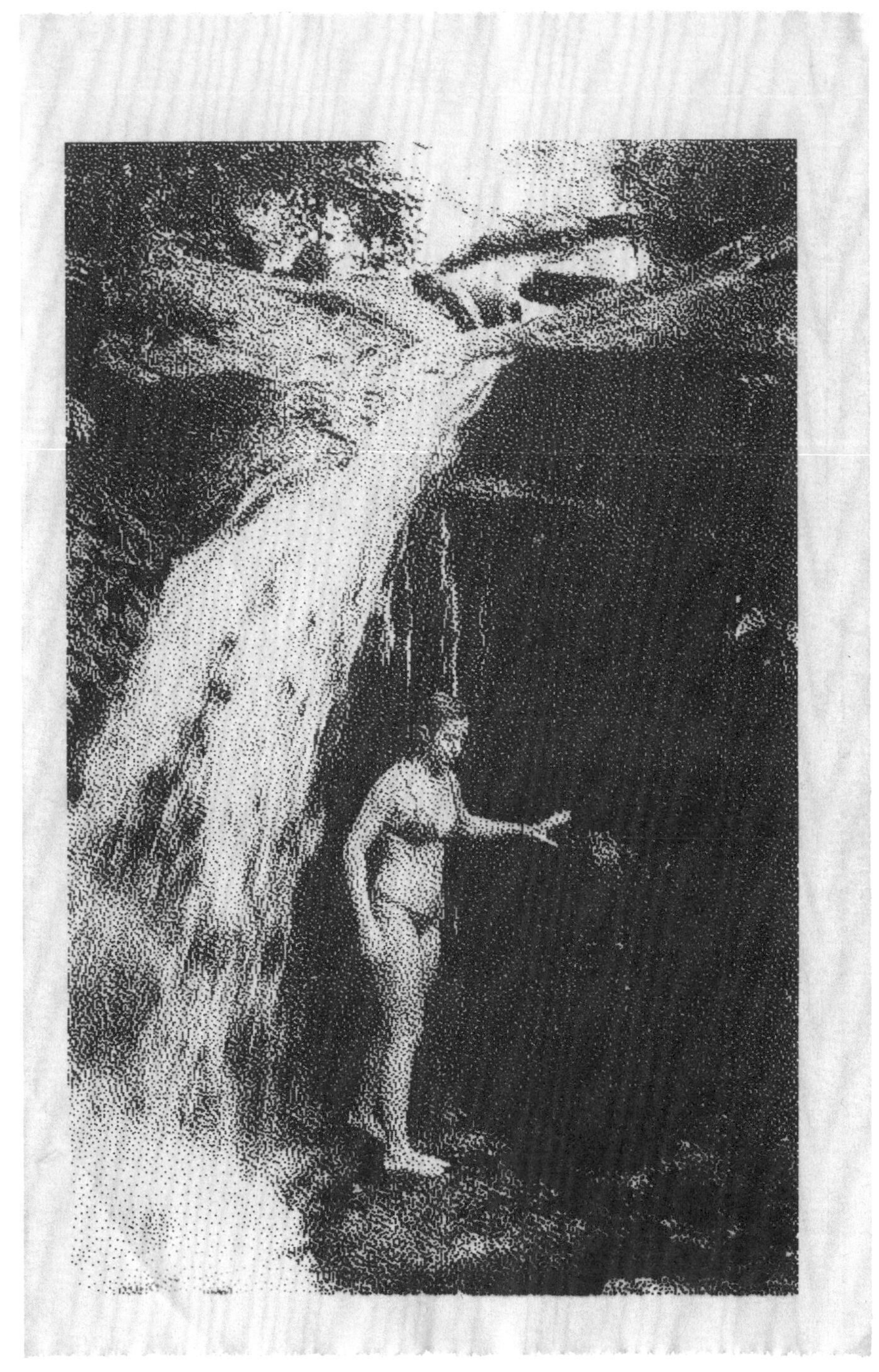

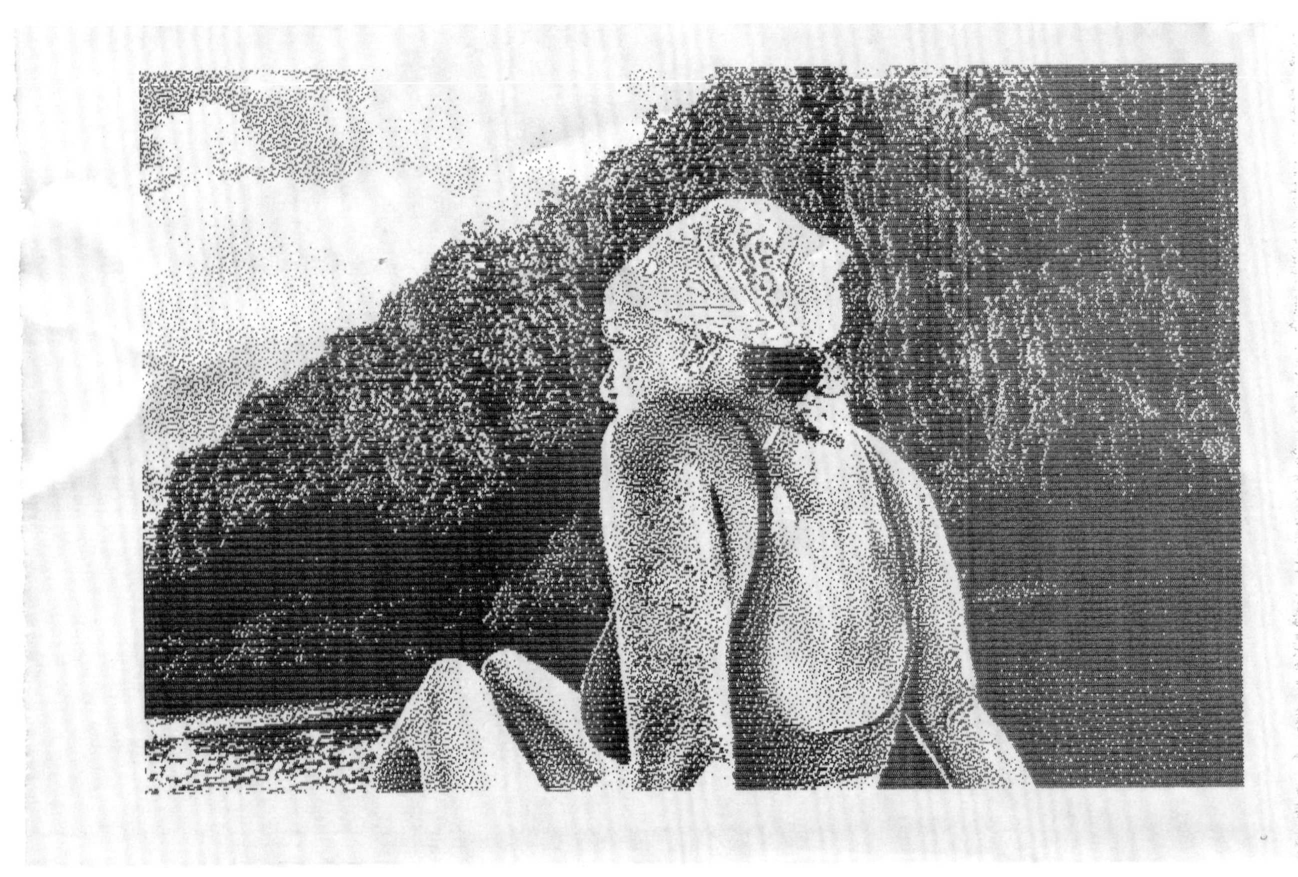

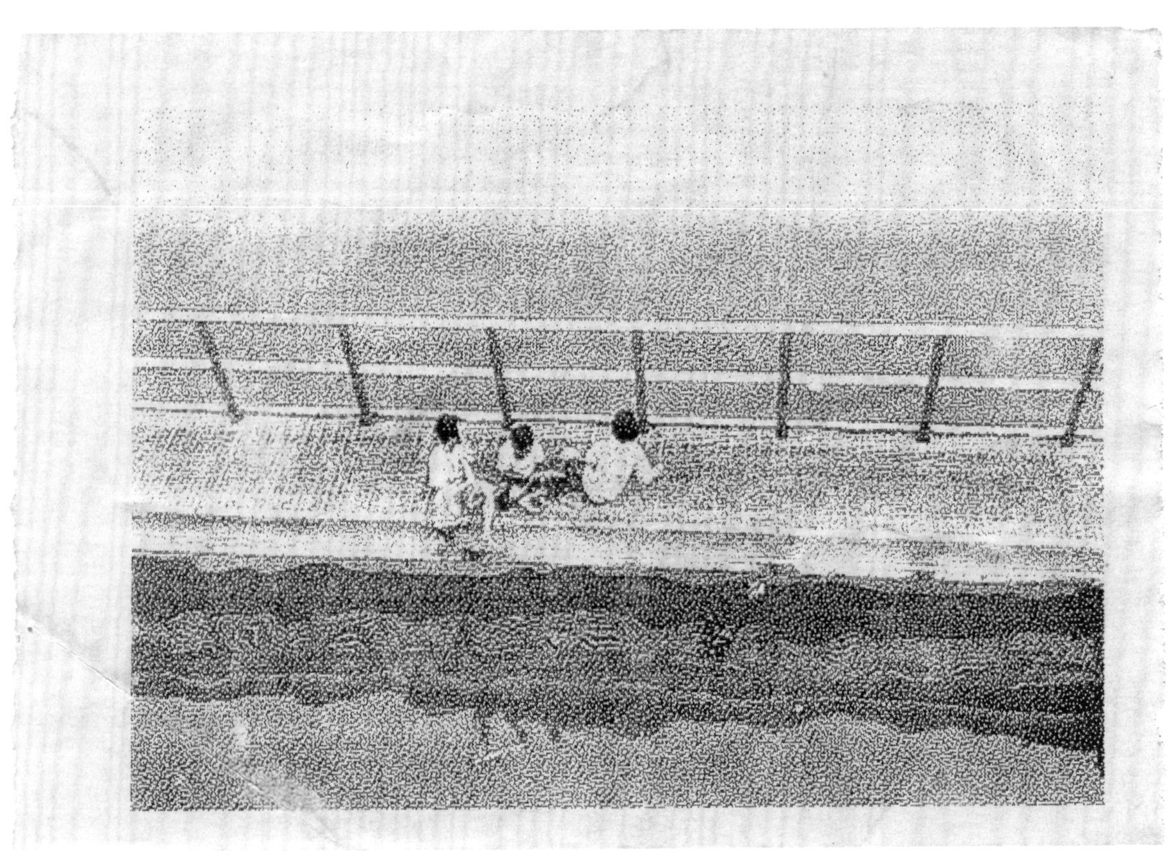

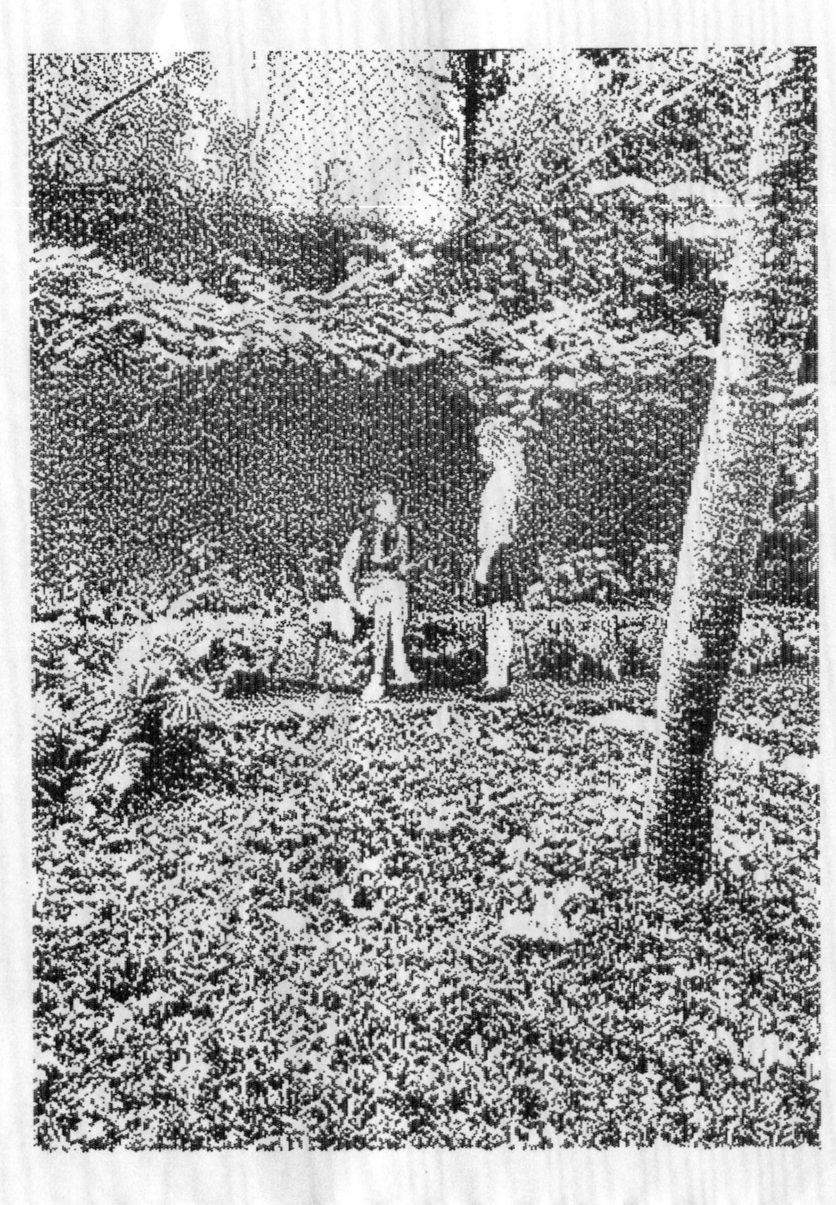

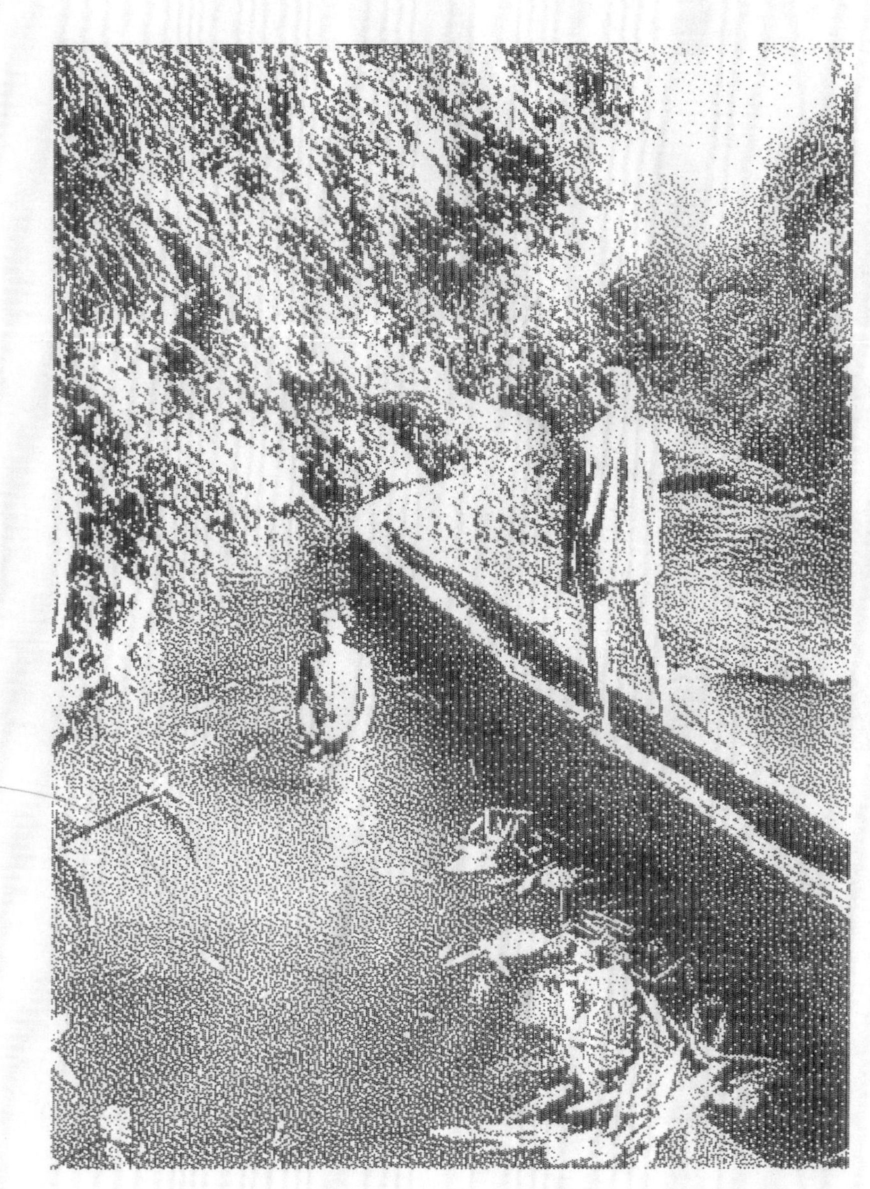

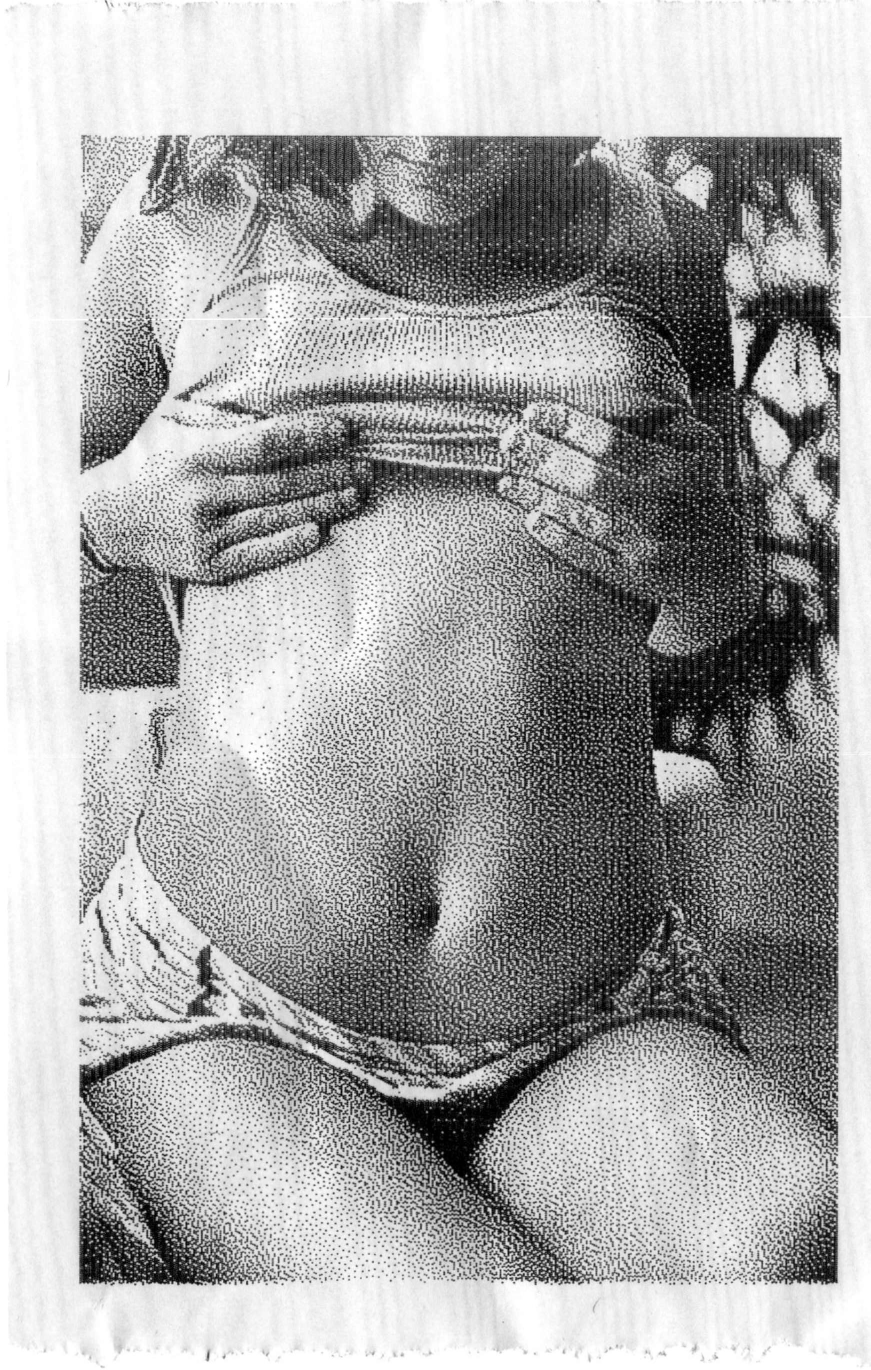

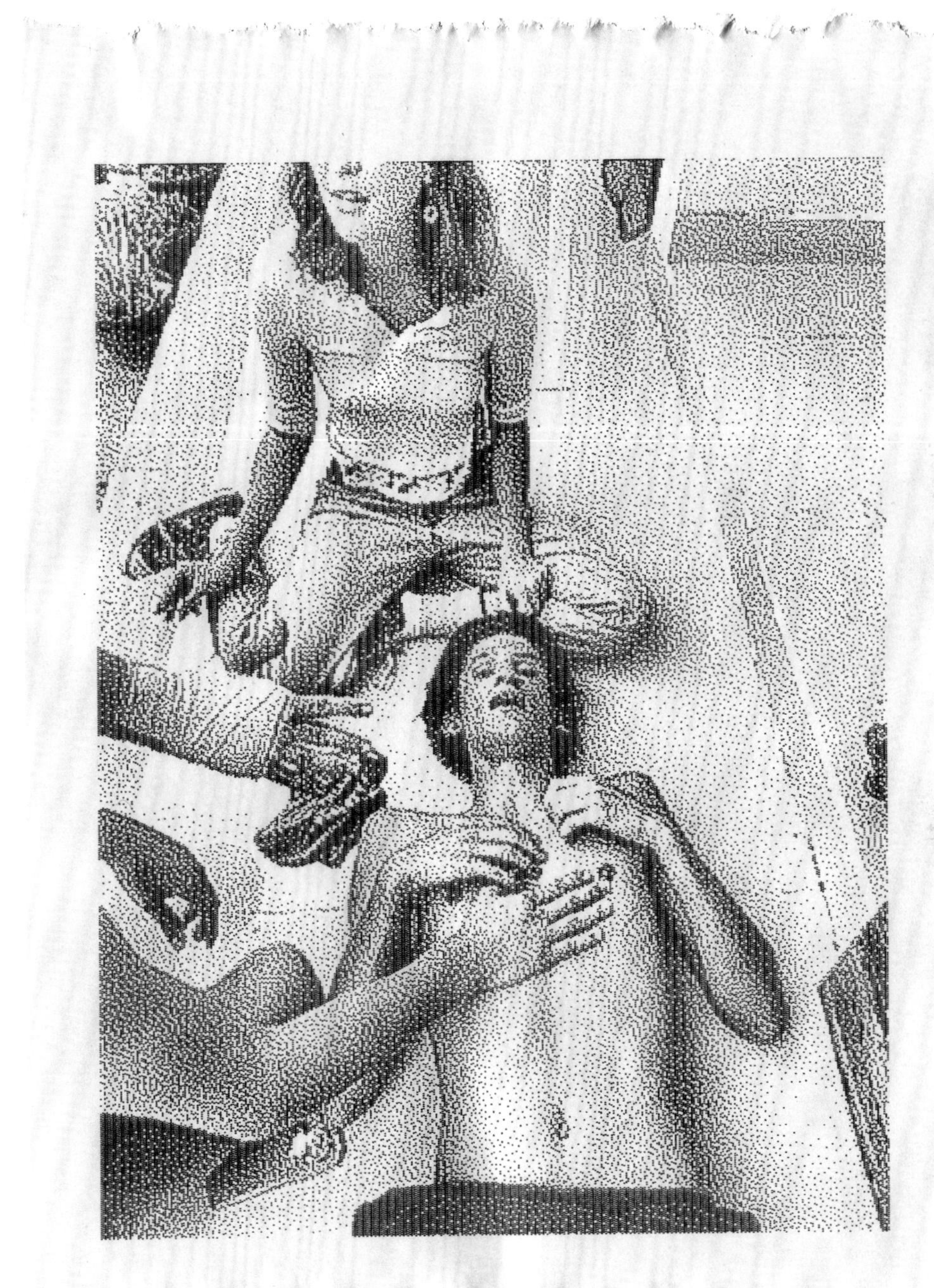

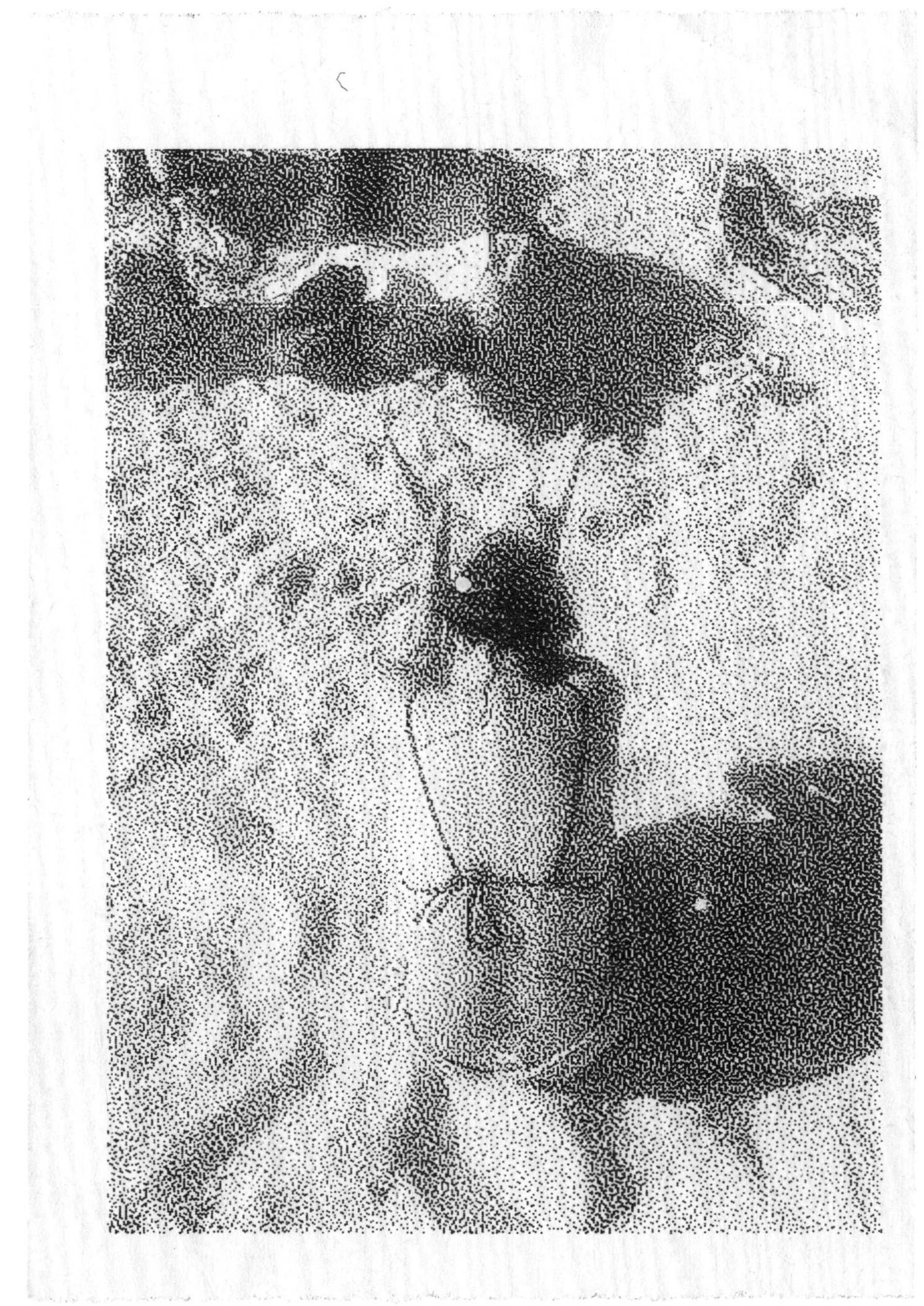

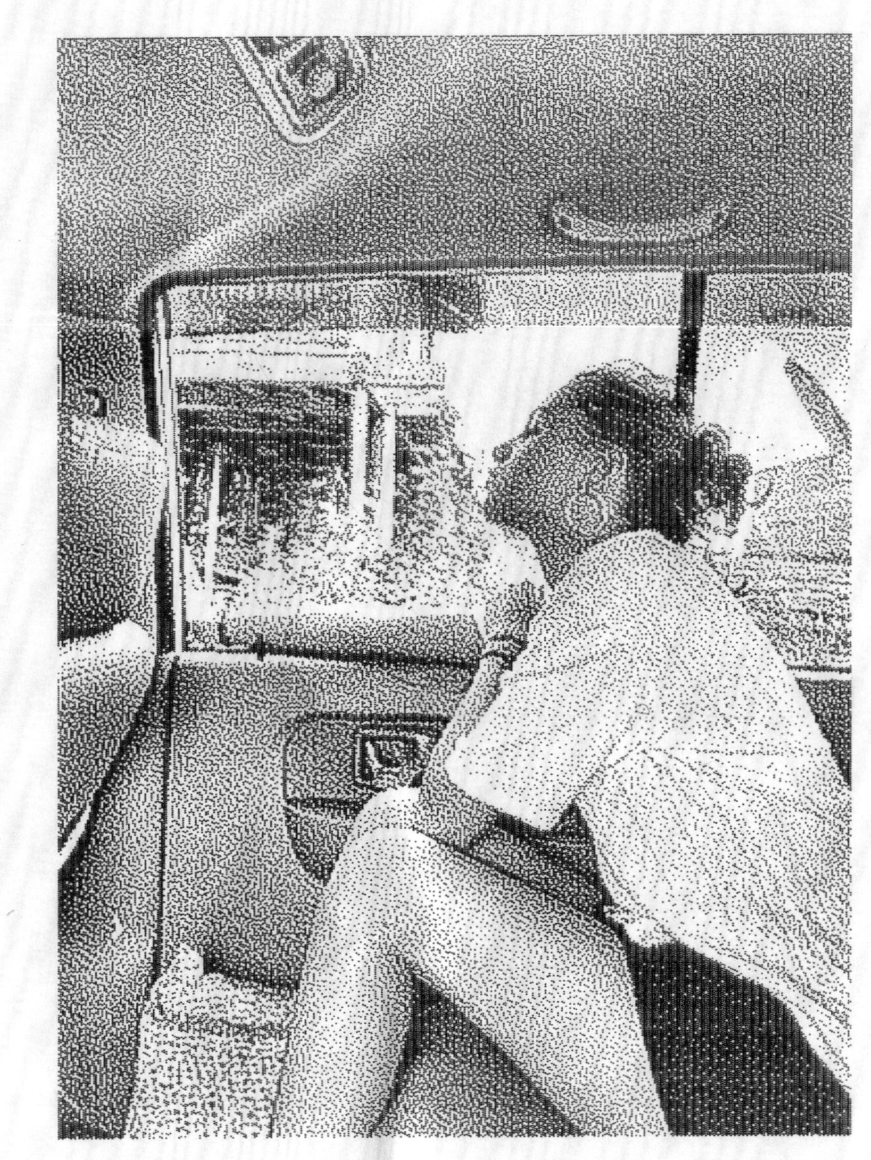

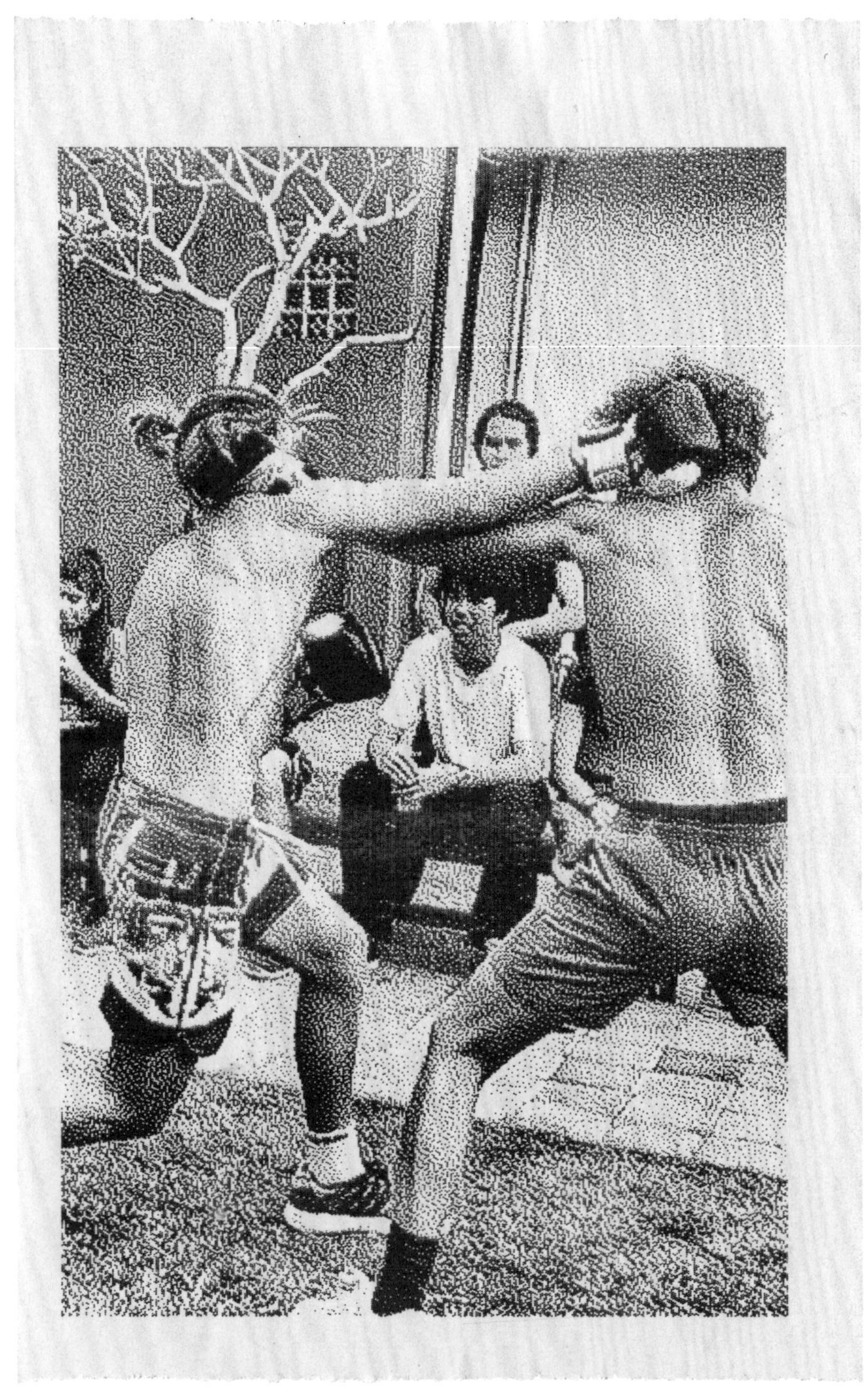

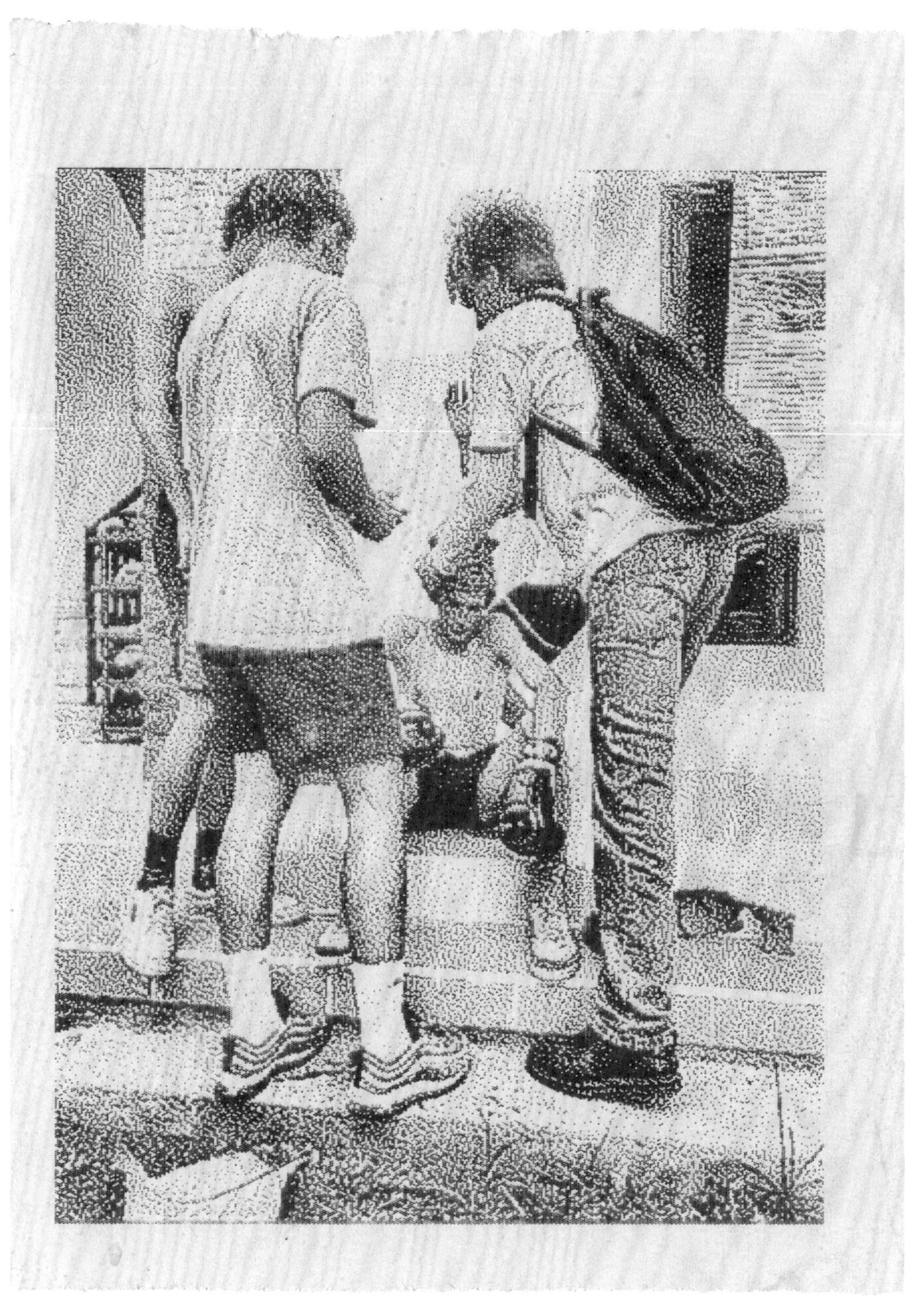

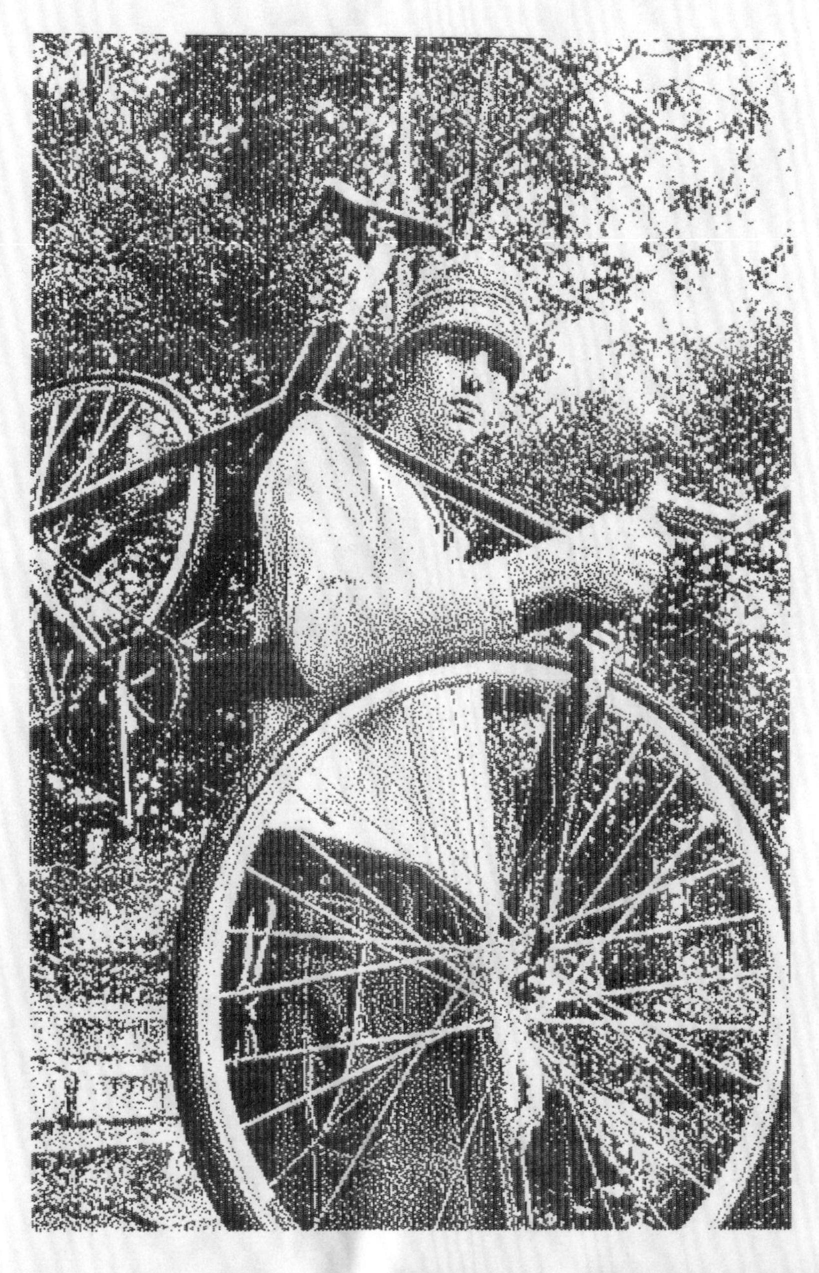

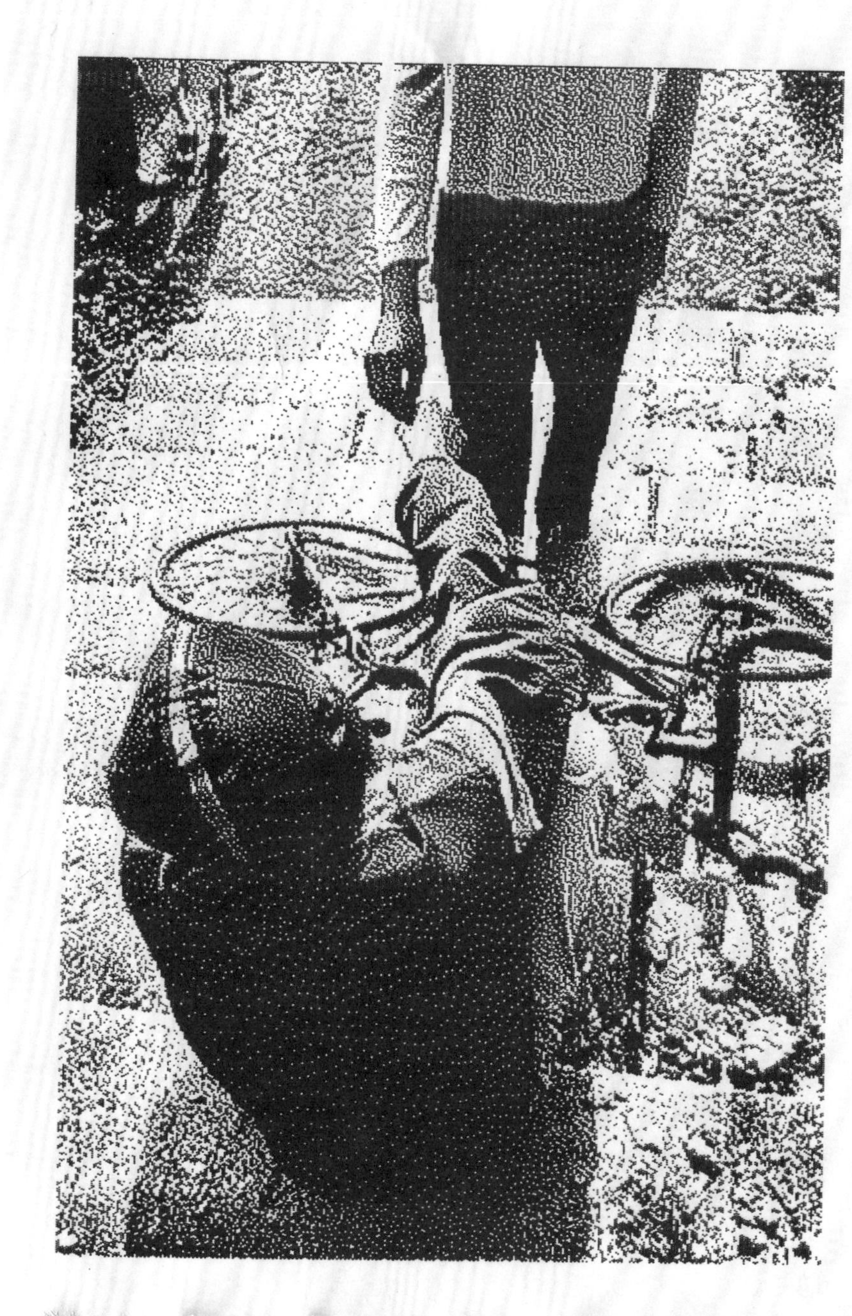

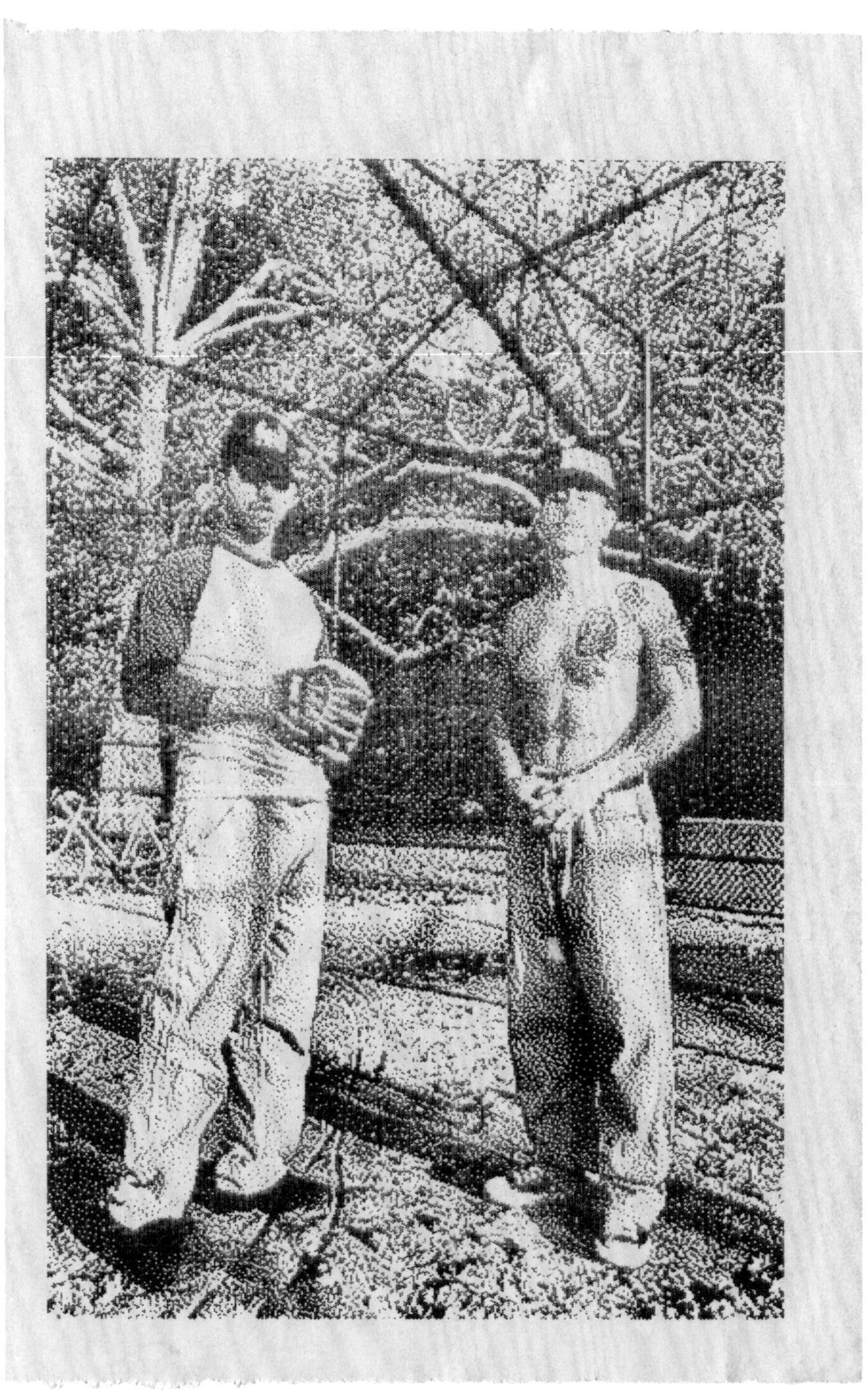

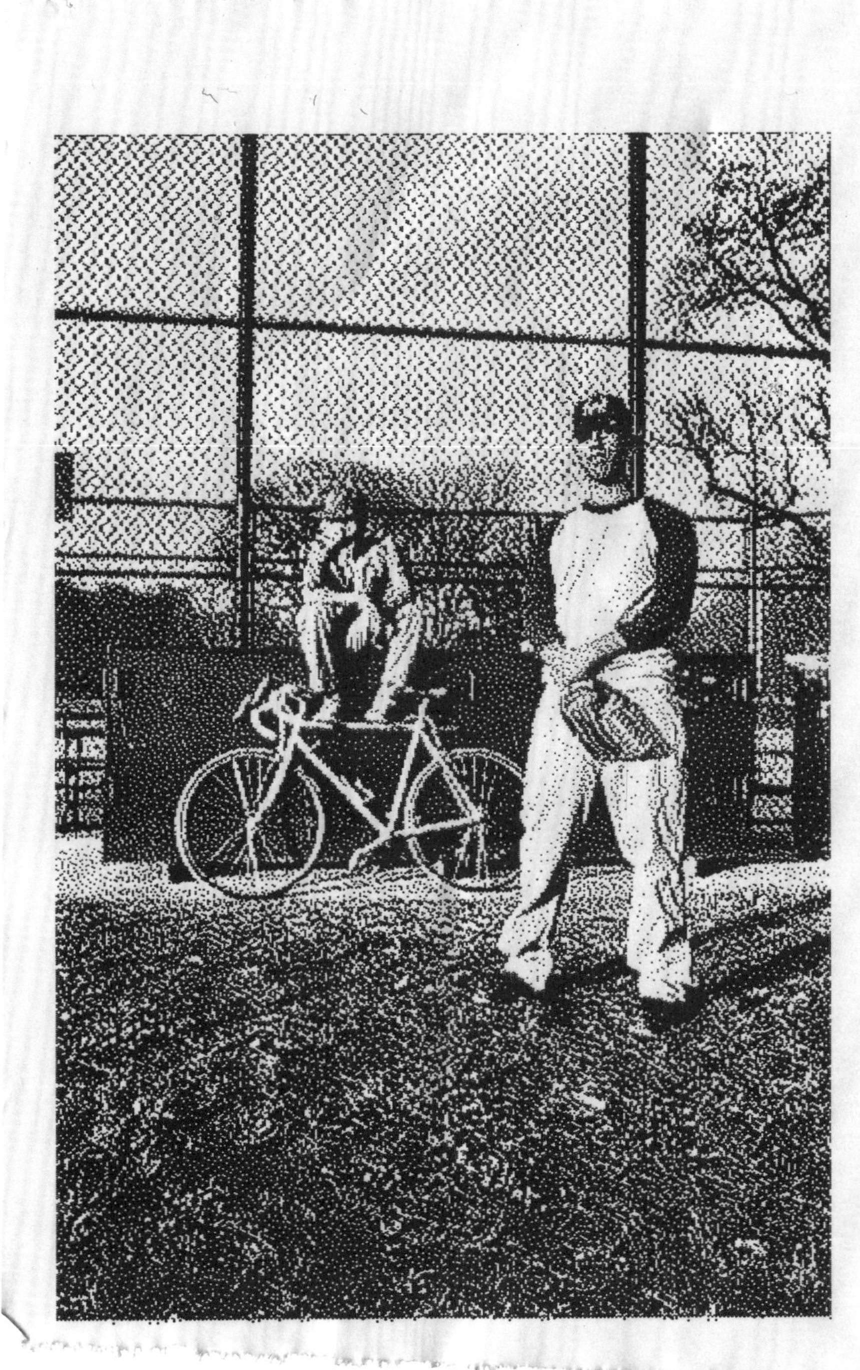

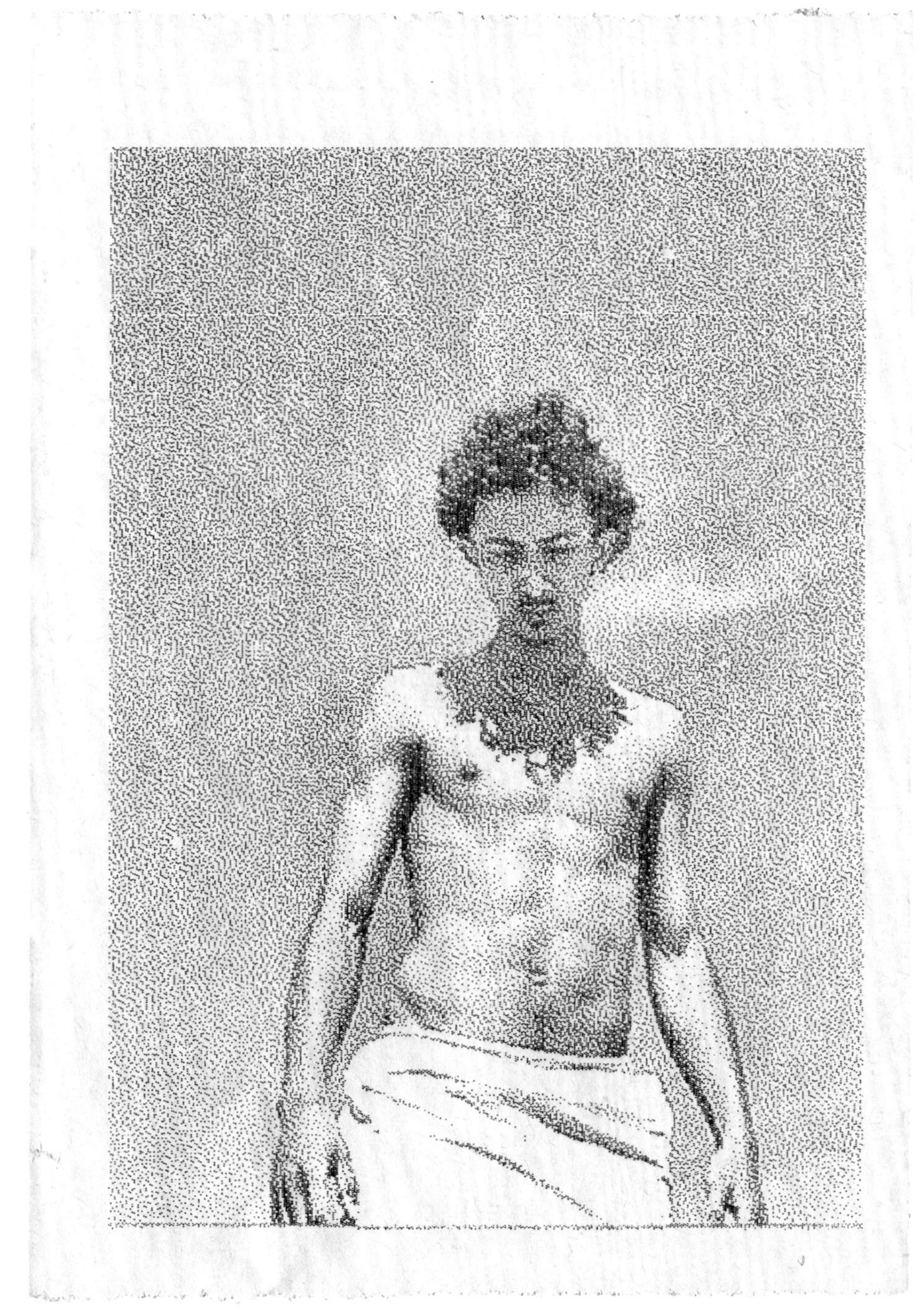

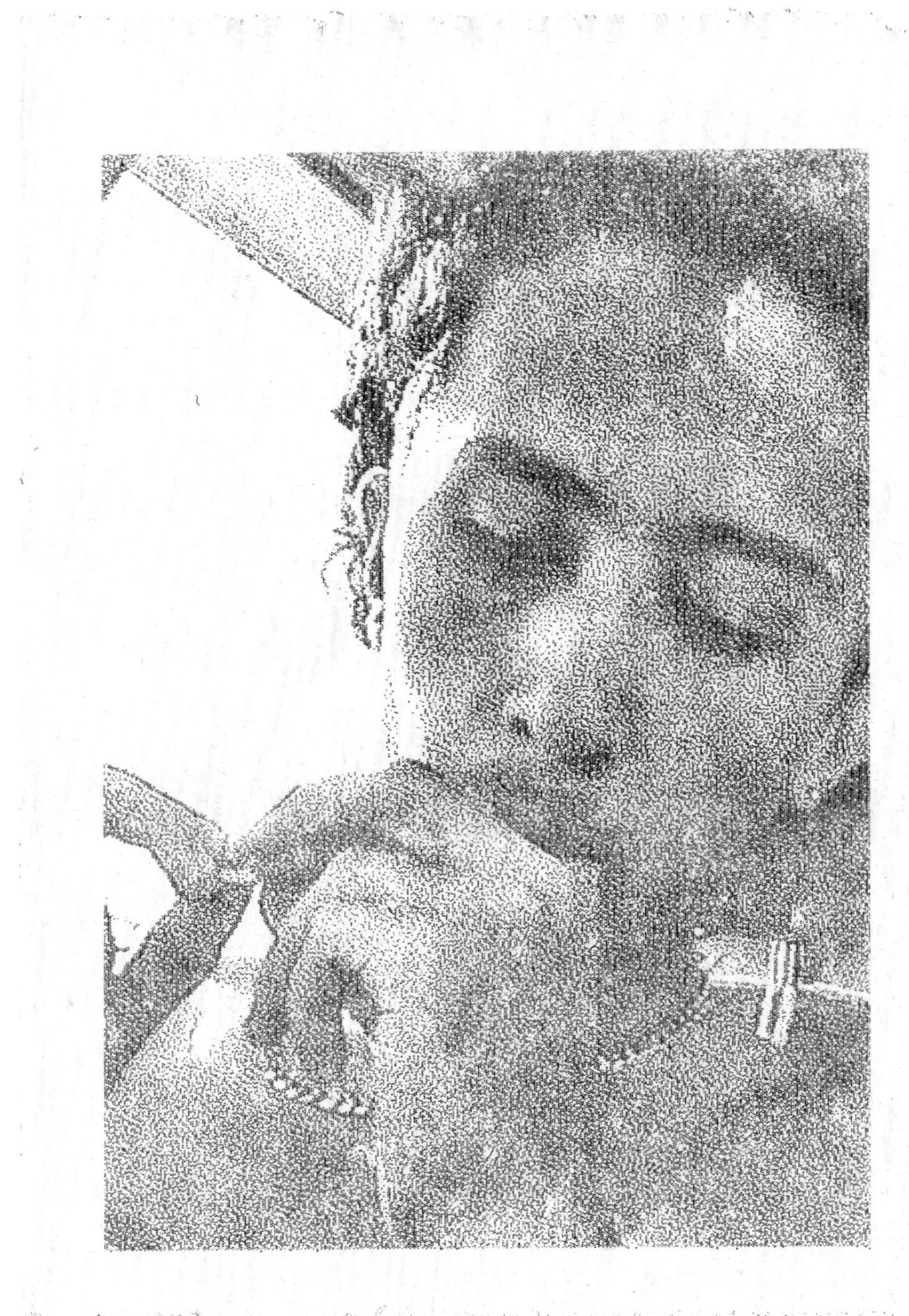

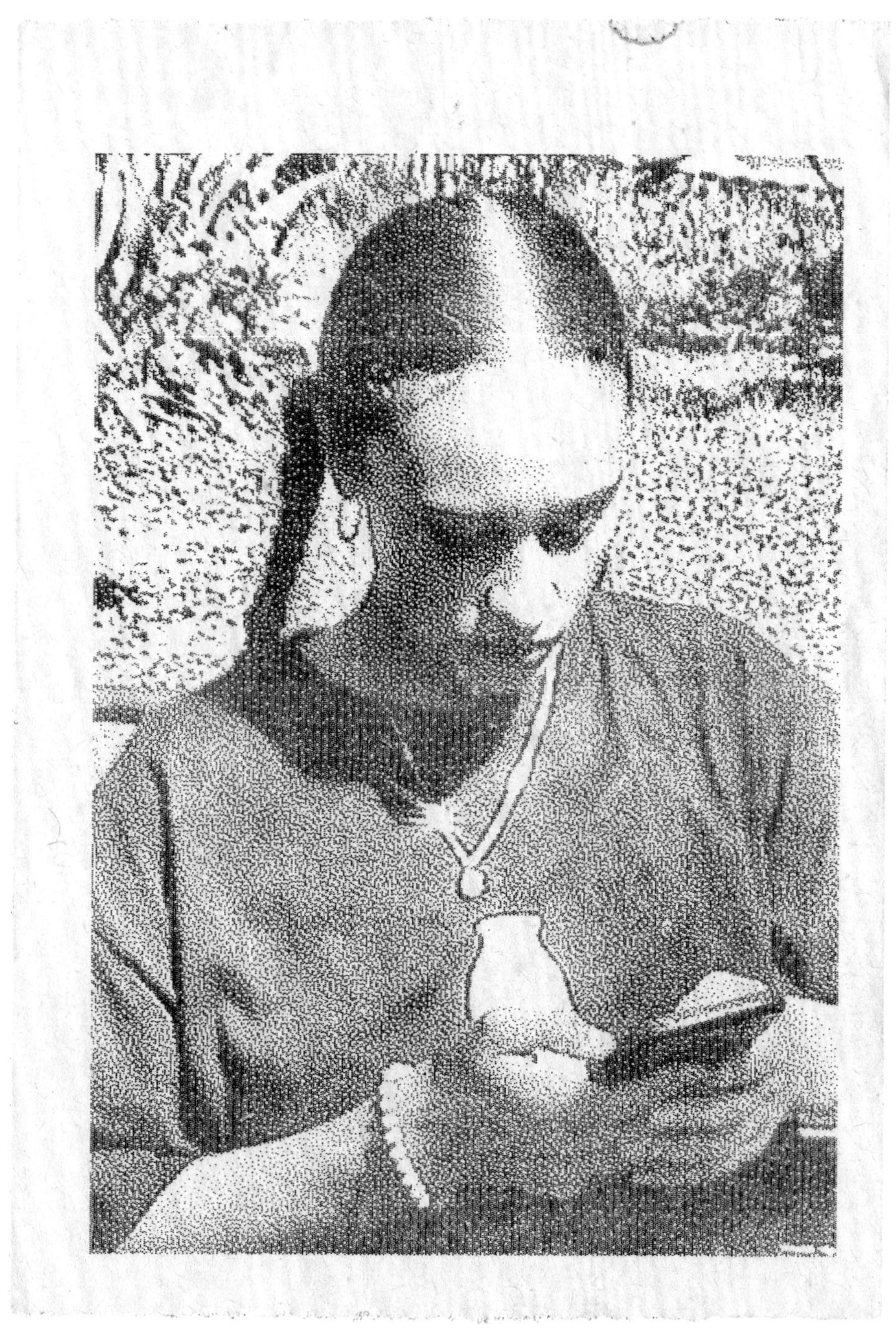

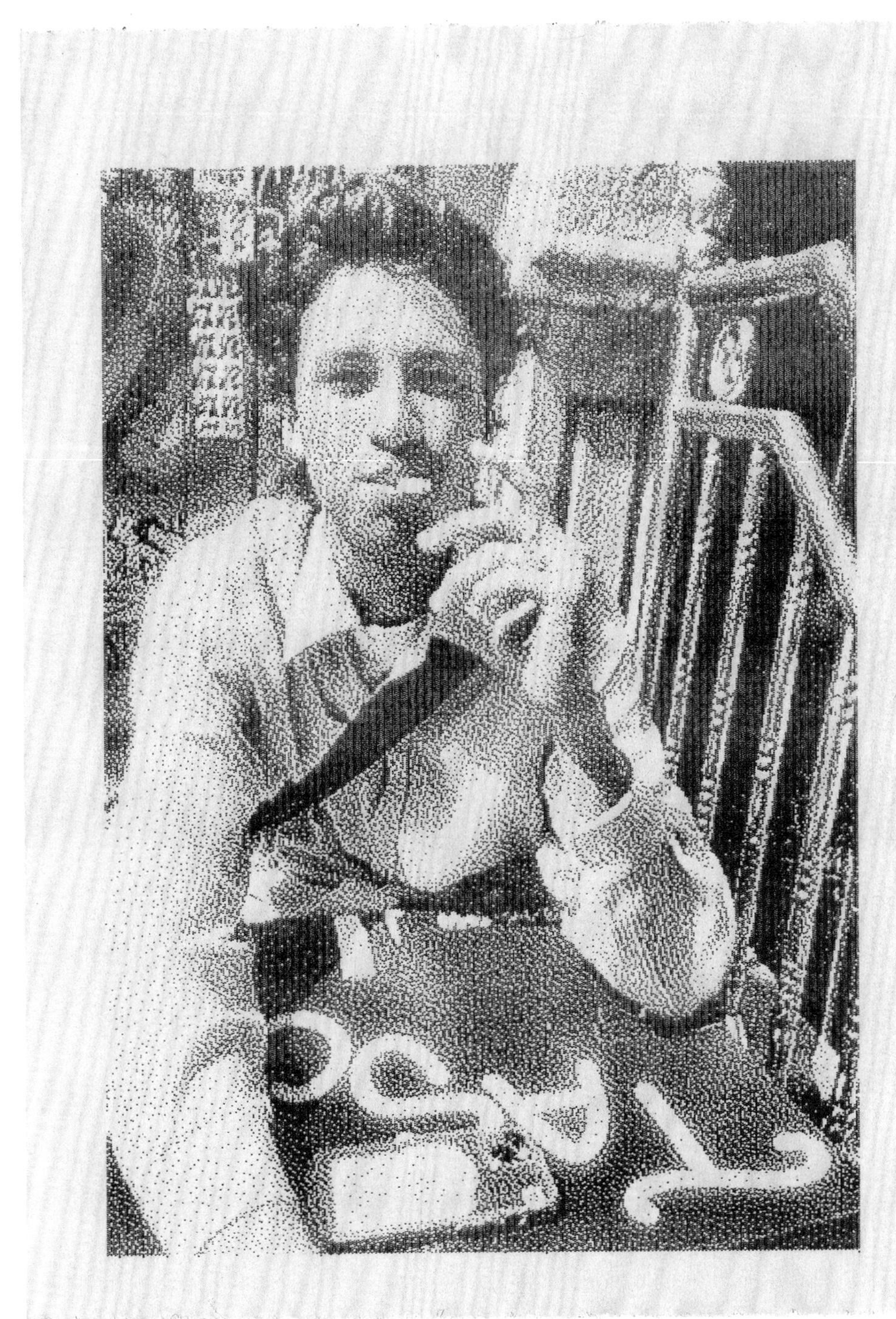

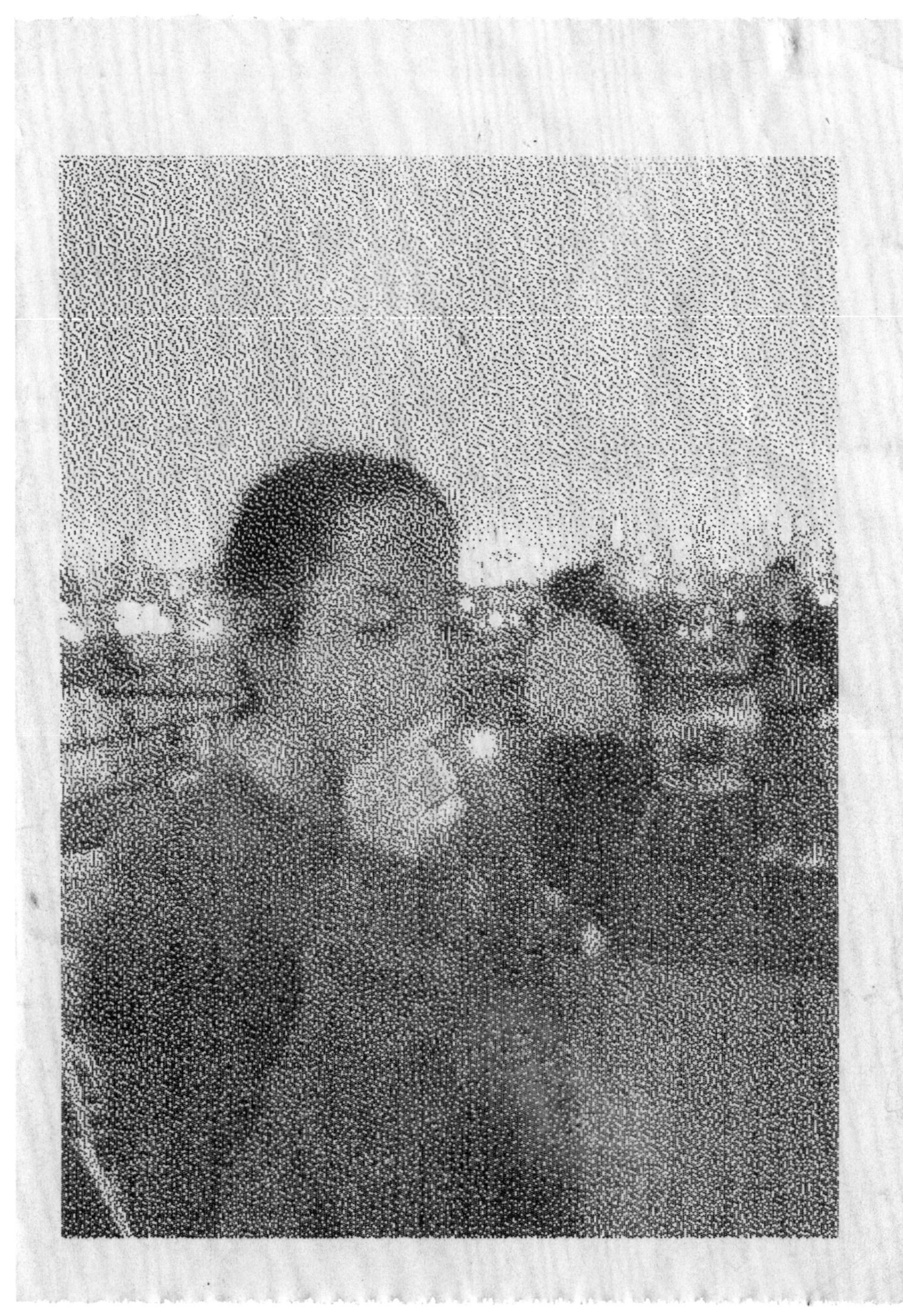

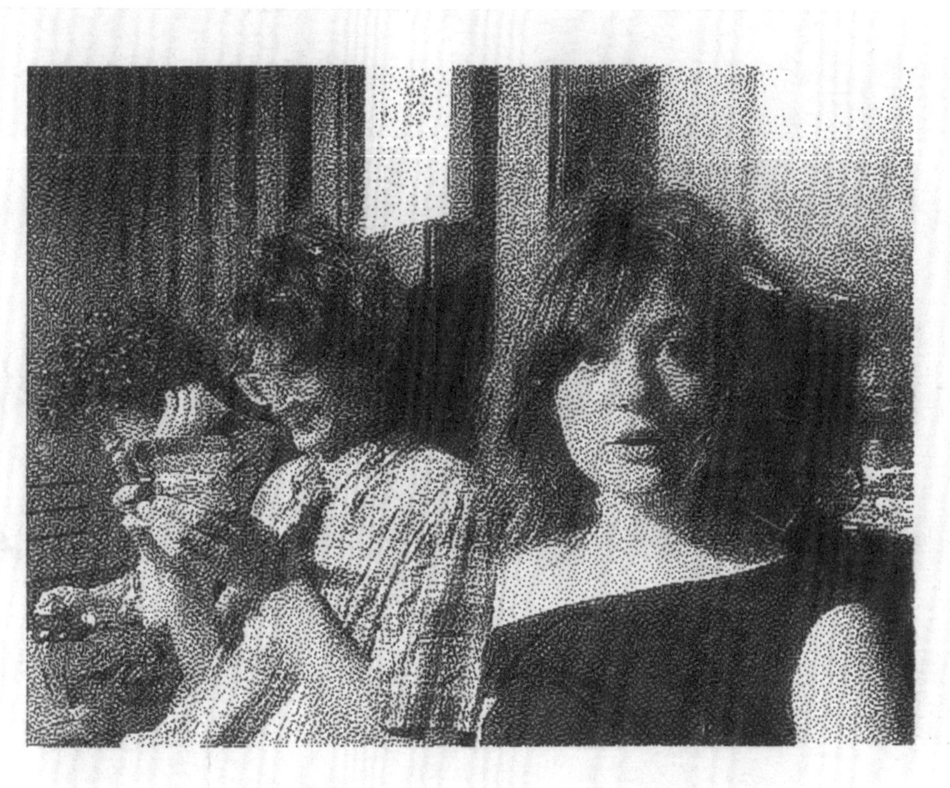

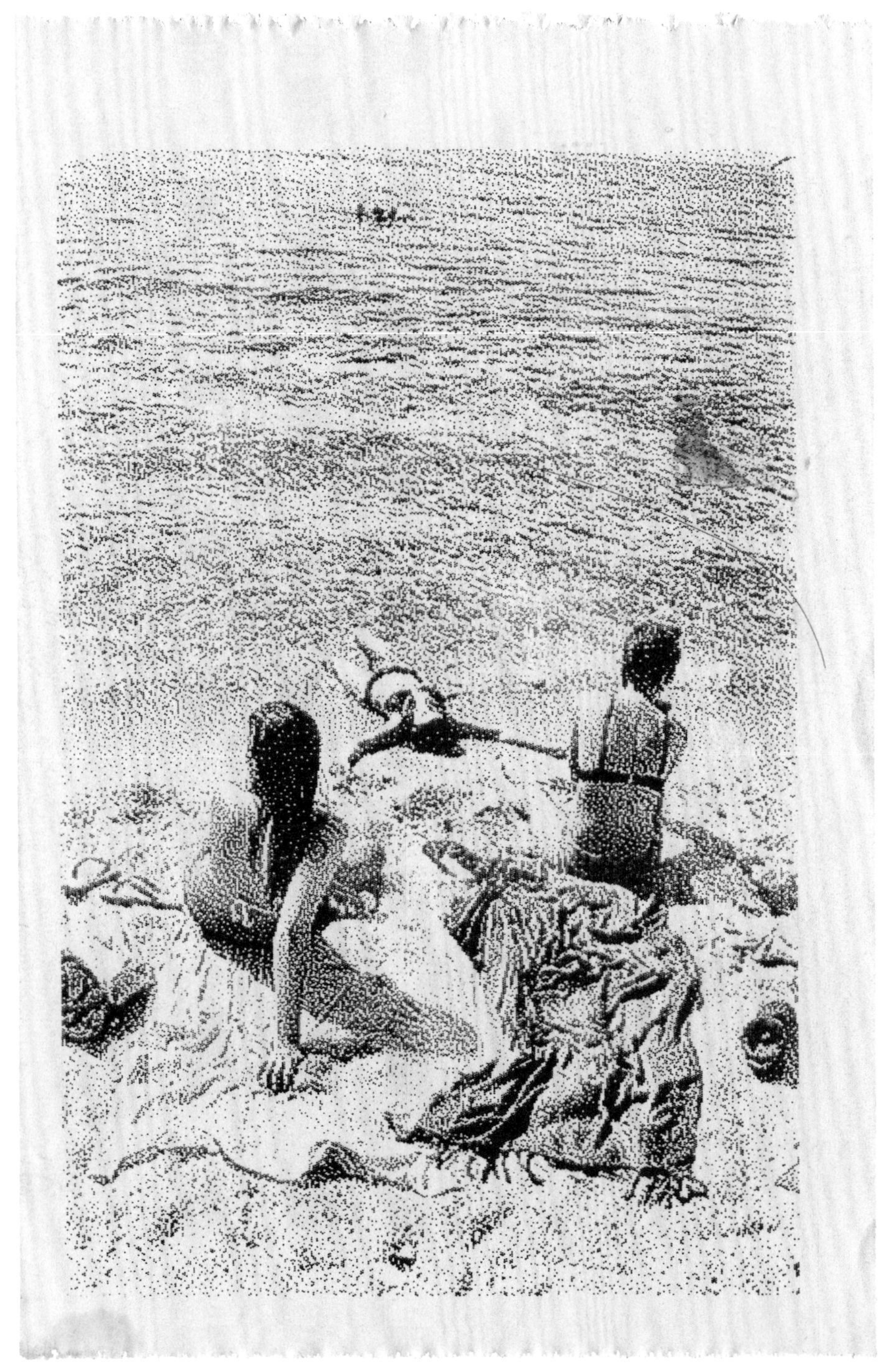

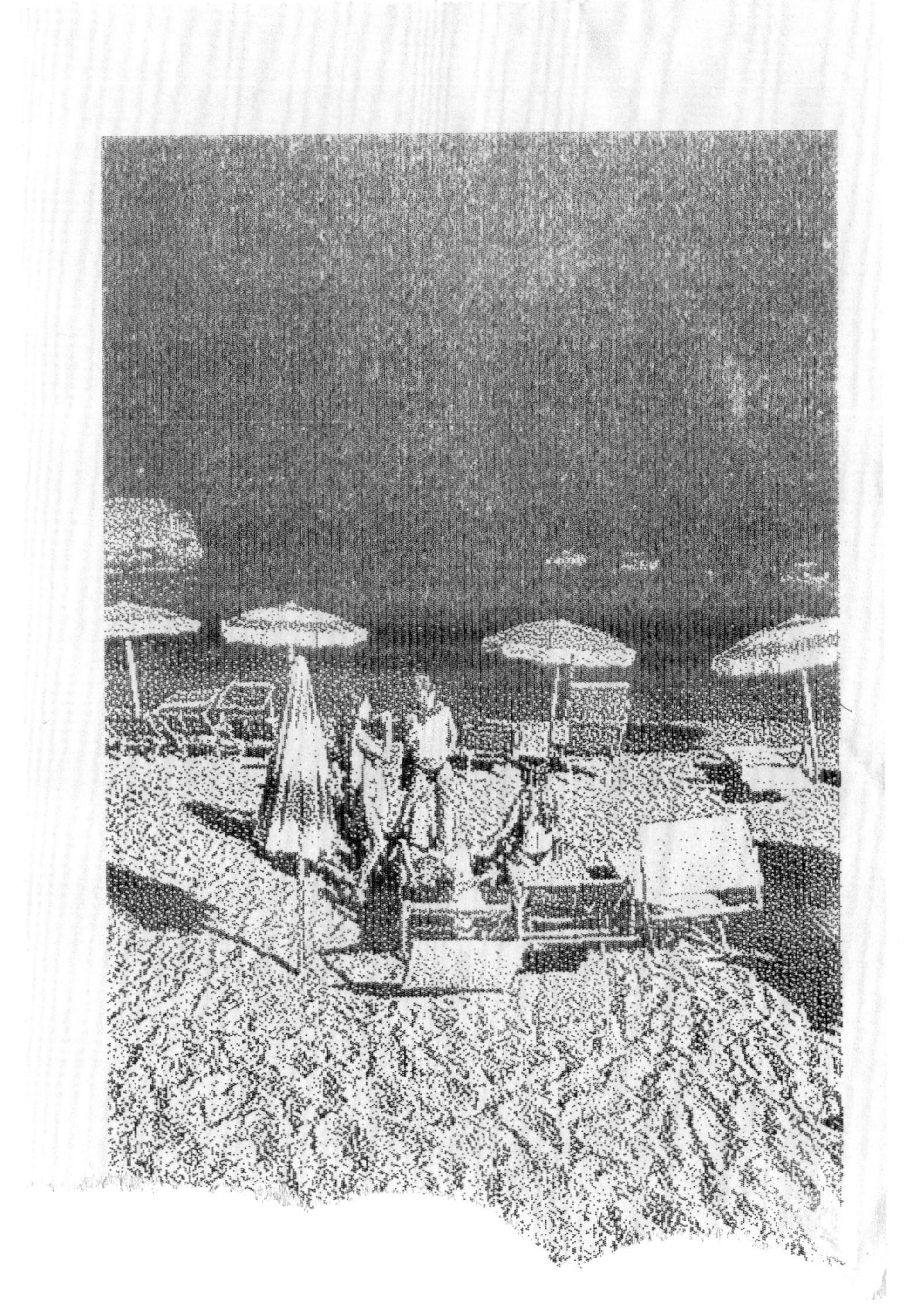

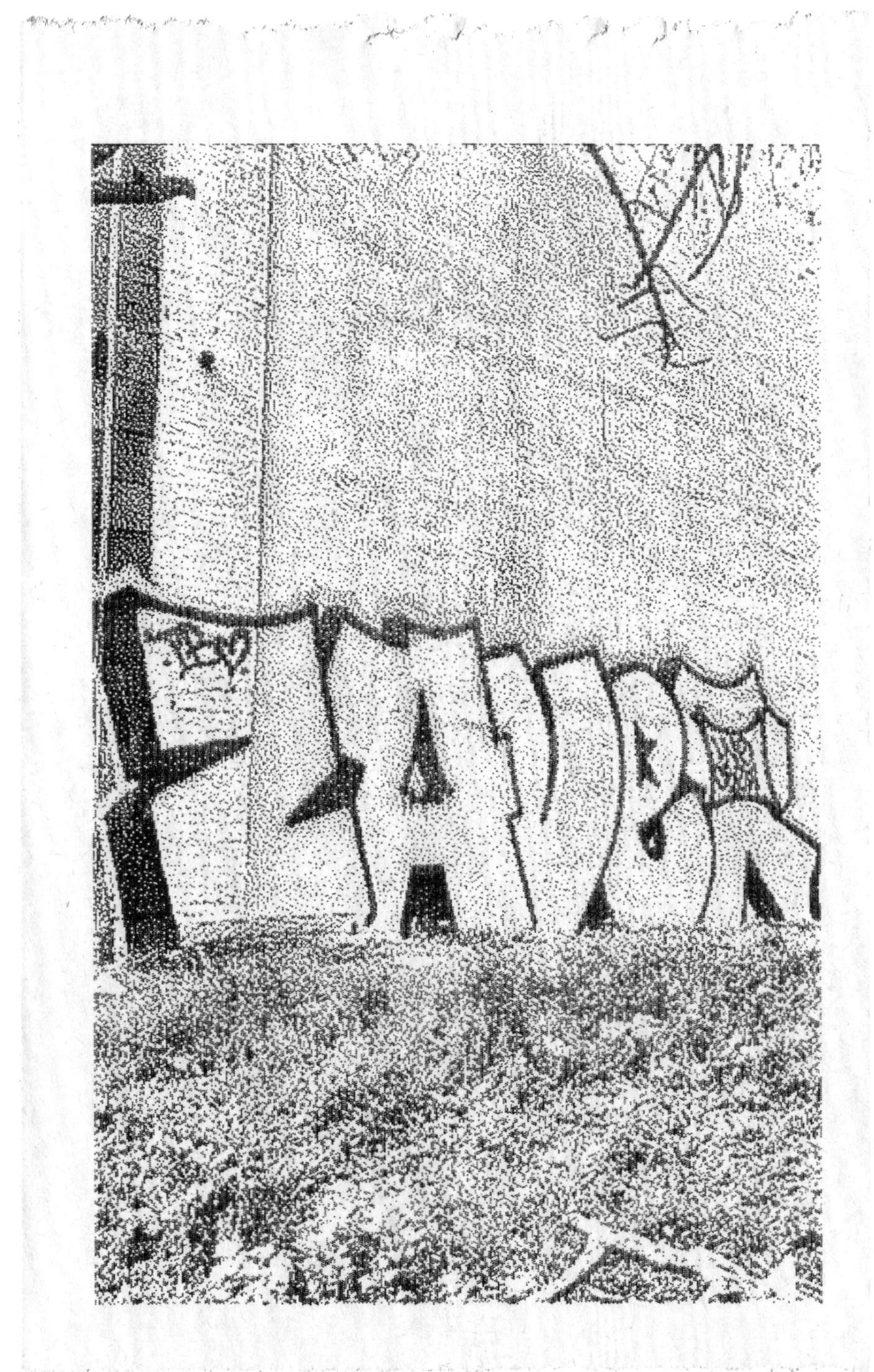

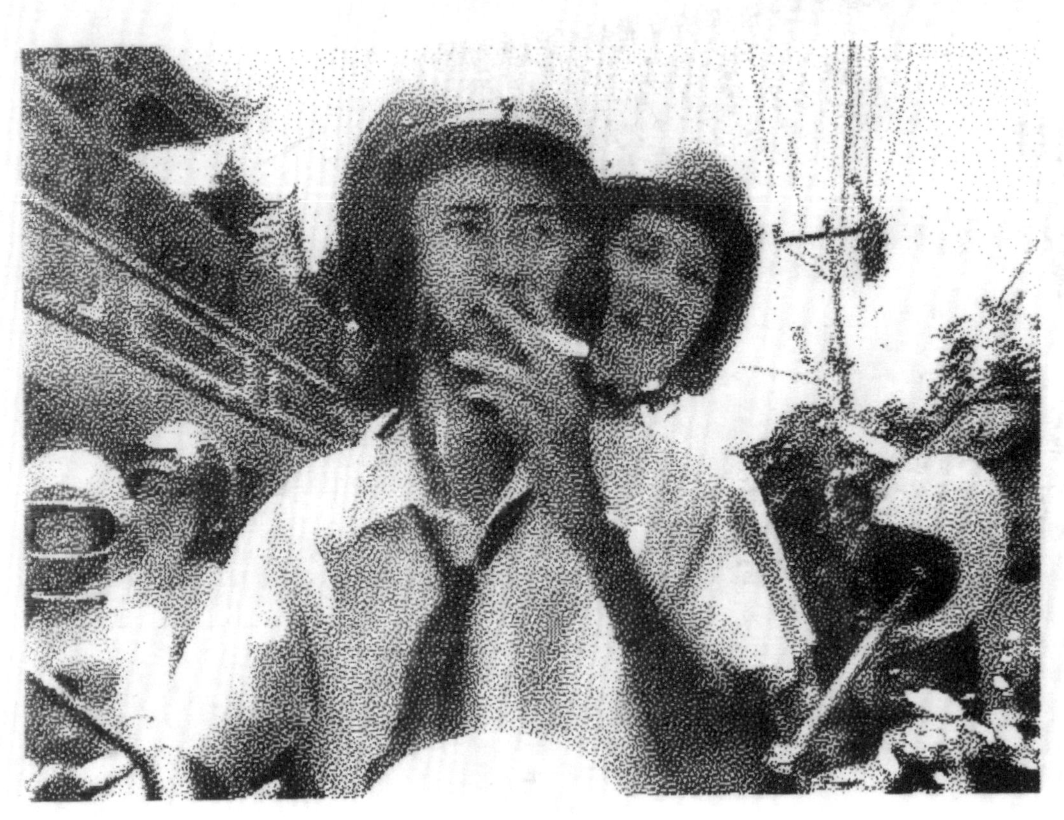

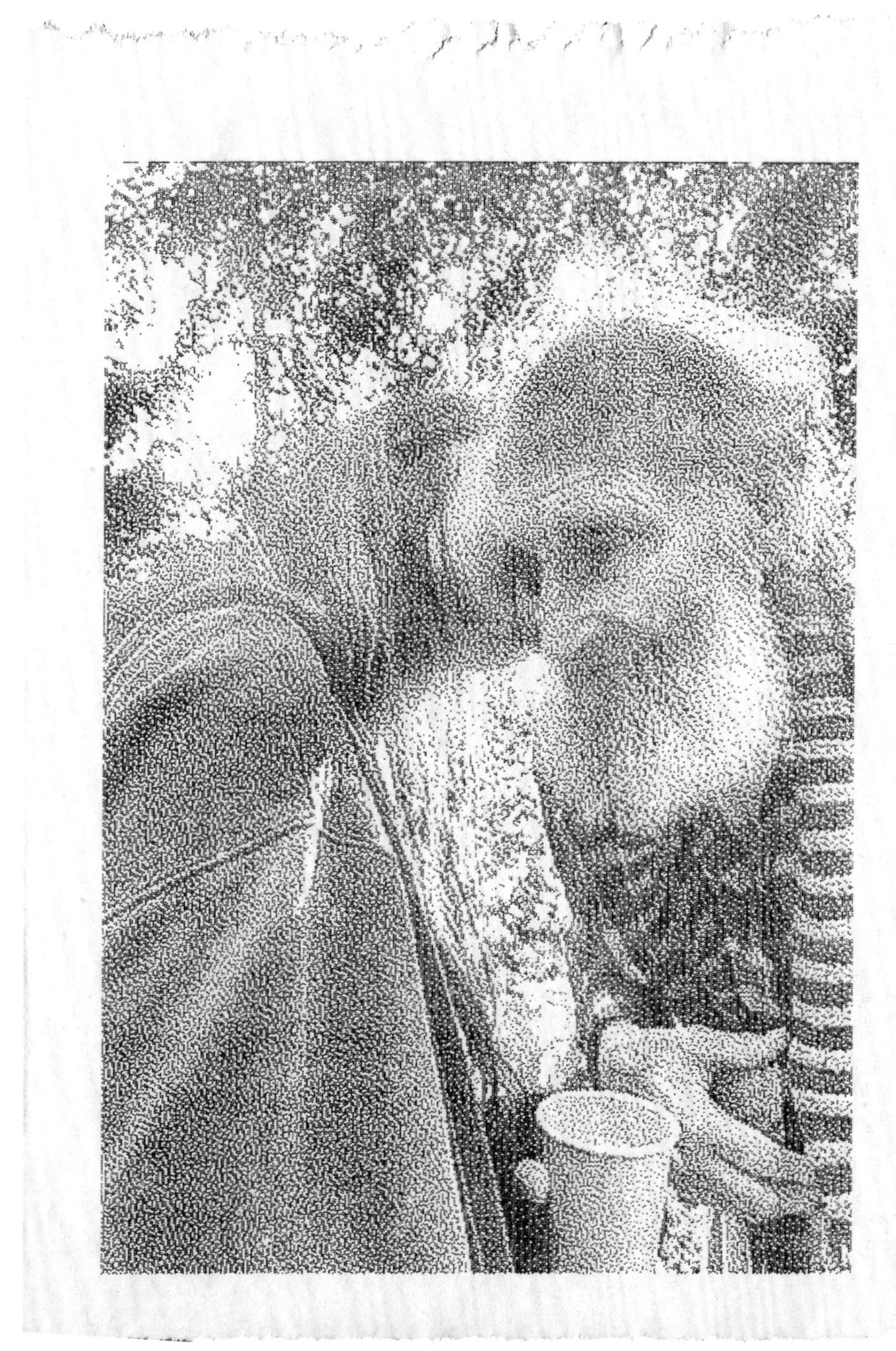

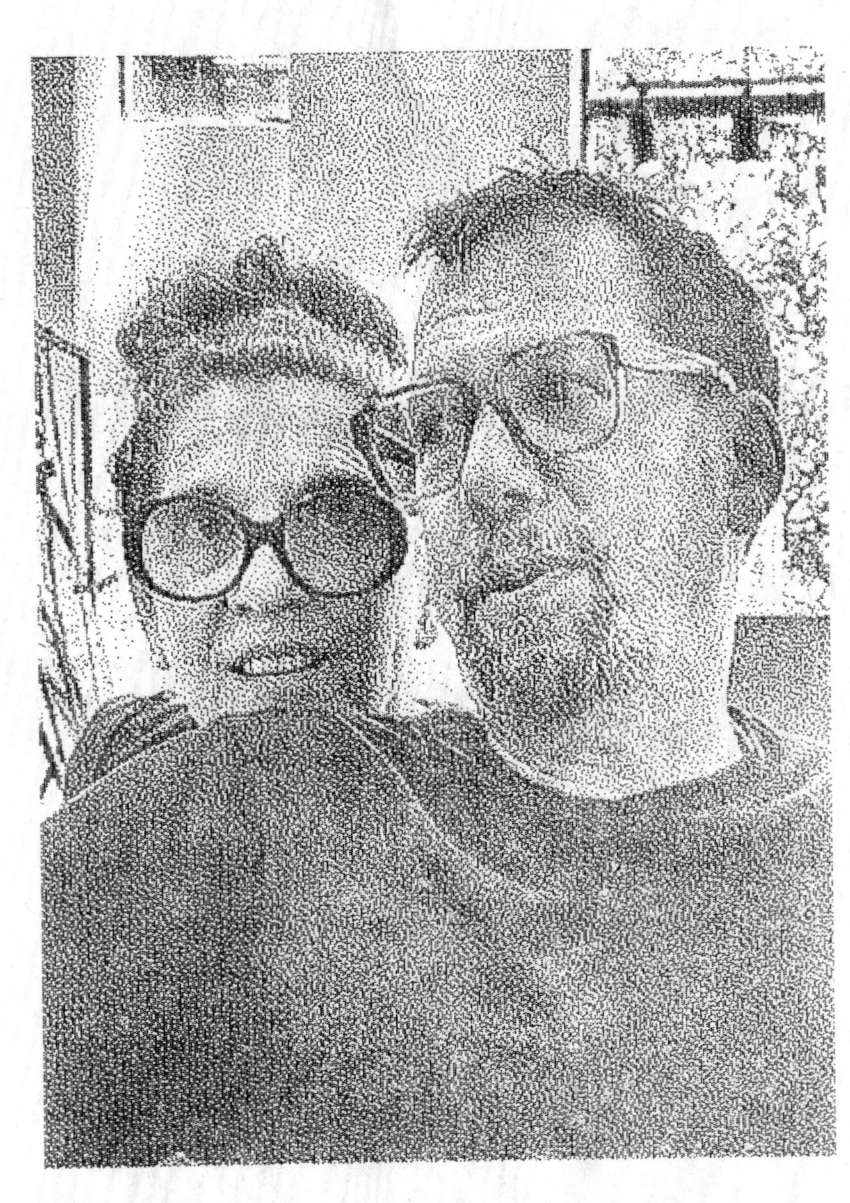

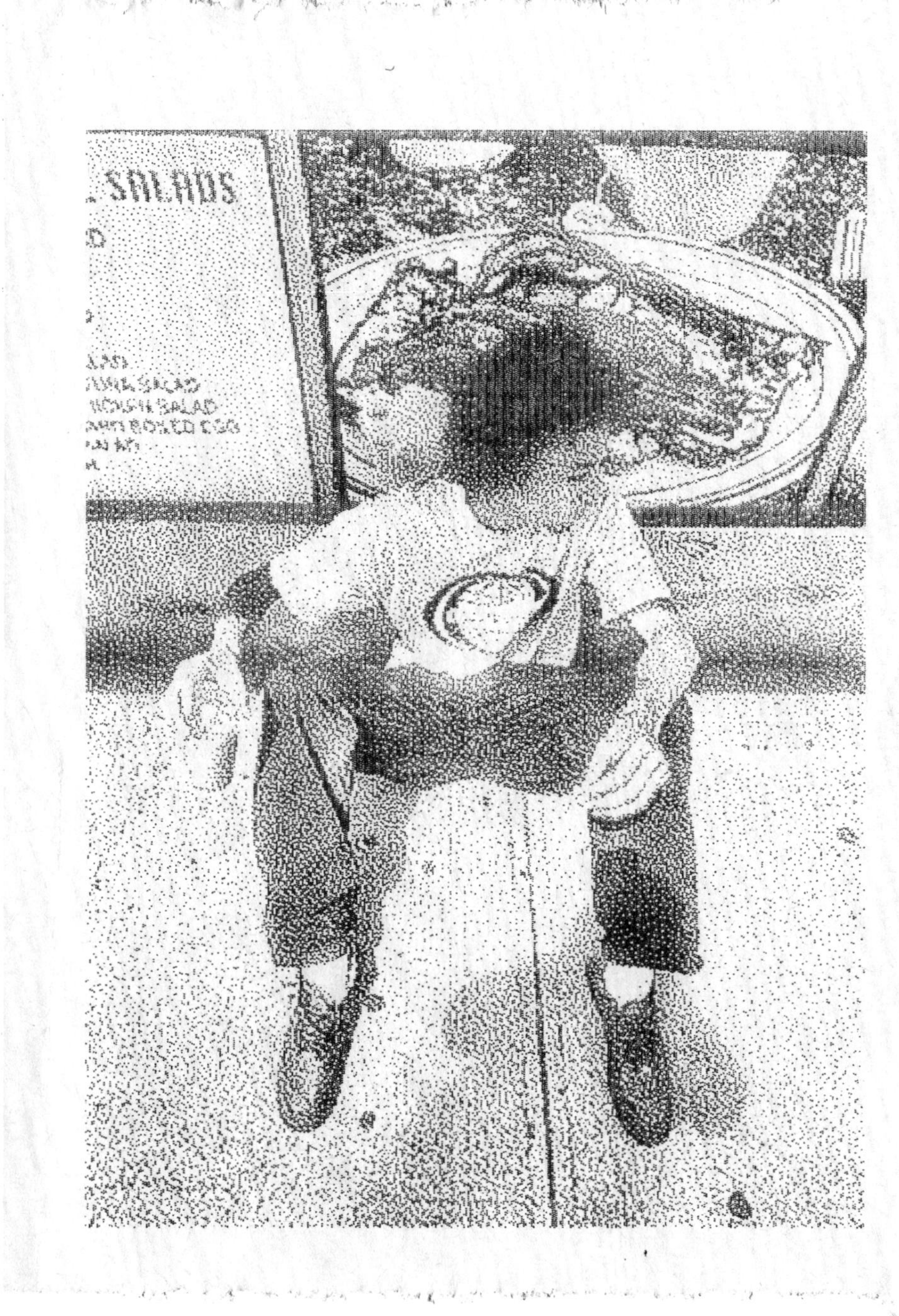
SALADS

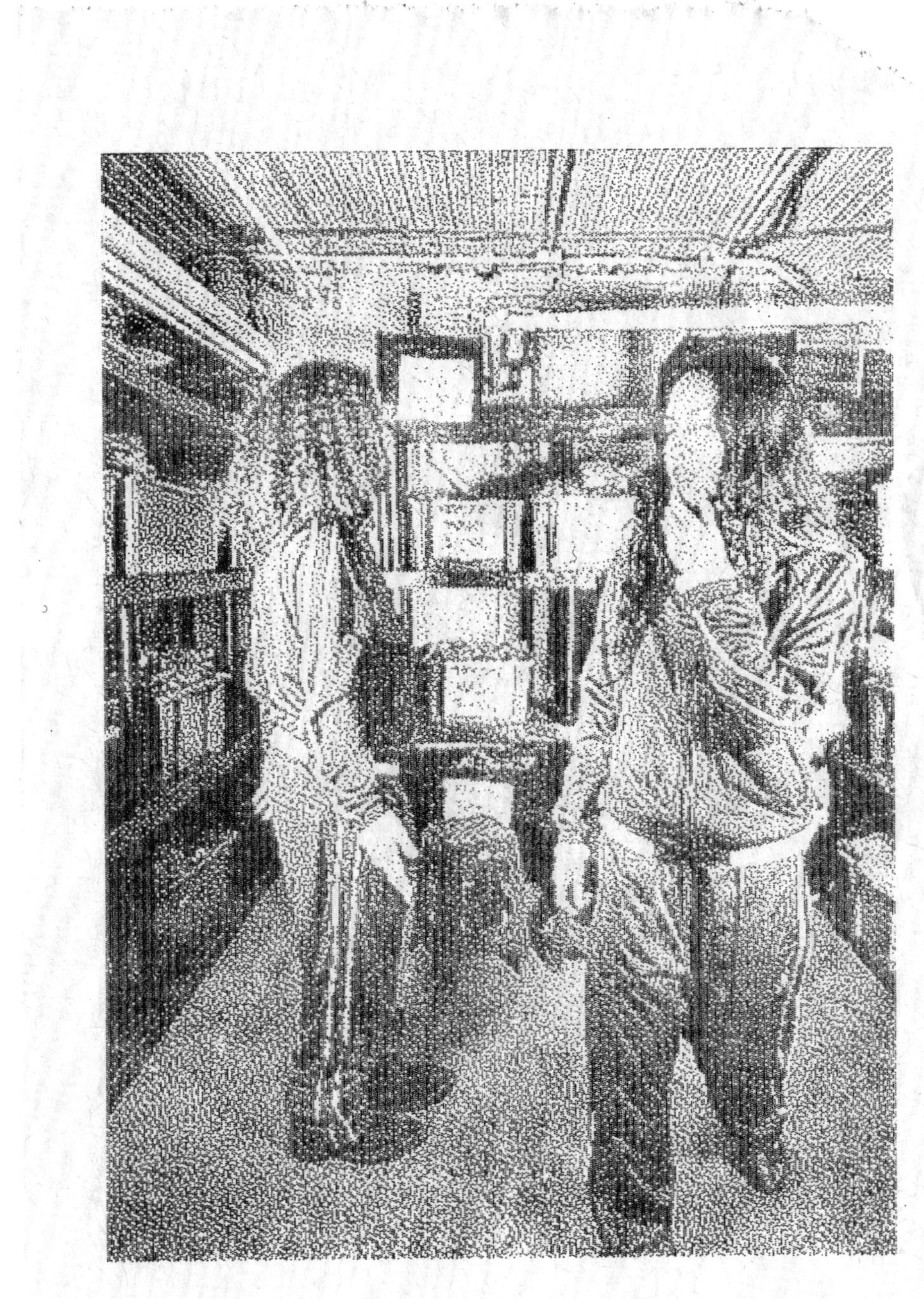

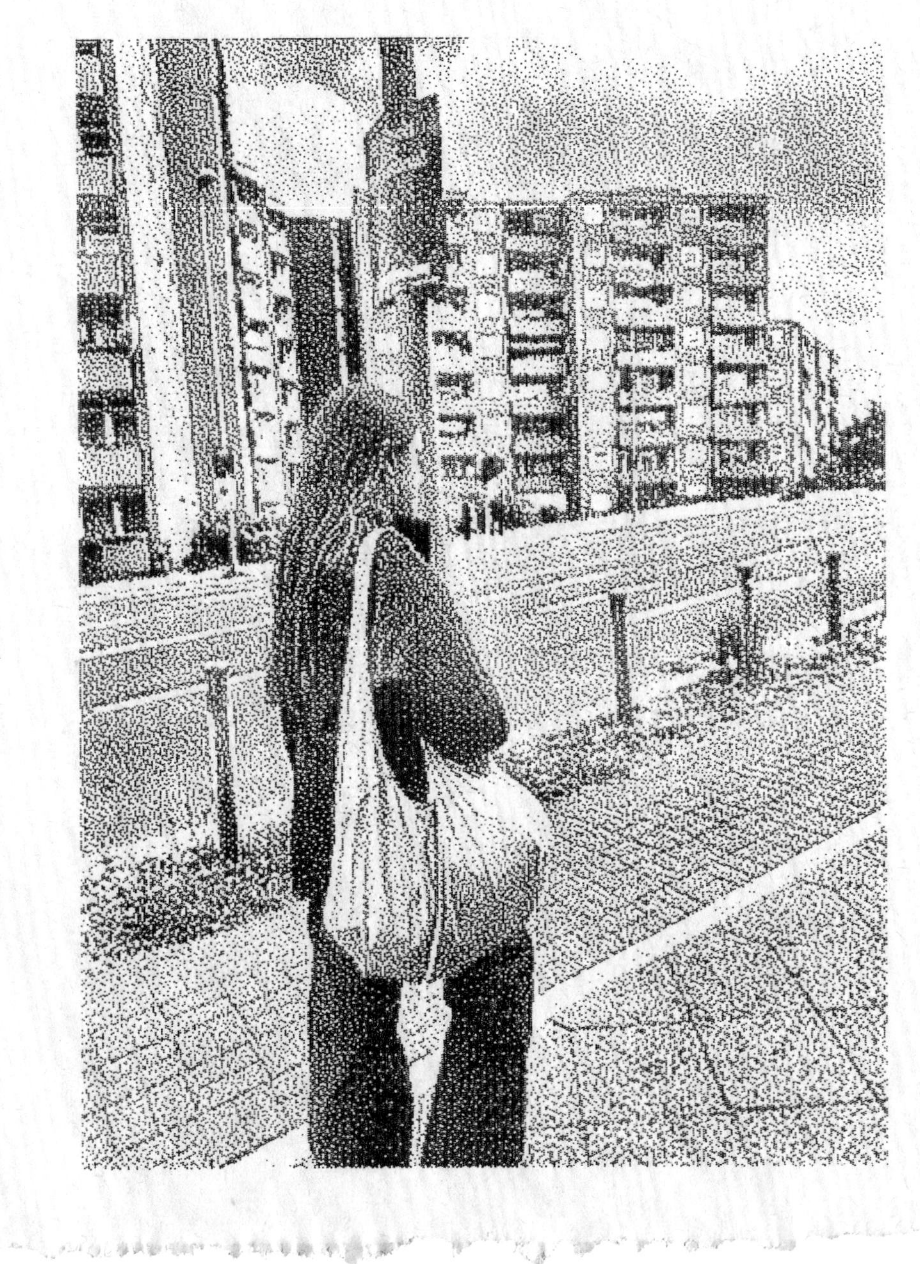

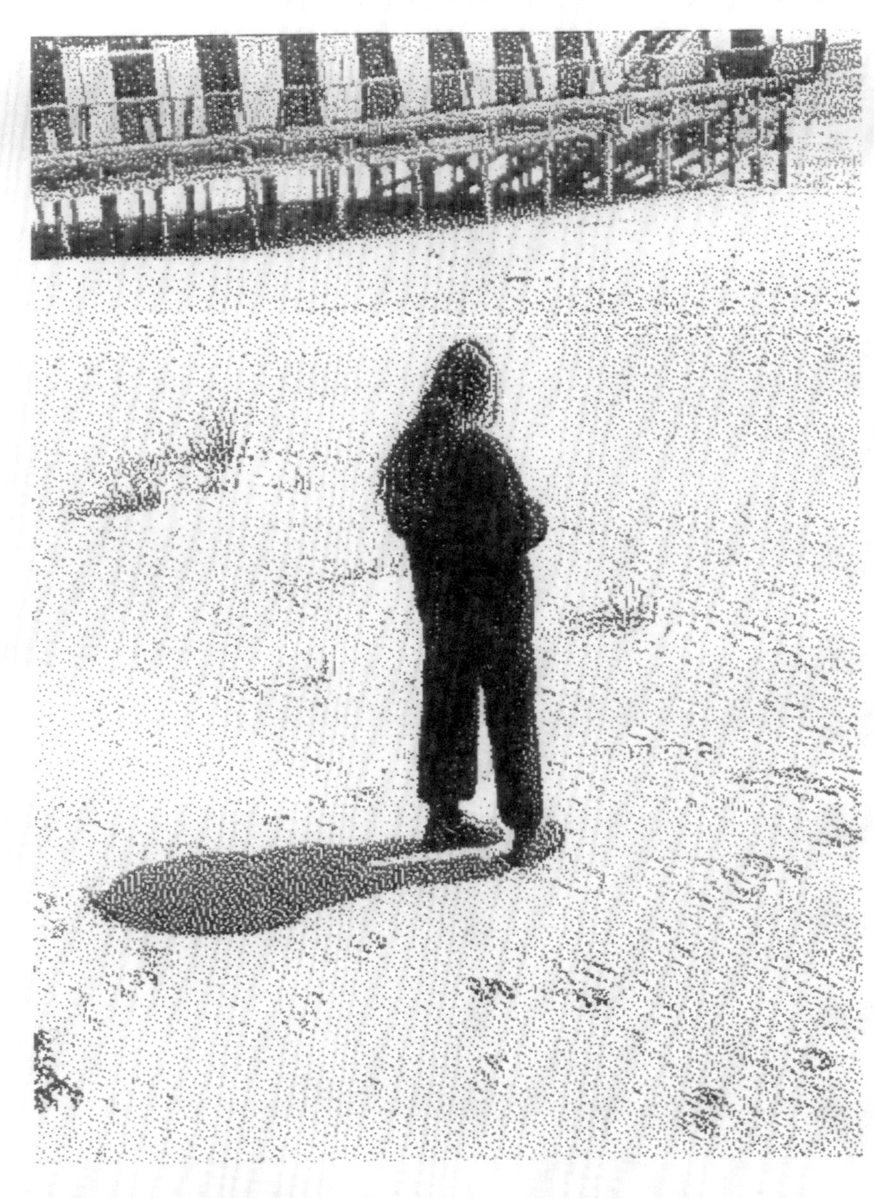

God grant me the Serenity
to accept the things I cannot change...
Courage to
change the things I can
and Wisdom to
know the difference...

RECEIPTS
TASCHI BELT

DESIGN & EDITING:
MAX BURKEMAN

SCANNING:
DEVLIN CLARO

EDITION OF 450

PRINTED IN UNITED KINGDOM

ISBN IS: 978-1-963814-15-6

LIBRARY OF CONGRESS CONTROL NUMBER: 2024921325

BLURRING BOOKS

WWW.BLURRINGBOOKS.COM